The Public Life of Cinema

The Public Life of Cinema

*Conflict and Collectivity in
Austerity Greece*

Toby Lee

UNIVERSITY OF CALIFORNIA PRESS

University of California Press
Oakland, California

© 2020 by Toby Lee

Library of Congress Cataloging-in-Publication Data

Names: Lee, Toby, author.
Title: The public life of cinema : conflict and collectivity
    in austerity Greece / Toby Lee.
Description: Oakland, California : University of
    California Press, [2020] | Includes bibliographical
    references and index.
Identifiers: LCCN 2020013470 (print) | LCCN 2020013471
    (ebook) | ISBN 9780520379015 (hardback) |
    ISBN 9780520379022 (paperback) |
    ISBN 9780520976481 (epub)
Subjects: LCSH: Phestival Kinēmatographou
    Thessalonikēs (50th : 2009 : Thessalonikē, Greece) |
    Independent films—Political aspects—Greece—21st
    century. | Film festivals—Greece—Thessalonikē.
Classification: LCC PN1993.5.G75 L44 2020 (print) |
    LCC PN1993.5.G75 (ebook) | DDC 791.4309495—dc23
LC record available at https://lccn.loc.gov/2020013470
LC ebook record available at https://lccn.loc.gov
    /2020013471

Manufactured in the United States of America

29 28 27 26 25 24 23 22 21 20
10 9 8 7 6 5 4 3 2 1

Contents

Illustrations

Acknowledgments

One of the paradoxes, as well as great pleasures, of researching and writing a book is that what often feels like a solitary journey is actually quite the opposite. Over the years, this project has gifted me with many friends, mentors, and helpful souls, without whose generosity and kindness this book could not have been completed. I come away from this process with many lessons learned, but above all else, with a profound sense of gratitude for the relationships and communities it has occasioned.

Before this project was a book, it was a dissertation, which was completed at Harvard University under the patient guidance of Michael Herzfeld, David Rodowick, Mary Steedly, and Lucien Castaing-Taylor. At Harvard, I was lucky enough to be part of a community of interlocutors and coconspirators that included Diana Allan, J. P. Sniadecki, Felicity Aulino, Stephanie Spray, and Ernst Karel. The time we spent together, both working and playing, was undoubtedly one of the best parts of graduate school, and they continue to be an inspiration.

The seeds for this project, and indeed for much of my scholarly trajectory thus far, were planted many years ago by Karen Van Dyck. I cannot adequately express my appreciation for her generous intellect, her sustained mentorship, and her friendship, which have so fundamentally shaped my life and my work.

I am deeply grateful to the many people I met in the field who graciously accepted my inquiring presence and allowed me to become a part of their lives: Kostas Aivaliotis, Eleni Alexandrakis, Vassilis Amoiridis,

Giannis Bakogiannopoulos, Giannis Chatzigogas, Elena Christopoulou, Michel Demopoulos, Dimitris Eipides, Notis Forsos, Marcos Holevas, Christos Karakepelis, Athina Kartalou, Stelios Kazadzis, Dimitris Kerkinos, Valerie Kontakos, Marineta Kritikou, Lia Lazaridou, Thomas Linaras, Vardis Marinakis, Lina Milonaki, Anna Milossi, Despina Mouzaki, Afroditi Nikolaidou, Nasia Pantazopoulou, Lilly Papagianni, Nikos Perakis, Angeliki Petrou, Maria Polyviou, Lucia Rikaki, Natasa Segou, Tasia Sempsi, Dimitris Sofianopoulos, Thanos Stavropoulos, Nella Tampouri, Ifigenia Taxopoulou, Themis Veleni, and Angeliki Vergou.

A number of organizations provided funding for this project at various stages of research and writing, including the Fulbright Foundation in Greece, Dan David Foundation, and Minda de Gunzburg Center for European Studies at Harvard University. Early on, this project was supported by a Dissertation Proposal Development Fellowship from the Social Science Research Council, which gave me the opportunity to develop my ideas in the context of a Visual Culture workshop. My thanks go to the leaders of the workshop, Vanessa Schwartz and Anne Higonnet, as well as to my fellow workshop participants, especially Aynne Kokas. Key support was also provided at later stages by fellowships at New York University's Global Research Institute in Athens and NYU's Center for the Humanities. As a Faculty Fellow at the latter, I had the great fortune of meeting George Shulman, whose intelligence and warmth have indelibly marked this book. This project has also benefited at different points in its development from the kind engagement and critical insights of Vangelis Calotychos, Efthymios Papataxiarchis, and Bonnie Honig.

It has been a pleasure to work with Raina Polivka at University of California Press; I am grateful for her careful work in shepherding this book, which is better for having passed through her capable hands. I would also like to thank Madison Wetzell, as well as my two readers, and especially Karen Strassler, whose sharp and incredibly thoughtful feedback provided much-needed perspective at a crucial moment.

At New York University, I am fortunate to have kind and supportive colleagues whose help and encouragement have been invaluable as I have worked over the past few years to bring this book to completion: Dana Polan, Anna McCarthy, Faye Ginsburg, Dan Streible, Allen Weiss, Karen Shimakawa, Bob Stam, Antonia Lant, Feng-Mei Heberer, Josslyn Luckett, and Laura Harris.

None of this would be possible, or worth it, without the cherished friendship and intellectual camaraderie of Pooja Rangan, Josh Guilford,

Sebastián Calderón Bentin, Fotini Lazaridou-Hatzigoga, Elena Mamoulaki, Efrosyni Plexousaki, Christina Thomopoulos, Kostis Kornetis, Tracey Rosen, Jeremy LaBuff, Jason Fox, Paige Sarlin, Tess Takahashi, and Laliv Melamid. The love and support of Francesca Aquino, Paweł Wojtasik, John Bruce, Steve Holmgren, and Christopher Allen have sustained me at key moments in the process.

The heart and ground of everything is my family: Suzy, John, Kihan, George, Lauren, and the little ones. This book is dedicated to the memory of my father, Kun S. Lee, and to Marc and our new family.

Note on Translation and Transliteration

Foreign quotations, whether from written or oral sources, are translated into English by the author, unless the reference itself is already taken from an English translation and cited accordingly. I also provide my own translation of foreign titles in the bibliography.

In the transliteration of Greek words, I have generally followed the phonetic system used by the Library of Congress with some slight modifications, primarily for visual purposes. In the transliteration of names and place-names, I defer to most common usage as well as to the way that individuals or organizations normally choose to render their names in Latin script.

Introduction

"Is Culture a Luxury?"

"Is culture a luxury?" This was the question posed in a small op-ed concerning the health of Greek cultural institutions that appeared in one of the main daily newspapers in Greece in early October 2009.[1] The op-ed was easy to miss, buried as it was among headlines shouting the more pressing economic and political news of the day: revised assessments of the soaring national deficit, emergency elections amid sustained civil unrest, and early indications of the sovereign debt crisis that would soon consume the country and the rest of Europe. Indeed, that October would prove to be fateful in the now well-known "Greek crisis": emergency elections ushered in a new government whose first order of business was to unveil the full extent of the country's economic troubles and begin negotiations with foreign lenders, starting a crushing cycle of debt and austerity that threw the country into deep depression and has lasted to this day.

Next to such sober matters, the op-ed writer's concerns about a number of arts institutions might have paled in comparison. The author acknowledges as much when, after calling for immediate solutions to the economic and organizational challenges faced by institutions such as the Thessaloniki International Film Festival and the National Film Archive, he writes: "In the brief pre-election campaign, which justifiably turned to economic issues, even references to culture were considered a luxury. But is culture a luxury? In the context of an economy that is struggling for survival, that might be the case. However, this luxury is supposedly one of our strongest weapons and a tool for the development of education."[2]

FIGURE I. 2009 Thessaloniki International Film Festival. Credit: Toby Lee.

In pondering the value of these cultural institutions, the author was participating in a larger public debate over the (in)significance of the arts at a time of economic and political exigency. Artists, critics, academics, and arts professionals, together with politicians, bureaucrats, civil servants, and the wider public, all grappled in different ways with the question of how the arts might justify their continued support by the state—or, as another op-ed a few days later put it, determine "some usefulness so that we might be able to understand, finally, what is culture and what is the job of the Ministry of Culture, which is considered to be the ugly stepchild of every government."[3]

I take up this question by reconsidering the political value of the arts, focusing on cinema as a field of cultural production, at a time when public life is increasingly threatened by the twin pressures of austerity and precarity on a global scale. In a rehearsal of perennial debates over the significance of cultural production, public funding for the arts is once again under fire, cast as superfluous or unnecessary against the backdrop of shrinking state budgets and crumbling social welfare structures. In the United States, the Trump administration's early and sustained attacks on the National Endowment for the Arts, among other agencies, are only the most recent in a long history of battles over state support for the arts. And the debates over public culture that took place in Greece at the onset of the economic crisis were just the beginning, as a massive wave of cuts to arts funding across Europe would soon follow.

In this book, I take a close look at the Greek case, focusing specifically on the world of independent film production and exhibition, starting with the Thessaloniki International Film Festival, one of the country's most important cultural institutions. In 2009, the state-sponsored festival was entangled in larger debates over public arts funding triggered by the country's economic troubles, at the same time that it became the target of a filmmakers' protest movement aimed at overhauling national film policy. The politicization of the Greek film world in those early years of the economic crisis is in keeping with the social history of cinema in Greece, where the independent film world has been variably aligned with the state, European Union (EU) cultural policy, and oppositional movements since the end of World War II. Understanding cinema expansively and diachronically, as a field of cultural production in time, I consider how it served as a site for agonistic encounters between different publics and counterpublics, between divergent political investments and conflicting agendas, and between the state and its citizens. What was often in dispute in these encounters was the "public thingness" of cinema: whether, in what ways, and to what extent cinema is what Bonnie Honig has called a "public thing."[4] At heart, these disputes are contests over the notions of publicness, hierarchies of value, and functions of the state that structure and organize collective life.

The stakes are particularly high in Greece, an apt site for investigating the relationship between state, citizen, and cultural production, and a bellwether of larger social and political dynamics at work around the world. Since 2009, when revelations of the country's insolvency marked the onset of the eurozone crisis, Greece has become the site of dramatic social upheaval, a testing ground for the neoliberal policies of the European Union and a key battlefield for those who oppose them. As successive governments implement deeply unpopular austerity measures dictated by foreign lenders, the state is forced to revise the terms of its social contract with its citizens, and the gap between citizen and state grows. Significantly, in a country where the state has traditionally functioned as the steward and patron of cultural heritage, the relationship between the state and cultural production is also being restructured as part of these struggles. Consequently, the arts have become one of the arenas in which people contest the terms of their engagement with the state and, in the process, renegotiate the terms of collective life. Moving away from a film-centric approach to understanding the politics of cinema, I trace the ways that multiple practices and discourses of publicness, citizenship, and political collectivity are being contested, imagined, and enacted within cinema's institutional and social spaces. Through such a reconsideration of its "public thingness," we may locate the political work of cinema and better understand the value of the arts to public life.

CULTURAL CITIZENSHIP

On a sunny October afternoon in 2009, I caught up with a filmmaker friend in a café overlooking the central square in the northern Greek city of Thessaloniki. Nicoletta was a perpetually active, lively figure who always seemed to be bustling from one project to another: leading film workshops at schools and festivals, teaching in the state film school in Thessaloniki, and working for hire as a filmmaker while also trying to get a half dozen of her own film projects off the ground. As she told me about the latest obstacles to getting her new documentary in production—she had applied for funding from both the Greek Film Center and ERT, the national television channel, but had been turned down by both—she lamented the state of public funding for the arts in Greece more generally. On the one hand, she complained about state institutions like the Film Center and ERT, which she characterized as inefficient bureaucracies and exclusive clubs, both impossible to penetrate. On the other hand, she said that the amount of public funding available was meager to begin with, and the economic crisis, the full magnitude of which was only beginning to become apparent in 2009, would only make the situation worse. Half-jokingly, she threw up her hands in mock surrender and quipped that soon she would have to leave Greece and seek work elsewhere as a "cultural immigrant" (*politismiki metanastis*).

It was a light-hearted remark, shared between friends in a small moment over coffee. We had both laughed at her clever play on the more commonly heard, and more "serious," categories of economic and political migration, which have figured prominently in different periods of modern Greek history and most recently in the ongoing migrant and refugee crisis. Indeed, part of the comic valence of her statement came from the sense of frivolity in the idea of cultural migration, compared to the often very dire circumstances that lead to economic and political migration.

Despite its levity, Nicoletta's statement lingered in my mind as I started to think through its deeper significance. By using the term "cultural immigrant," she was highlighting her relationship as a filmmaker to the Greek state. Underlying her comment was the assumption that the state was responsible for supporting the country's cultural producers, and because it was not providing the conditions necessary for her cultural work, she would have to find another state that would. In this sense, the half-serious notion of the "cultural immigrant" points to its flip side, the figure of the "cultural citizen," and to rather more serious questions of state responsibilities, citizens' rights, and the place of both within cultural economies.

The concept of cultural citizenship has traditionally been understood in a much broader sense. Across a number of disciplines, including film and media studies, cultural studies, sociology, and anthropology, cultural citizenship has come to denote myriad forms of mutual engagement between states and subjects that fall outside the purview of the strictly civil, legal, political, and economic. In one dominant strain of this scholarship, cultural citizenship encompasses "the right to symbolic presence, dignifying representation, propagation of identity, and maintenance of lifestyles."[5] Nick Stevenson adds to this formulation the ideas of "cultural inclusion," "the opportunity to be heard," "rights of communication and dialogue," as well as "the right to be different" and access to "the possibility of lifestyle experimentation and new possibilities for selfhood."[6] Similarly, Renato Rosaldo and the Latino Cultural Studies Working Group understand cultural citizenship in terms of the rights of individuals to cultural difference as protected by the state; here, cultural citizenship means full enfranchisement of cultural minorities, the sense of fully belonging as a member of a polity without fear of cultural oppression.[7]

Another approach understands cultural citizenship in less empowering terms and more as a form of governmentality. In this articulation, cultural citizenship refers to the ways in which individuals learn or are trained to be total subjects of the state, not only legally or politically, but also socially and culturally, and how they take on or resist such training. Writing in this vein, Aihwa Ong argues that the rights-centered understanding of cultural citizenship "attends to only one side of a set of unequal relationships," and offers another definition of citizenship as "a cultural process of 'subject-ification,' in the Foucauldian sense of self-making and being-made by power relations that produce consent through schemes of surveillance, discipline, control, and administration."[8] Toby Miller writes about cultural policy as one such technology of governance, which aims at "the formation of cultural citizens, docile but efficient participants" in capitalist democracies through, for example, state regulation of television, or the institutionalization of literary studies and critical reading practices in secondary education.[9]

The primary difference between these two formulations of cultural citizenship concerns the power dynamics between the citizen and the governing cultural-political system, and where critical attention is focused within those relations of power. As Lok Siu describes it, the first approach "treats cultural citizenship as a process by which subordinate groups assert cultural rights and political claims in society," thus attempting to "transform the cultural-political system by expanding notions of national belonging and political participation," while the second takes cultural citizenship to be a process of subject formation through negotiations between state and subject, in which the balance of power skews heavily toward the former.[10] Despite these differences, what is common to both approaches is a rather broad definition of culture. For example, Ong's definition includes notions of morality, taste, and economic and consumer practices; Miller's encompasses "artistry and ethnicity . . . language, heritage, religion, and identity"[11]; and Rosaldo's is described as "how specific subjects conceive of full enfranchisement,"[12] referring to larger belief or value systems and their attendant notions of respect and dignity.[13]

In this book, I trace a different notion of cultural citizenship. Rather than working from a very broad definition of culture as "morality," beliefs, or value systems, I start from Pierre Bourdieu's more narrowly defined "fields of cultural production," or the social conditions for the production, circulation, and use of symbolic goods, with literature, visual arts, and theater being of primary concern. Each field constitutes a complex system of interests, motivations, forces, conflicts, currencies, values, and goods, as well as the "the structural relations . . . between social positions that are both occupied and manipulated by social agents which may be isolated individuals, groups, or institutions."[14] Taking the world of Greek independent cinema as such a field of cultural production, I examine how it served as a site for multiple forms of engagement—alternately empowered, resistant, complicit, overdetermined, dissenting—between citizens and the state, at a time of intense political turmoil. It is in this sense that I understand the term *cultural citizenship,* as the forms of citizenship—that is, how subjects engage with and position themselves in relation to the state and to political collectivity—that arise where fields of cultural production meet the practices and discourses of the state.

In this delimited sense, cultural citizenship could be seen as resembling "artistic citizenship," a term used in the field of art and public policy to refer to the ways in which artists and their work operate within larger social and political worlds. Some treatments of the concept risk slipping into universalizing humanist terms, conceiving of artistic citizenship as art-making that aligns with vague notions of "civic responsibility" and "virtuous action," contributing to even vaguer notions of "shared humanity," "positive change," and "personal and collective flourishing."[15] A more nuanced and useful elaboration of the concept is offered by Randy Martin, who uses the term "artistic citizenship" to refer to "art's worldly effects" and "the artist's civic capacities," attending not only to their potentialities but also to their inherent frictions.[16] For Martin, the social and political dimension of art's work in the world lies in the dynamic relationship between art and publicness, which is made especially apparent in the case of civic monuments and memorials, public installations and happenings, and other forms of public art that function as "a means to realize and recognize the commons, a medium for people to gather together to reflect on the very idea of being together."[17] Such work brings into high relief the fact that "public making, calling the people together, is one of the operations of art."[18]

Martin goes further, however, by complicating the idea of "public" itself, imagining it as agonistic, representing disparate and even conflicting social and political positions, investments, attachments, and identifications that, when gathered together, "challenge the consensus conception."[19] In this cacophonous public life, the work of artistic citizenship is not to resolve these dissonances but rather "to make these fissures legible as matters available to common rumination."[20] What is more, Martin contends that art has the potential to destabilize our very understanding of publicness. Here again, a useful case is public art. The controversies that tend to surround public art works are often a symptom of their ambiguous status as both "serious," in their associations with the state or in their civic functions, and "frivolous," a "luxury incompatible with republican values."[21] Thus, what is often being contested is not simply the content or thematics of the work in question, but more importantly, the notion of what is properly public in the first place, that is, what rightly deserves public funding and state support, and what should or should not be in public or be considered part of a shared, public life. In this sense, disputes concerning contentious public art works "have much to teach us not simply about how artists are perceived by the public but also about the very nature of what we take *public* to mean."[22]

Martin's formulation of artistic citizenship—as the friction that occurs where art "rubs up against the state" and participates in the creation or contestation of publicness and collectivity—provides a helpful framework for understanding the debates circulating in and around the world of Greek cinema at the onset of the economic crisis.[23] However, I insist on the term "cultural citizenship" rather than artistic to broaden the scope of Martin's underlying terms, which are ultimately limited to the individual artist and the work of art. Decentering the artist-filmmaker and the film as object, art work, or text, I attend instead to the wider sphere of social actors, institutions, and political and economic processes that constitute the cinematic field of cultural production, circulation, and engagement. This book aims to understand how independent Greek cinema, conceived more expansively, served as an occasion for agonistic public-making and for wrangling over the very definition of publicness in relation to the state, citizenship, and collectivity.

My use of the word "cultural" rather than "artistic" also reflects the complexity of the Greek word *politismos,* and the related *politis* and *politeia,* roughly translated as "culture," "citizen," and "polity," respectively. All three derive from the archaic Greek term *polis,* which, often translated as "city-state," in its original usage evoked more the sense of a political entity ruled by its members or citizens, and even the body of citizens itself, rather than the city proper, in the sense of the urban built environment. In Modern Greek, *politis* is defined as "a citizen of a state with all the rights and obligations thereof," but layered onto that definition are the alternate meanings of "inhabitant of a city," "private citizen, as opposed to figures of state/authority," and "nonmilitary civilian." *Politeia* also has multiple, overlapping meanings of "state," "body politic," and "government," with the connotation of "city" or "place." All of these semantic shadings inform the numerous, overlapping definitions of *politismos.* It can be used to mean "civilization," both in the sense of a society or culture in a particular area—for example, the ancient Greek or Egyptian civilizations—and in the more value-laden sense of development, sophistication, refinement, or modernity. It is also commonly used to mean "culture" in the more narrowly defined sense of Bourdieu's fields of cultural production, evident in its common usage as the title for the "Arts and Culture" section of most Greek newspapers; in this sense, it contains the notion of art, *techne,* or the fine arts, *kales technes.* As it is used in the designation "Ministry of Culture" *(Ypourgeio Politismou),* the term expands to include matters such as archaeological heritage; traditional folk music, dance, crafts, and dress; and even sports. Sometimes it is used interchangeably with the word *koultoura,* a Latin borrowing, but *politismos,* unlike *koultoura,* is colored by its etymological association with *polis, politeia,* and *politis* and thus carries the sense of the political, as Hannah Arendt would understand it, as something public, experienced in common and collectively held.[24]

Another distinction that exists in the Greek language, but for which there is no clear corollary in English, is between the adjectives *politismikos* and *politistikos*. They might both be roughly translated as "cultural," but in relation to each other, *politismikos* takes on more of an association with vernacular or popular culture, while *politistikos* refers more to high culture. Traditionally, the Greek state has privileged the latter over the former, allocating significant resources to support the fine and performing arts, classical music, opera, architecture, and prestige forms of literature, theater, dance, and cinema, with a particular emphasis on proximity to the classics, ancient Greek culture, and Western European traditions. This state investment in the arts and cultural heritage has been economically and politically strategic, especially beginning in the late 1970s and early 1980s, as the country developed its tourism infrastructure and began its bid for entry into the European Community in earnest.[25] As cultural producers and institutions came to depend on and even expect this public funding, the role of the state as steward and patron of "high" cultural production in Greece was cemented.

The term "cultural citizenship," as I use it in this book, thus refers to this complex nexus of the state, publicness, and cultural production, in relation to which my friend's comment about "cultural immigration" takes on new meaning. Embedded in her story about the obstacles she faced with her latest film is an expectation that the state should fund her cultural work—indeed, that public funding is the only possible way to get her film made—and this expectation is foundational to her understanding, and her practice, of cultural citizenship. Nicoletta's quip was a response to what was beginning to be felt at that time as an unraveling of this assumed relationship, or social contract, between state and cultural citizen that was most directly associated with the onset of the economic crisis and the shrinking of state budgets, but which, in fact, was part of a larger social and political destabilization, as was the economic crisis itself.

NARRATIVES OF CRISIS

The word "crisis" has come to be so ubiquitous in characterizing life in Greece over the past decade that it has nearly become meaningless, a catch-all term that can refer to everything from sovereign debt, poverty, and austerity to political instability, far-right extremism, and migration.

In *Anti-Crisis*, Janet Roitman takes a critical distance from the term to think through its discursive functions as a "second-order concept." Referring specifically to the U.S. subprime mortgage crisis, she writes: "When does a credit (asset) become a debt (toxic asset)? How do we distinguish the former from the latter? . . . When does the judgement of crisis obtain? We see, by putting these questions to contemporary crisis narratives, how crisis, in itself, cannot be located or observed as an object of first-order knowledge. The observation 'money' is a first-order observation based on a distinction (money/not money); the statements 'I lost money' or 'Lost money is a crisis' are second-order observations."[26] Understood not as an "object of first-order knowledge" but rather as a secondary narrative operation, enabled by and enabling particular understandings of history, the notion of "crisis" occupies a double temporality. It is both "a signifier for a critical, decisive moment" in history, and at the same time a term indicating a "protracted historical and experiential condition . . . an ongoing state of affairs."[27] And the same crisis can be narrated as multiple moments, or as variable histories, depending on who is telling the story, and why.

As the discourse on the "Greek crisis" matures, scholarship has taken up Roitman's terms of analysis, reflecting critically on how the trope of "crisis" and its multiple temporalities condition and shape the production of knowledge concerning the situation in Greece today. In the afterword to *Critical Times in Greece: Anthropological Engagements with the Crisis,* Evthymios Papataxiarchis warns that "when we analytically adopt the term 'crisis,' we indirectly acknowledge the dramatic upgrading of the present vis-à-vis the past that the acceleration of economic and political time has produced. Yet we face the danger of ignoring the historicity of the manifestations of the 'crisis.'"[28] He suggests that we add to our analytical vocabulary Judith Butler's concept of "trouble," which he understands to be "a multi-dimensional trope that allows the simultaneous consideration of many different facets—economic, social, political, ideological, mental/psychological—in the production of antagonism."[29] Rather than indicating a decisive moment, "trouble" stands for a broader "political disorder, materialized in actions destabilizing the normative political arrangements, and producing disarray in the dominant taxonomy of actions, rules, and representations . . . a structural unsettlement of all those powers subsuming individuals in the political order."[30] The important thing about "trouble" is that it "has been around for a long time and that it preceded the 'crisis'" and thus, as an analytical concept, it helps us escape the pre-

sentism of much of the crisis literature and attend to the longer historical processes in which the current moment is positioned.[31] Papataxiarchis argues that attention to "trouble" is an integral part of a balanced
approach to understanding the Greek predicament, one that combines
what he refers to as the "short-term approach," which defines it primarily in terms of rupture or a break with the past, and the "long-term
approach," which considers it in a much longer historical context and
looks for historical continuities and transformations.

This two-pronged approach mirrors my own experience of the "Greek
crisis," which was similarly one of mixed temporalities, comprising both
marked events or moments in time and a growing awareness of broader
conditions with longer histories. While many locate the start of the crisis
in 2010 with the arrival of the International Monetary Fund (IMF) and
other foreign lenders, and others look further back to public revelations
of sovereign debt levels in October 2009, for me the crisis exploded violently into public life when, on the evening of December 6, 2008, fifteen-
year-old Alexis Grigoropoulos was shot and killed by police in the
Exarcheia neighborhood of Athens. What ensued was an unprecedented
eruption of protest and collective rage, led by urban youth, that ripped
across the country. For weeks following the shooting, the streets of Athens and other cities—large and small, on the mainland and the usually
sleepier islands, close to the capital and out in the *perifereies* or more
remote districts—were filled with thousands marching in protest. Students occupied middle schools, high schools, and universities nation-
wide, and teachers' unions and other labor groups called for strikes in
solidarity. While some protests were peaceful, albeit tense, many ended
in rioting and violence, with vandalism of both public and private prop-
erty, hundreds of arrests, and bloody clashes between small armies of
riot police and the infamous *koukouloforoi,* a term meaning "those who
wear hoods," used to describe protesters hiding behind masks or hooded
sweatshirts who are often portrayed, particularly in mainstream media,
as hoodlums responsible for instigating violence. Police responded to
protests and rioting harshly, using tear gas and other chemicals, and
beating protesters, photographers, and journalists, which aggravated
public anger and led to further protests and violence. In the first few days
after the shooting, more than five hundred shops in the centers of Athens
and Thessaloniki were damaged or looted, resulting in an estimated €50
million in damages.[32] Hundreds of protesters and police were injured,
government buildings and police stations were firebombed, cars and
dumpsters burned in the streets, and even the towering Christmas tree in

Athens' central Syntagma Square, directly opposite the Parliament building, was set ablaze in a potent and very public symbol of the outrage
triggered by the teenager's death.

Out of a swirl of rumors, news reports, and counter-reports that circulated in the days following the shooting, the details of what happened
quickly began to emerge: Grigoropoulos, a hard-working student from an
affluent northern suburb, was visiting a friend in the Exarcheia neighborhood when they got caught up in an altercation between two policemen
and a larger group of youth. What began as an exchange of insults became
violent when one of the boys threw a glass bottle in the policemen's direction; one of the cops snapped, drew his gun, and shot into the crowd,
hitting and killing Grigoropoulos, who happened to have been standing
between the police and the larger group. Other versions of the events also
circulated. In an early report, Grigoropoulos was cast as a *koukouloforos,*
anarchist, and troublemaker, the implication being that he was at fault for
provoking the policemen; according to another version, the teenager had
been killed by ricochet bullets from warning shots that were not aimed to
kill. But these reports were quickly dispelled, and the two policemen
involved were eventually found guilty and convicted of murder.

While the police shooting of an innocent teenager was tragic and
unjust, it was not the sole reason behind the widespread civil unrest and
destruction. As the protests continued and grew in intensity, it soon
became clear that the incident had larger social significance, unleashing
broader frustrations and grievances that had been building up over
years. When I arrived in the field in mid-2008, a series of government
scandals dominated headlines, the two largest involving bribery of government officials by the German communications company Siemens
and sweetheart land-swap deals between the state and the Greek Orthodox Vatopedi monastery, both of which implicated figures across the
political spectrum and are estimated to have cost the public billions of
euros. In addition, a series of devastating forest fires the year before had
stoked public outrage over state incompetence, and possible culpability,
that was still palpable. Everyday conversations revealed the general sentiment that such high-level state scandals were part of a much larger
culture of corruption and lack of transparency that characterized the
public sector in Greece. It was widely acknowledged that nepotism, clientelism, and outright bribery were the modi operandi, not just in the
halls of government but in universities, hospitals, courts, and other public agencies and institutions. The circulation of *fakelakia,* or "little
envelopes" full of cash exchanged for services or favors, and the reli-

ance on a *meson,* a family connection or personal intermediary, to ensure a favorable outcome are common when people apply for a permit, vie for a job as a civil servant, or even try to get a medical procedure at public hospitals.

Alongside this acknowledgment of widespread corruption was a simmering frustration, particularly among Greeks in their twenties and thirties, over their lack of earning power and sense of limited professional horizons. The phrase "The 700 Generation" was commonly used to describe highly educated professionals who were only able to find work for which they were overqualified and underpaid, the average salary hovering at about €700 a month. The scarcity of suitable jobs was an early indication of the economic crisis that was already in motion; well before the country's insolvency became public knowledge, people were already feeling the effects of recession in their everyday lives as the economic bubble of the 1990s and early 2000s in Greece quickly deflated. This financial and professional uncertainty, together with the government scandals and entrenched corruption in the public sector, led to underlying frustration with and distrust of the state, which was seen as having abused the country's finances for the benefit of a few elites, and in the process failing to provide for citizens' economic and social welfare. The shooting of Grigoropoulos was a lit match to this larger tinderbox of social discontent, which exploded in public expressions of collective fury.

Greece is no stranger to protest. In a country where political graffiti is ubiquitous, and where national holidays mark dates of historic uprisings and resistance, strikes and public protests can be so common as to seem common*place*.[33] But the sustained unrest in December 2008 and January 2009 was different. It felt unusual in its ferocity, but more importantly, in the kinds of public discourse that grew around and from it. The marches, occupations, and riots were accompanied by an ever-growing discursive field that aimed at collective action and fundamental change in the political and social status quo. In the December 2008 issue of *Synchrona Themata,* a scholarly and political journal published in Athens, an entire section was dedicated to an initial accounting of some of this discursive output, including slogans on protest banners, graffiti, and public statements made by activist groups and professional organizations, as well as individual comments and discussions on blogs, Twitter feeds, Facebook pages, alternative media sites, and both Greek and international websites. In an introduction to this collection of material, the authors argue that this public discourse went "beyond the narrow temporal and geographical boundaries of the event" by harnessing the speed and wide reach of new media and electronic communication for the purposes of resisting state actions and narratives, countering reports made by state-sanctioned mainstream media, and getting people out into the street in organized and coordinated movements.[34] While the authors found that as a whole this discourse was polyphonic, heterogeneous, and even disorderly, expressing a wide range of ideological positions, it was nevertheless coherent in its expression of "the deep feeling of dysphoria in the face of a seemingly 'dead-end' situation, the demand for real sociality, the criticism of commercial and consumer society and a strong anti-establishment attitude."[35]

In the months following the shooting, as this discourse of civic rights and responsibilities emerged online, I noticed that the same themes and language dominated my everyday conversations. Nearly everyone I knew or spoke to was affected directly or indirectly by the political, social, and economic instability that cast an ever-present shadow on all aspects of life: they were either out of work or waiting for late paychecks, struggling through an ill-equipped public education system badly in need of reform, frustrated by clientelism and nepotism, or unable to find adequate medical care. Conversations and interviews would inevitably turn to a discussion of the "uprising" (*exegersi*), the ongoing strikes and protests, party politics, and the shortcomings of the state. Some would talk about the lack of transparency (*diafaneia*) and accountability (*ypefthinotita*) in government and the public sector; others lamented what they saw as the lack of civic participation and a sense of responsibility for collective welfare; and for many, the two went hand in hand. One longtime festival employee addressed the economic crisis in terms that brought together the economy, the state, and the individual:

> All of this is connected to the "kickback," with this mindset of the "*meson.*" Ultimately it's all political—you do things to ensure state support, state money or a public-sector position. In the past, let's say in the 1970s, Greeks had honor [*filotimo*], which had to do with trustworthiness, not cheating other people. Now, Greeks have changed. We've lost this sense of honor, and Greek society has been taken over by this "lifestyle" mentality, consumer culture. . . . While the crisis is economic, it's more of an ethical crisis, that has to do with how you set your priorities, your values.[36]

Notable in his observations is the way in which state and citizen are both seamlessly woven into the larger narrative. In his account, the loss of *filotimo* or honor—that is, an honorable way of dealing with others and living collectively—is part of a larger way of life in which consumerism rules and the relationship between citizen and state has been perverted into one of cynical opportunism and the selfish pursuit of economic advantage. The unethical citizen and the irresponsible state are ultimately to blame for the crisis, an opinion I encountered often during my field-work. Even the political parties themselves strategically adopted the terms of this civic discourse, and in the emergency national elections of October 2009, the center-left opposition party PASOK (Panhellenic Socialist Movement) roundly defeated the incumbent center-right New Democracy party with a campaign built on a rhetoric of transparency and accountability, and a promise to right the relationship between state and citizens.[37]

As is now well known, the PASOK government neither solved the country's problems nor quelled public unrest. Instead, the situation only grew worse. A few weeks after winning the elections, the new govern-ment revealed the true extent of Greece's economic woes, adjusting the projected budget deficit to nearly double that of the previous govern-ment's estimates. The economy soon unraveled, with credit-rating agen-cies quickly downgrading Greek sovereign debt to junk status, and talk of default and bankruptcy starting to circulate. In 2010, the infamous "troika" of foreign lenders—the European Union, the European Central Bank (ECB), and the International Monetary Fund—began to intervene, to much public protest. The 2010 *mnimonio* or memorandum, which spelled out the terms of the EU–ECB–IMF bailout of the Greek govern-ment, was the first in a series of such agreements stipulating harsh aus-terity measures in exchange for funds the country needed to pay its debts to foreign creditors. This cycle of debt and austerity was accompanied by a revolving door of short-lived governments, both elected and appointed, across the political spectrum, adding to the chaos that was overtaking the country. And while Greece officially exited the last of these bailout programs in 2018, the sense of precarity remains, with the country still under EU financial supervision, unemployment levels still high, and the "structural adjustments" imposed by the troika over the past decade continuing to strain everyday life. For the rest of the world, this drama of economic collapse and rescue is what most people think of as the "Greek crisis." However, as is clear from the narrative of crisis I have presented here, within Greece it was experienced equally, and perhaps more importantly, as a manifestation of a larger social and political "trouble," rumbling beneath the surface of everyday life long before the first revelations of the economic "crisis."

TROUBLING THE PUBLIC

At the heart of this trouble was nothing less than publicness itself, in its many dimensions. In *Publics and Counterpublics,* Michael Warner outlines the wide range of possible definitions of the term "public," including "open to everyone," "state-related; now often called public sector," "political," "official," "national or popular," "international or universal," "in physical view of others," "circulated in print or electronic media," "known widely," "acknowledged and explicit."[38] He also lists different definitions of "public" as a noun ("the public," "a public," "the public sphere"), as well as the notion of "publicity . . . not merely publicness or openness but the use of media, an instrumental publicness associated most with advertising and public relations."[39] In the turbulence that followed the events of December 2008, many of these definitions of "public" and "publicness" became topics of heated debate. With the onset of the economic crisis, civil unrest, and the growing civic discourse of responsibility, accountability, and transparency, more people began to think critically about the negative effects of private interests and consumption—economic inequality, state corruption and indifference, clientelism—on the quality of public and collective life. The bailout agreements were also understood in this light, widely seen as both a consequence and a continuation of the dysfunctional relationship between state and citizen. Among the reforms required by the bailouts was a sharp reduction in the size of the Greek public sector, commonly referred to as the *dimosio,* which for decades has been one of the main mechanisms of the clientelistic state-citizen relation.[40] Another unpopular bailout mandate was the privatization of national industries and the selling of state assets, which protesters decried as a fire sale with little oversight, accountability, or concern for the effects on Greek citizens. And those who opposed the bailout agreements more generally accused the "troika," as well as the governments of Western European countries involved in the negotiations, of infringing on Greece's national sovereignty.

In these early stages of the "Greek crisis," it became clear that a larger "trouble" was brewing in the terms and conditions of public, collective, and political life. Significantly, this trouble did not represent a historical rupture but rather was borne of complex and uneven processes of neoliberalization, political and economic Europeanization, and the growth of state patronage that were set in motion in the postwar period. The economic crisis crystallized this trouble and brought it to the surface of social life in debates over the role, function, and reach of the state, both in relation to its citizens and in a larger transnational sphere, as well as the rights of citizens to make demands of the state and their responsibilities to one another. These concerns would eventually carry over into the *Aganaktismenoi* or "The Indignant" movement, which started in May 2011 with a group of protesters occupying Parliament Square in the center of Athens. This was inspired by and in solidarity with other anti-austerity and anti-government protest movements emerging at the time, such as those in Egypt, Spain, and Portugal. What was clear from the rapid rise and proliferation of these mass movements was that the issues at the heart of the "trouble" in Greece—the relationship between state and citizen, the contested value and status of publicness, and the "right" way to live collectively—were concerns that had captured, with urgency, the wider public imagination, not just in Greece but around the world.

Exploring this "trouble" and its reverberations in the world of the arts and cultural production in Greece, I consider the changing conditions of, and possibilities for, public life and political collectivity in the face of neoliberalism's economizing logic. The use of the term "neoliberalism" to name the perceived source of a wide range of frustrations and anxieties has become so prevalent in Greece in recent years as to render the term nearly meaningless. In my use of the concept, I follow Wendy Brown, who understands neoliberalism to be "a distinctive mode of reason, of the production of subjects, a 'conduct of conduct,' and a scheme of valuation" that "configures all aspects of existence in economic terms."[41] While it takes diverse forms wherever and whenever it appears, according to the particular social, cultural, and political context, a universal effect of neoliberalism is that "economic framing and economic ends replace political ones, a range of concerns become subsumed to the project of capital enhancement, recede altogether, or are radically transformed as they are 'economized.'"[42] For Brown, this is equivalent to the gutting of public and political life, as "the foundation vanishes for citizenship concerned with public things and the common good," that is, the "neoliberal vanquishing of *homo politicus* by *homo œconomicus*."[43]

While the neoliberal takeover of public life may appear to be total, diverse resistance movements counter this totalizing view, fighting to preserve, revive, or forge altogether new forms of public life, often by utilizing modes of publicness. For example, an important aspect of recent mobilizations such as the anti-austerity movements in Europe and the Occupy movement in the United States is the use of persistent public appearance and sustained assembly, or the collective exercise of "the right to appear."[44] In her discussion of these movements, Judith Butler emphasizes the significance and power of collective appearance, when bodies gather in space to appear, both to each other and to the world at large. Butler argues that the claims such movements make are "not only spoken or written, but [are] made precisely when bodies appear together, or, rather, when, through their action, they bring the space of appearance into being."[45] Here, Butler draws on Arendt, for whom appearance, or "being seen and heard by others as well as by ourselves," is the basis for the existence of the public realm, without which political action would not be possible.[46] Similarly, this book attends to the various forms of gathering and collective appearing occasioned by cinema and its institutions in the context of the Greek "trouble." Starting with the 2009 Thessaloniki International Film Festival and then moving out from there in both space and time, I investigate the relationship between assembly, appearance, and publicness as they come together in multiple configurations within this field of cultural production. Some configurations enable forms of political collectivity and resistance, as described by Butler. Others, however, actively participate in neoliberal cultural economies, as when the appearance of being public becomes co-opted as symbolic capital by individuals, institutions such as the festival, or the state. Examining the political functions of, as well as people's investments in, different modes of publicness in cinema's social spaces, I attempt to show how the arts and cultural production can variably facilitate and hinder the practice of public life.

One of the modes of publicness under consideration in this book is that of the public sphere, articulated most famously by Jürgen Habermas and subsequently elaborated in numerous alternative formulations, understood as essentially discursive and constituted through communicative rationality and collective deliberation. This normative mode tends to dominate, both within cultural institutions such as the film festival and in scholarship on such institutions. By contrast, the modes of publicness at work in protests arising within the space of the festival or in response to it, both historically and in the early years of the recent economic crisis, are more embodied and performative, aimed precisely at disrupting such reasoned communication. In this, they are closer to what Warner describes as counterpublicness.[47] I am interested in the ways that dominant or sanctioned forms of publicness, predicated on discourse and dialogue, come up against these more unruly, oppositional forms. Key to my understanding of these oppositional publics, and of publicness more generally, is the concept of agonism, or the idea that public life does not tend toward agreement or consensus, but rather is inherently discordant and incomplete. In this, I draw on Arendt's formulation of the public realm as a space of plurality, difference, and contention. Countering the tendency in film and media studies and in public sphere theory to take Habermas as a starting point for discussions of publics and publicness, I apply Arendt's ideas on political collectivity, read through feminist theorists such as Honig and Chantal Mouffe, in thinking about the cinematic field of cultural production, to see how they might better attune us to the value of agonism and dissensus in public life.

Another key concept in this book is Honig's notion of "public things," a term which she uses to refer to the material and concrete elements of a shared world.[48] For Honig, public things such as infrastructure, natural resources, and public institutions are the "holding environment[s]" of public life, objects around which people gather and through which collective life is constituted, "press[ing] us into relations with others" and serving as "sites of attachment and meaning that occasion the inaugurations, conflicts, and contestations that underwrite everyday citizenships and democratic sovereignties."[49] Significantly, the collective life that these things bring into being is characterized not by unity or consensus, but more often by difference and conflict, as people with divergent investments and worldviews tangle over the meaning, management, and future of the world they share. It is precisely in providing opportunities for people to appear to one another, disagree, and contend with each other that such public things foster a robust, democratic public life, and it is this public life that is endangered by the increasing neoliberal privatization of public things. Extending this line of thinking, I ask how cinema might function as such a public thing, and what a consideration of the arts and cultural production might contribute to our understanding of public life.

"IS CULTURE A LUXURY?"

By 2009, the social and economic turmoil that was destabilizing many aspects of everyday life in Greece was having an equally troubling effect on the arts, and the same public sentiments concerning state corruption and incompetence, lack of transparency, and the relationship between state and citizen were circulating in regard to all fields of cultural production. Around the emergency elections in October 2009, numerous articles in the press called attention to major problems within the Ministry of Culture and the severe challenges faced by dysfunctional cultural institutions and initiatives. On September 27, 2009, the newspaper *To Vima* featured a series of articles collectively titled "The open battle-fronts of culture" (*Ta anoichta metopa tou politismou*), examining the state of affairs in various cultural fields: "A ministry in despair" (*Ena ypourgheio se apognosi*), "The theater suffers, money is nowhere to be found" (*To theatro stenazei, to chrima apousiazei*), "The National Opera on a tightrope" (*Ethniki Lyriki se tentomeno schoini*), "A divided climate in cinema" (*Klima dichasmou ston kinimatografo*). Each article pointed not only to the lack of adequate state funding but also to the overgrown and convoluted bureaucratic structures of the Ministry of Culture and the cultural institutions it supports; the apathy of cultural administrators in tenured civil-servant posts; and the static introduced by personal ambition and party politics. Many echoed this sentiment in major newspapers, calling for an overhaul of the ministry, more transparency in its dealings, and increased public funding for the arts.[50] Underlying these demands is the assumption that the state is financially, legally, and administratively responsible for the health of cultural fields. Whether because of the structures of public funding, without which the majority of cultural organizations and institutions in Greece could not survive, or because of policies and legislation, which often determine the parameters within which cultural producers and institutions can function, cultural production in Greece has long been dependent on and inseparable from practices and discourses of the state.

One of the most high-profile cultural institutions to be caught up in this turbulence was the Thessaloniki International Film Festival (TIFF), the largest in the country and a cultural centerpiece of the city, the second largest in Greece after Athens. Begun in 1960 as a small weeklong showcase of Greek films, it is now one of the largest international film festivals in Europe, screening more than two hundred films annually. Alongside a full roster of screenings, master classes, panel discussions, exhibits, and performances, the festival also has a robust Industry Center, which houses a film market, a coproduction forum, and, until 2010, a Balkan script-development competition. Started in 2006, the Industry Center has raised the international profile of the festival and transformed it into a destination for film industry professionals, an important stop on the fast-paced international film festival circuit, with filmmakers, producers, sales agents, distributors, and film programmers from around the world coming to Thessaloniki to watch, buy, and sell films.

In 2009, the year of its fiftieth anniversary, the festival found itself swept up in the larger trouble that was overtaking the rest of the country, in large part because of its close ties with the state. Although a legally independent private entity, it received most of its funding from the Greek Ministry of Culture, and the position of festival director was largely considered to be an unofficial political appointment, with each change of government bringing a new director and key staff.[51] Thus, the unfolding economic catastrophe, political instability, and shrinking of state budgets threatened the festival with financial insecurity and organizational uncertainty. The festival's close connection to the state also made it the target of a high-profile boycott by a large group of prominent Greek filmmakers, including some of the country's most established directors and the most promising among a new generation. Calling themselves "Filmmakers of Greece (FOG)," the group's members decided to withhold their films from the 2009 festival as a protest against what they saw as incompetence, corruption, and lack of transparency in the formation and implementation of national film policy. They vowed to boycott the festival until new legislation was passed to meet their growing demands, which included an overhaul of state funding structures, increased support for domestic film distribution, and improvements in film education. For the festival, the boycott was potentially disastrous, threatening the possibility of a fiftieth anniversary without Greek films, a prospect especially troubling in a year distinguished by Greek filmmakers' breakthrough success at important international festivals abroad.[52]

At the same time that the festival was thus facing crises on multiple fronts, it was also continuing to prepare for its fiftieth edition, a milestone anniversary for this oldest and most important of film institutions in Greece. Despite mounting economic pressure and a larger atmosphere of fiscal restraint taking hold across the country, the festival continued to spend ferociously, planning a full slate of lavish parties, VIP guests, commemorative publications, and special programs and exhibitions. It was as if the festival, annually presented as a celebration of cinema, could not be caught skimping on the most important occasion for celebration in its institutional history. The incongruity between the severity of the national economic crisis and the extravagance of the fiftieth-anniversary events provoked public criticism. Complaints about the festival's budgets and spending were not uncommon before this period, especially after the organization and programming expanded and took a more commercial turn beginning in 2005. However, in the context of the crisis and the newly current discourse of civic responsibility, these complaints became more pointed and insistent, turning into accusations of corruption and waste. These accusations were all the more serious precisely because state funding made up more than two-thirds of the organization's annual income: it was public money that was being wasted. Yet others raised the larger question of whether or not the arts should continue to be funded at all, given the severity of the economic crisis. With steep cuts to state budgets affecting hospitals, schools, and other basic social welfare institutions, many asked the question, "Is culture a luxury?" Underlying the debate over whether or not the arts should be supported by public funding is a more fundamental question concerning the value of the arts and cultural production to public life, and the criteria by which that value is to be determined.

In her defense of the "holding environments" of public life, Honig focuses primarily on the kinds of public things that are more conventionally understood as valuable, necessary, and deserving of collective concern, such as universities, libraries, natural resources, and even the state itself.[53] Traditionally, those who advocate for public arts funding tend to do so by casting the arts in similarly weighty terms, often taking one of two approaches: either essentialist, understanding the arts as national cultural heritage in need of protection, or economic, as a potential source of capital, whether economic or symbolic. The problems with both arguments are especially clear in the Greek context, where the current situation has led to the rise of a fascist political right wing based on notions of ethnic purity, on the one hand, and a disastrous economizing of the relationship between state and citizen, on the other.

This book offers an alternative to such approaches. Looking at how the Greek film world served as an arena for imagining, contesting, and enacting different forms of citizenship and collectivity, I propose an understanding of the arts that rethinks their value in terms of their "public thing-ness," or the particular forms of public life that they enable. In doing so, however, I insist not on the significance of the arts, but rather on their *in*significance within dominant hierarchies of value. With the question "Is culture a luxury?" as starting point, I ask what happens if we take seriously the notion of mereness contained in the oddly dualistic notion of luxury, which connotes something both highly valuable and entirely dispensable. Embracing the oft-maligned mereness of fields of cultural production, I propose that it is precisely this distance from the supposedly more "serious" and "consequential" areas of social life that might allow them to harbor more radical, agonistic, and dissenting forms of collectivity. Under the twin pressures of austerity and precarity wrought by neoliberalization, fields of cultural production may offer alternative forms of public life appropriate to these troubled times.

The chapters that follow represent a selective itinerary through one such field, the world of independent Greek cinema, starting with the Thessaloniki Film Festival as a central point of orientation in my navigation of this troubled terrain. Chapter 1 serves as an introduction to the festival as an event and as an institution, situating it in a larger social, cultural, and political landscape, as well as in longer histories of cinema, cultural policy, modernization, and Europeanization in Greece in the twentieth and twenty-first centuries. In thus locating the festival in space and time, this chapter also traces the complex ways in which different publics and forms of publicness have intersected with multiple scales of circulation, significance, and cultural economy over the course of the institution's history.

Chapter 2 takes a closer look at how some of these publics and forms of publicness come together within the festival, focusing on the fiftieth-anniversary edition. While the festival is a space for a multiplicity of publics, I discern a particular and singular form of publicness that dominates interactions within that space, leaving little room for oppositional practices, overt conflict, or unruliness. In 2009, many of the crises that the festival was facing, including the filmmakers' boycott, were largely swept under the rug, and this avoidance of conflict was particularly conspicuous in the larger context of protests and uprisings taking over the rest of the country. Here, Arendt's understanding of public life as agonistic and discordant helps to illuminate the distinctions between the forms of publicness active in the festival and the stakes of their varying deployment.

In the past, agonism and conflict had played an important role at key points in the festival's history, particularly in the 1970s and 1980s, when the festival was a space of political opposition, resistance to the military dictatorship, and a growing counterculture. Chapter 3 examines some of these past moments through the lens of how the history of the festival was variably remembered by different individuals, groups, and the institution itself on the occasion of its fiftieth anniversary. Drawing out the differences between these divergent practices of historiography and collective memory, I consider how the remembering of past conflicts and forms of "counterpublicness" functions as an intervention in the present moment, reintroducing agonism and agonistic collectivity as valued terms in the context of the larger civil unrest growing at the time, and more specifically in relation to the FOG boycott.

Chapter 4 focuses on this boycott and the filmmakers' larger protest movement. Analyzing the group's activities as well as their rhetoric, I discuss the movement as a counterpublic practice, part of the larger climate of protest and collective resistance that has taken root in Greece since the beginning of the economic crisis. In the context of the film festival, the protest had the effect of reviving that historical sense of the festival as a space for the practice of an oppositional cultural citizenship and agonistic collectivity. However, the movement's ultimate capitulation to the economizing logic of the neoliberal state had the effect of undermining and limiting its counterpublic impulse. Following the emergence and dissolution of the filmmakers' protest movement, I consider what forms of citizenship and publicness were being proposed, enacted, and obstructed in the process.

In the closing chapter, I return to the question "Is culture a luxury?" by elaborating on Honig's theorization of "public things" and applying the concept to fields of cultural production. In particular, I look at some of the more recent developments in the arts in Greece, particularly the growing importance of private foundations and large cultural institutions, such as *documenta 14* in Athens in 2017, in contrast to smaller and less visible art and film initiatives. I then discuss at length an example of one such small initiative, an annual documentary workshop in Athens. Reflecting on the particular social world and forms of collectivity the workshop engenders, as well as its position in larger cultural economies, I consider how the public and political value of the arts and cultural production may lie precisely in their mereness.

A WORD ON METHODOLOGY

Since I began traveling to Greece in 1999 as a student of Modern Greek, I have witnessed the country undergoing a series of rapid and dramatic transformations: from the sudden economic and social changes following the country's entry into the eurozone in 2001; to the economic bubble of the first half of the 2000s; to the post–2004 Olympics euphoria; and the economic, social, and political instability of the past ten years. Specifically, this book is based on twenty-two months of fieldwork that took place in Thessaloniki and Athens between 2005 and 2010, with the bulk of the research taking place in 2008–10. My primary methodology was sustained participant observation, which allowed for a closer look at the complex and meaningful micro-interactions that take place within the social space of the festival and the larger field of cultural production in which it is located. It also afforded a sense of social familiarity that facilitated more intimate conversations with fieldwork subjects, which I supplemented with formal interviews. The main portion of my fieldwork was greatly shaped by a decision I made early on concerning the direction of my research. Having started in the festival's main offices in Athens, I quickly realized that I was less interested in what would usually be considered the "center" of the institution—the offices, core staff, the work of the festival director, programming decisions—and more in what might be considered its "periphery," where the festival interacts with the other institutions, businesses, individuals, and publics that constitute the broader social and cultural field in which it operates.

As I developed close relationships with people in the field, learning about their deeply personal ties to the festival, the dynamic between individual and institution also became an important part of my research. People's personal histories of the festival, their loyalties, and their professional, political, and emotional investments all put flesh on the bones of institutional structures, constituting the institution as lived experience. This is tricky terrain, where the personal and the political are mapped onto each other, and in learning to navigate this, I not only became acutely aware of the intensely political nature of social life in Greece, in the sense of both party politics and micro-politics, but also had to become a political being myself, carefully considering my alignments, how they might be perceived, and what doors would open or close accordingly. Although my position as a foreign academic afforded me some neutrality, there were moments when my inquiries were met with silence or politely declined; in some cases, these silences were telling in and of themselves, and I learned to listen for and incorporate them, when possible, in my analysis. As an academic, I also shared a connection with the considerable number of scholars who work in or around the festival, and an important part of my fieldwork comprised long conversations with these subjects, colleagues, and friends. Together, we discussed and debated the topics and questions considered in this book, which owes a great deal to their insights and generosity.

CHAPTER I

Locating the Festival

First encounters, in retrospect, always seem fateful. My first brush with
the Thessaloniki International Film Festival was far removed in both
space and time from the troubled cultural terrain of austerity-era Greece,
but that early experience left me with lasting impressions and larger questions that would later become central to my investigations of that terrain.
That first encounter took place in the spring of 2000, when an abridged
version of the festival's Greek and Balkan programs from the previous
year was traveling around the world and made a stop at New York's
Anthology Film Archives. I had recently started studying Modern Greek
language and culture, and a professor had suggested that I attend one of
the screenings as an exercise in language immersion. It was thus that I
found myself in a dark theater in the East Village, watching *See You in
Hell, My Darling* (1999), an obscure film by Greek cult director Nikos
Nikolaidis. The film—a bizarre, noirish erotic thriller with little plot and
lots of shock value—certainly left an impression, but what I found most
striking was the screening itself, and the fact that such an obscure Greek
film was playing to a full house in a theater far from the traditionally
Greek immigrant neighborhoods in and around New York. Looking
around at the audience, I began to wonder what kind of public was being
constituted in that moment. How were linguistic and cultural identity,
shared history, and notions of ethnicity and nationality intersecting
with transnational aesthetic traditions, viewing practices, and forms of

FIGURE 2. Opening night. Credit: Toby Lee.

cinephilia? What was the particular sense of social or cultural collectivity that was being forged in the process? And in what ways did this public shift as the program traveled from Thessaloniki to London, New York, Chicago, and Los Angeles, its itinerary mapping the Greek diaspora?

Thus, my first experience of the Thessaloniki festival crystallized two important ways in which international film festivals operate. On the one hand, they articulate scales of circulation and belonging, functioning as points of connection or conflict between the local, the national, the regional, and the global. On the other hand, they gather complex publics, serving as spaces for negotiating diverse forms of publicness and collectivity. In this chapter, I attend to these two operations as I introduce the Thessaloniki Film Festival as event and institution. Tracing the festival's entanglements with local, national, and transnational histories of cultural production, modernization, and Europeanization, as well as histories of publics and public life as these have evolved in Greece over the past half-century, this chapter highlights the complex nature of the institution and its position in the country's cultural landscape. On another level, this chapter also begins to sketch the outlines of a larger relationship between notions of scale and publicness, to be elaborated in subsequent chapters.

TANGLED LOCALITIES

In the years following that initial encounter at Anthology, with my curiosity piqued by the questions it raised, I began to research the Thessaloniki festival in earnest. This research would lead me to return to the festival year after year, each time deepening both my engagement with the institution and my appreciation of its social and cultural complexity. By the time I arrived in Greece for a more extended period of research, in the lead-up to the festival's landmark fiftieth anniversary, I had come to understand it as being much more than the relatively bounded, coherent event that it is understood to be in popular conceptions of film festivals. Far beyond films and screenings, the festival marks a sprawling and variegated social space, defined as much by its porous periphery as by its supposed centers, and crisscrossed by diverse agendas and investments—social, cultural, political, and economic—that connect it to other spaces, times, and fields of discourse and practice. To help get our bearings, I begin this introduction with an ethnographic "tour" of its 2009 jubilee edition, deliberately focusing on spaces, practices, and institutional structures rather than films, screenings, or programming in order to focus on the festival as a larger social field.[1] By no means comprehensive or exhaustive, this tour is meant to serve as an entry point into a field site that, compressed as it is both spatially and temporally, can feel dense and disorienting. At the same time, the tour also aims to trouble our sense of place and location, bringing into relief the festival's complicated relationship to space and scale.

Given this latter aim, it is fitting that our tour starts rather far from Thessaloniki: about 300 miles south, in the center of Athens. Here, in the festival's main offices, the staff are busy packing large cardboard boxes with DVDs, stacks of folders, binders, books, posters, hard drives, even computer towers and monitors. With less than a week before the festival is to begin, the organization is not moving office, at least not permanently. Rather, they are preparing for their yearly migration north, when the Athens branch of the festival organization—which includes the offices of the festival director, all the major programming departments, the film market, the coproduction forum, the script-development fund, publications, and domestic and foreign press offices—packs up and relocates north. Joining the festival departments that are permanently located in Thessaloniki, including the production team, public relations, and educational programs, the Athens staff set up in rented offices, move into hotel rooms, and settle in for the duration of the festival, only to pack up again at the end and return to Athens.

Thus, we begin with a story of center and periphery: Athens, definitively the cultural, economic, and political center of Greece, bursting with more than a third of the country's population, and Thessaloniki, less than a third of the size of Athens, pushing up against the country's far northern border. In Greece, Athens is the dominant, unmarked category. While one often hears Peloponnesians stereotyped as being shrewd and cunning, Cretans as proud and violent, and Thessalonicans as laid back or even lazy, one is hard-pressed to come up with such blanket characterizations of Athenians. It is not unusual for Athenian friends and acquaintances to tease me about my slight Thessaloniki accent, with its drawn out *l*'s and grammatical shortcuts, but one rarely hears such remarks going in the opposite direction. In most respects, Athens is assumed to be the standard, the center against which Thessaloniki, the country's second-largest city, is often marked as provincial *(eparchiaki)* and peripheral *(perifereiaki)*. But with the festival staff in Athens hurriedly preparing for their annual trip north, we see that this story of center and periphery is not a static one, as the center moves to the periphery, literally but also figuratively, with Thessaloniki taking over as the center of festival operations, and the center of the Greek film world, for the ten days of the festival's duration.

Within Thessaloniki, the festival has its own centers and peripheries. One center is undoubtedly the Olympion, the institution's main building, located at one of the most prestigious addresses in the city, on central Aristotelous Square overlooking the waterfront. The Olympion houses the festival's Thessaloniki offices, which are open throughout the year and primarily handle the logistics of festival production, as well as the year-round screenings in the building's two theaters. The main theater is a stately, old-fashioned cinema that goes by the same name as the building itself. Spacious, with everything lined in sumptuous red velvet, two levels of balconies, a large stage, and crystal chandeliers, the Olympion theater is the most coveted of the festival's spaces for screenings and presentations. On the fifth floor of the building is a smaller screening space, named after the festival's founder, Pavlos Zannas. Also on the fifth floor is the entrance to a fashionable café with an impressive view of the square and the sea beyond, which serves as a meeting place not only for festival-goers but for stylish city residents year-round. Throughout the year, the building tends to see a steady stream of people, owing to the almost nightly screenings in the two screening halls; the various educational programs, conferences, meetings, and workshops that take place there, either organized by the festival or by other organizations renting space from the festival; and the regular flow of Thessaloniki residents who frequent the building's two cafés. But during the ten days of the festival, the Olympion is busier than ever. The production, logistics, and accounting teams are located in offices on the upper floors, and the most important events of the festival—opening and closing ceremonies, screenings of films with top billing, the awards ceremony, and special events honoring the most important festival guests—all take place in the Olympion theater. On numerous occasions during each festival, the lobby becomes packed with standing-room only crowds awaiting a film or hoping to slip into a particular ceremony. At other times, it fills with photographers and television crews awaiting stars and special guests: directors, producers, politicians, the heads of major local businesses and organizations, and socialites who make their way past the crowds outside and down the red carpet.

However, it was not at the Olympion that I started my day on the morning of November 13, the first day of the 2009 festival. Well before the commotion of the opening ceremony that would officially mark its beginning later that evening, I made my way to a small public high school, half-hidden on a quiet pedestrian street a few blocks east of Aristotelous Square. There, a handful of graffiti artists were busy spray-painting a large, colorful mural onto a wall enclosing the school yard. One artist was painting a tower of old television monitors, with eyes peering out from the screens; another was outlining blocky letters that spelled out "CINEMA." At the far end was spray-painted "50th Thessaloniki International Film Festival," together with the 2009 festival slogan, "Why Cinema Now?" The artists, speckled and smeared in colorful paint, wielding aerosol cans and dirty rags, made for an odd sight in the morning light. People on their way to work paused to do a double take, while others, holding bags of groceries or strings of worry beads, lingered, looking puzzled. A woman stopped to take photographs of the developing mural, and she asked one of the artists what they were doing, to which he replied, "We're part of the film festival." She raised her eyebrows in slight confusion, took a few more pictures, and went on with her day.

Indeed, they were part of the film festival. Before the opening ceremony, before any guests had arrived, even before a single film had been screened, one of the festival's sidebar programs, called "Street Cinema" (*O kinimatographos stous dromous tis polis*), had already started popping up around Thessaloniki. Conceived especially for the fiftieth-anniversary edition, Street Cinema was a program in which the festival commissioned local art, music, and performance groups to stage happenings and installations in public spaces throughout the city, starting a few days prior to the opening of the festival and extending through the full ten days. As I will discuss in more detail in the following chapter, the program was designed to strengthen and make more visible the connections between the festival and its host city, and to foster a greater sense of public engagement, or at least an appearance of it, particularly at a time when it was facing criticism for what many perceived as its lack of engagement with issues of increasing concern to the public. Street Cinema was one of countless such sidebar programs that year which gave the festival its sprawling character, blanketing the city with events and exhibits, some of which seemed only tangentially, if at all, related to cinema, and which were often produced in conjunction with many other local, national, and international organizations and agencies. These sidebar programs included art, photography, video, and even jewelry exhibitions in venues throughout the city; a full schedule of concerts, talks, master classes, roundtables, and open discussions; an environmental program that included participatory public art works, tree-plantings, and recycling and green transportation initiatives; and student volunteer programs organized with local educational institutions. Given this size and spread, not uncommon for the festival but notably increased for its fiftieth anniversary celebrations, it is no wonder that the average attendee would have trouble getting her bearings and navigating the festival, or even discerning its boundaries.

Anticipating the crowds that would soon overtake the festival, I left the graffiti artists and quickly made my way to the accreditations office to pick up my badge. The office is located on the city's old port, or *palio limani*, which for most of the year occupies a rather peripheral position, about half a kilometer west along the waterfront from Aristotelous Square. On a long strip of land reaching out into the Thermaic Gulf, a series of renovated warehouses sit on either side of a cobblestone street, administered by the municipality and the Thessaloniki Port Authority. For most of the year, these warehouses remain empty; foot traffic in the old port is limited to the occasional visitor to the Cinema Museum, Photography Museum, or the small Center for Contemporary Art, which are housed in some of the renovated warehouses. But every year since 1999, the festival has rented the empty warehouses for a couple of weeks each November, transforming the usually sleepy *limani* into a buzzing center of operations. Some of the warehouses are used for screenings, master classes, panel presentations, and open discussions, while another houses the offices of the Athens staff and serves as the administrative and social hub of the festival. Here, we find the office of the festival director, all the programming departments, publications, the press office, print traffic, accreditations, and guest services, as well as a large, airy café that serves as one of the main gathering spots for both staff and festival-goers. The cavernous ground floor of this warehouse—lined with the information kiosks of Greek television channels, film organizations, and funding bodies—serves as the stage for press conferences, as well as for the main concerts and parties that take place throughout the course of the festival. With the festival occupying so much of the old port, the *limani* becomes one of the city's most bustling areas, with audiences streaming in and out throughout the day; staff members hurriedly shuttling between warehouses; news crews roaming the cobblestone streets; and industry professionals, such as producers, directors, sales agents, and distributors, making their way from one meeting to another. Vendors set up stands selling roasted chestnuts and hot spiced drinks; teenagers pass out flyers for concerts, parties, and local businesses; and festival-goers meet friends and see familiar faces at screenings, at the various cafés temporarily set up in the warehouses, and in passing on the street. Thus, the picturesque port, which usually occupies a peripheral position in the city's social and cultural landscape, is transformed into a central location for the festival.

At the accreditations office, I met a film sales agent from Germany and a screenwriter from Bulgaria, who are were also there to pick up their badges, and together we walked over to the Industry Center, housed that year in a large warehouse at a distance from the others. Inaugurated in 2005, the Industry Center is an umbrella department whose primary purpose is to support and foster the business of filmmaking, which it does through a number of industry-oriented activities and services aimed at film professionals from Greece, throughout Europe, and around the world. In 2009, these included the Agora, or Film Market, where the 250 films showing at the festival that year, plus a handful of films selected only to be part of the Market, were available for viewing by accredited industry professionals to facilitate sales of both Greek and international films to domestic and international markets. Another Industry Center program that year was the Balkan Fund, a script-development competition open to film projects with directors or producers from Balkan countries; in 2009, ten films were competing for a number of cash prizes, as well as introductions to potential funders, coproducers, sales agents, and distributors. In the Crossroads Co-production Forum, which supports Mediterranean and Balkan films in more advanced stages of production, filmmakers from seventeen different projects were given the opportunity to pitch their films to a variety of industry professionals, with one project ultimately chosen to receive a cash award and free accreditation in the Producer's Network program at the 2010 Cannes Film Festival. Finally, in the Salonica Studio program, part of the EU MEDIA Program's educational initiatives, students from film schools across Europe participated in an intensive workshop to develop and attempt to secure funding for their proposed projects, with access to all the resources of the larger Industry Center.

But all of these activities, events, meetings, and competitions were still to come. When we arrived on that first day, the warehouse was nearly empty and the Center was still being built. A construction crew was erecting walls to partition off rooms and offices in the raw, open space; an electrician was wiring lighting fixtures and outlets; another work crew was setting up furniture, computers, and the Film Market's complicated audio-visual equipment; all while Industry Center staff members gathered in whatever cleared spaces were available to prepare for the crowds that would soon arrive. Looking onto this scene, I was reminded of the previous year's festival when, working as a volunteer for the Balkan Fund, I had witnessed a similar scene, greeting guests and handing out information packets while construction crews were still hard at work. This last-minute scramble is an annual phenomenon, as the festival does not own these spaces but rather rents them year after year, usually for the minimum amount of time possible in order to save money. Similarly, staff members from Athens also travel north at the last moment possible, usually just a day or two before the festival opening, or sometimes even that same day, and as soon as the festival comes to a close, they return to Athens, and these spaces are once again disassembled.

The Industry Center crystallizes the festival's complicated sense of locality and its tangled relationship to place and geographical scale. To begin, it is here that the festival's international character is most evident. In the programs and activities that it houses, we can see the concrete ways in which the festival is embedded in networks of circulation at scales beyond the local and the national. For the international film industry professionals who frequent the Center, particularly from the Balkan and Mediterranean regions, the festival functions as a crossroads of diverse global currents of media, people, ideas, and capital. For the same reason, the Center has great national significance, as it annually presents one of the most important opportunities for Greek film industry professionals to access sources of funding and other support for domestic film production. For both of these constituencies, the Center puts Thessaloniki on the map professionally. However, as we see in the above scene of construction crews hard at work on opening day, the Center's location and its relationship to its host city are anything but straightforward, split as it is between Thessaloniki and Athens. What is clear from this initial glance at the Industry Center, and from this introductory snapshot of the festival more broadly, is the extent to which the festival is a much larger and more multifaceted phenomenon than simply a film exhibition event, with complex social, economic, and political dimensions. Each stop on this ethnographic "tour" demonstrates how various forms and scales of operation, circulation, and identification become entangled within the space of the festival.

HISTORIES OF SCALE

In the last fifteen years, the field of film festival studies has emerged to provide a scholarly language for thinking critically about such a complex phenomenon. This interdisciplinary field has developed in response to the rapid growth of film festivals around the world; their growing social, political, and economic significance; and their increasingly important role in all aspects of the global film industry and film culture, from distribution, exhibition, and practices of spectatorship and cinephilia, to the development, financing, and production of films themselves. One of the earliest publications in this new field, Thomas Elsaesser's "Film Festival Networks: The New Topographies of Cinema in Europe," articulates many of the terms and concepts that have come to dominate the literature. Elsaesser's essay considers the international film festival in the context of a larger discussion of what he refers to as the "post-national" in contemporary European cinema—in other words, the nation understood not in essentialist or constructivist terms but as a "second-order concept," a set of ideas and practices "reintroduced for external use, so to speak, while suspended within the European Union."[2] For Elsaesser, the international film festival functions as yet another site of the post-national. Although he acknowledges that film festivals began in the first half of the twentieth century as nationalist vehicles, he states that they have since developed into an international network that provides "another way of transcending the national for European films."[3] Taking up the vocabulary of modern systems theory, Elsaesser considers the role of the festival as a node in a network or circuit, emphasizing the "network effects that international film festivals now realize for the global media markets," in the functioning of film and tourism industries, but also in the formation of audiences and aesthetic expectations and evaluations.[4] While he does attend to the relationship between festivals and their historically specific locations, it is the global network that is of primary concern to Elsaesser, who focuses on aspects of the film festival that can be considered systemic, shared by all festivals within the network, or even necessary to the functioning of the network as such.

This emphasis on the global characterizes much of the early foundational research on film festivals, evidenced by a quick look at the *Film Festival Yearbook,* an annual collection of festival scholarship. The inaugural edition (2009) takes as its overarching theme "The Festival Circuit," and its editors state that their goal is to move "above and beyond specific socio-geographical dimensions" and focus "primarily on the international dynamics of festivals, on defining the place of festivals in international film distribution, exhibition, and production, and on identifying the underlying forces that drive the growth of the festival phenomenon within the system of global culture."[5] The second edition (2010), employing the theme "Film Festivals and Imagined Communities," similarly emphasizes the "global view" in its focus on diasporic communities and "a wider range of transnational formations related to the economics and the politics of those film festivals engaged in promoting a cause or a concept that transcends state borders through assisting the circulation of moving images in supranational spheres."[6] While sharing this emphasis on the global network, other early contributors to the field qualify it in important ways. For example, Julian Stringer highlights the uneven power dynamics that characterize this network, envisioning it not as a system of smooth flows, connections, and exchanges, but rather as one in which prestige, value, and access to capital are continuously being contested—a "contact zone for the working through of unevenly differentiated power relationships."[7] Similarly, Marijke de Valck sees the festival circuit as comprising "unequal geopolitical power relations," an instantiation of what Michael Hardt and Antonio Negri describe as the new deterritorialized and heterogeneous spatial order that nevertheless continues to be determined by the exercise and contestation of power and dominance.[8] My own approach to the Thessaloniki Film Festival is to see it as such a contact zone or space of contestation, where identities and investments across the scales of the local, national, and transnational encounter each other, variably falling into alignment, coming into conflict, or becoming otherwise articulated with each other in complex ways.[9]

Greece is a particularly apt place for considering such entanglements of scale. Here, the agonistic negotiation of varying interests, identities, and publics across the local, regional, and global has had a long history, and narratives of national history and identity have often been constructed as much for foreign as for domestic consumption.[10] Since the late eighteenth century, the very idea of modern Greece as an independent national entity was largely determined by ideas, interests, and forces that were bred and set in motion from faraway, in the intellectual centers of Western and Central Europe and Russia. The struggle to establish a sovereign Greek state was driven by an imported ideology, a combination of Romantic nationalism and a fervor for a classical Greek ideal, elaborated and promoted by Greek scholars and writers who, while living and studying abroad, were exposed to Enlightenment ideas and inspired by the French Revolution. Their vision for a Greek nation-state, liberated from Ottoman rule, was centered on an assumed (or actively constructed) continuity between present-day Greeks, on the one hand, and the glorious cultural and political heritage of ancient Greece, on the other.[11] While this vision conflicted with native, "Romeic" understandings of Greek identity—a nationalist ideology that centers on the importance of Orthodox Christianity, as well as linguistic and cultural forms that developed over four centuries of Ottoman rule—it was supported by European philhellenes and intellectuals of the Greek diaspora, and served as the ideological basis for the Greek War of Independence (1821–32).[12] The notion of cultural continuity between modern and ancient Greeks was offered not only as a justification for Greece's independent statehood; Greek intellectuals and the political elite also hoped that the attainment of sovereignty based on this ideology would allow Greece to claim a position in the Europe, understood as both political entity and cultural ideal, that was taking shape in the eighteenth and nineteenth centuries. As Michael Herzfeld notes, "the partially western origins of their vision hardly dismayed the Greek intellectuals, for whom all European wisdom was Greek by definition and derivation."[13] By thus arguing their way into the origin myths of Europe, the intellectual leaders of the Greek Revolution were positioning the fledgling nation in two places at once, both temporally and spatially: on the cusp of modernity and at the heart of an ancient origin, at the margins of Europe and at its very center. In this double vision, Greece is presented both as a culturally specific national entity and as the source of a transnational, even universal, cultural legacy; indeed, it is precisely this universal legacy that is offered up as the culturally specific justification for Greek sovereignty. Ultimately, it was only with the diplomatic intervention and military and financial support of foreign powers that the Ottomans were defeated and a tenuous political stability was established. Thus, the emergence of Greece as a modern nation-state was predicated on the complicated intertwining, on the one hand, of local cultural and historical specificity, and on the other, ideologies and aspirations, interests and interventions, that were foreign in origin and transnational in scope.

Such complex articulations of the local, national, and transnational have continued to characterize Greek history over the past two centuries, owing to the country's precarious but strategic position between Europe and Asia, on the doorstep of the Middle East and North Africa, as a front in the Cold War, and most recently on the frontlines of the eurozone and global migration crises. Time and again, Greece has served as a critical site not only for foreign and international investments and mobilizations, but also for local investments in and mobilizations of "the foreign" and "the international." These entanglements of scale shifted and intensified in the 1970s and 1980s, as the country emerged from the shadows of World War II, the Greek Civil War (1946–49), and the far-right military dictatorship (1967–74), and began to orient itself to a changing Europe, joining the European Community in 1981. That same year, the election of the social-democratic PASOK government marked the beginning of a broader national project of modernization and Europeanization, political and economic, but also cultural. If, in the early nineteenth century, it was an ancient cultural heritage that was leveraged to support the young nation's claims to modernity, then in the late twentieth century the state also began to mobilize contemporary cultural forms to stake out a place in an increasingly integrated Europe, by bringing itself up to speed and into alignment with public culture and cultural policy in the European Union.[14]

The Thessaloniki Film Festival is emblematic of this larger project of cultural Europeanization and the entanglement of scale that this project represents more generally. From the very beginning, in the festival's prehistory and the story of its inception, we can see the coarticulation of the local, national, and transnational at work. Originally, the festival was a project of the Macedonian Art Society "Techni" (*Makedoniki Kallitechniki Etaireia "Techni"*), a local organization formed in Thessaloniki in 1951 by a small group of academics, writers, artists, and intellectuals who wanted to revive the arts and public culture in their city after the ravages of World War II and the Greek Civil War. The two wars in quick succession had not only damaged the country economically, politically, and infrastructurally, but they had also weakened public life and frayed the social fabric. Zannas, an early Techni member, described the initial motivations of the Society's founders: "It started with the idea that within its ranks would gather the art-loving public of Thessaloniki, and that this public must fight for Thessaloniki to achieve an artistic and intellectual life, which it did not have. At the same time, it must demand that the State develop intellectual activity in this city which always has the large and grandiose title *co-capital,* but which was and unfortunately still is a province in relation to Athens."[15] Zannas's description makes clear the imbrication of the local and the national: by fostering the arts in the city, Techni wanted to help create a stronger and more active local public and cultural life, but specifically in order to raise the city's national profile, and significantly as a project of the state. Also important to note here is another kind of imbrication, that of geopolitical scale and different notions of publicness: the cultivation of a local public is seen as the means by which to achieve national standing, which requires public funding and other forms of state support.

Zannas is a key figure in the history of the Thessaloniki festival, which he is generally credited with envisioning and inaugurating. His involvement in the Techni Art Society and in the founding of the festival introduces another scale, that of the European, into the story. Zannas, whose family was originally from Thessaloniki, returned to his hometown in 1954 after living and studying in Geneva for seven years. As a student abroad, he had been immersed in the burgeoning culture of cine-clubs and film festivals that blossomed in Western Europe in the postwar period, and his goal upon returning to Thessaloniki was to develop a local film culture along the lines of what he had experienced in Geneva. To that end, he joined Techni and, under its auspices, started a local cinema club in 1956. Just as the goal of the Society was "the organization of regular cultural events, in order to create a sensitized public," similarly Zannas's primary motivation in starting a cinema club was "the formation of an informed and cultivated cinema public."[16] In a 1988 interview, Zannas describes the cinema club, or *leschi,* at length:

I remember well how the Cinema Club started. A second-run theater offered us the opportunity to hold screenings in the evening. Thus we were able to invite people to come watch films at 10 in the evening. And because it was of course a good time for the socialites but also for the students, on opening night the cinema was packed. Socialites were all mixed up with non-socialites, and there were the ladies who thought that finally they would see the important films with Hollywood stars. But they found themselves in front of a black and white movie that startled them: *Los Olvidados* by L. Buñuel. Maybe it was too strong and hard a dose for the first contact. One lady fainted and had to be taken outside. Nevertheless the public that filled the theater ensured the success of the events. And the screenings continued.

The Club went through many hard times. Sometimes the theater was full, and then suddenly it would empty. You had the feeling that the public wasn't following. You would present great classic works of silent cinema and the public would sulk. They didn't understand why they had to put up with three hours of a film by Griffith or a masterpiece by Eisenstein. They didn't yet have the education/knowledge. They hadn't yet understood what these works meant for the history of cinema. At one point, I held a screening and only two spectators came. I insisted and the screening continued. Of course, at the end, the three of us in the theater discussed the film.

Gradually, the changing public—because each year we had 200–300 new member registrations and primarily many students—became familiar with cinema. The introductions [to the films] were written with greater attention and care. The public, which at first was "stuck," started to participate in the discussions and become more of an important presence. . . . Sometimes the Club had very few members, sometimes it had many. The last few years, the following that attended the screenings exceeded 200 or 300, even 400 members. And I admit that it made an impression on me when, after many years, I heard experienced directors telling me that they learned many things about cinema attending those screenings.[17]

What is most striking about the way Zannas describes the *leschi* is the extent to which he narrates its history and significance in terms of its public. His memory of opening night is dominated by his impressions of the audience and their reactions, and he measures the club's success and the various stages in its development by the size of the public and the level of engagement of its members, both with the films but also with each other in postscreening discussions. On occasion, he even ran the club like a classroom, showing a film twice and presenting an analysis of the film illustrated with slides between the first and second screenings, or giving lectures on film form or production.[18] He stated that the goal of the club was to make possible "a 'cinematic edification' of the public, which will learn to distinguish (and to support) good cinema."[19] Zannas also understood the role of film criticism, particularly as published in Techni's monthly journal, to be similarly pedagogical. The inaugural issue states that the goal of criticism is "to educate. To guide the public in the difficult realm of art, to orient it and to sharpen its artistic sense."[20] In the same issue, Zannas writes, "We hope that the film criticism which will happen in this column . . . will help the friends of Cinema to watch the films that are shown in our city with a more critical eye and with more artistic criteria."[21] While Zannas was in many ways a classic cinephile for whom a critical cinema and the language of film were of utmost importance, it is also clear that for him, creating a knowledgeable, critical public around and through the films was just as important. Significantly, this particular idea of a public was, like the films he favored, largely imported from Euro-American contexts. It was a public imagined in the classic bourgeois formulation: informed, "cultivated," organized around notions of good taste, and conceived as local, but at the same time articulated with the nation-state and modeled after Western European notions of the public sphere. After the destruction and divisiveness of consecutive wars, such a public, as well as the cinema and cultural institutions that occasioned it, could be seen as reparative.

Out of this early work of Techni and its cinema club, the Thessaloniki Film Festival was first conceived. In 1960, the Thessaloniki International Trade Fair organization (*Diethnis Ekthesi Thessalonikis,* or HELEXPO) solicited proposals from the Techni Art Society for cultural events in celebration of HELEXPO's twenty-fifth anniversary. In response, Zannas put together a proposal for a film festival, based on his experience running the *leschi,* which was immediately accepted.[22] Already at this early point of conception, the festival was seen as operating on multiple scales. On the one hand, the proposal suggests that the festival would be nationally oriented. It would begin primarily as a showcase of Greek films, and it ties the festival to the state administratively and financially, pointing out that a new national film law about to be introduced for debate in parliament already contained legal and financial provisions for such an event and institution. Moreover, under the parent organization of HELEXPO, itself a subsidiary of the Greek Ministry of Industry, the festival would technically be a state institution. On the other hand, the proposal also includes the larger goal of eventually building the festival into an international organization of the size and scope that would merit accreditation by the International Federation of Film Producers (FIAPF). In the proposal, Zannas argues that the festival would have a two-fold benefit: first, it would bring foreign interest to Thessaloniki and to HELEXPO, as countries would want to show their films in Greece and potentially expand the market for their national film production, and second, it would be the best way to promote Greek cinema internationally, showcasing it among the best films from around the world to an audience of international guests and industry professionals. Of course, these lofty goals were far beyond the scope of what was possible in the first year. In September 1960, the inaugural "Week of Greek Cinema" was limited to Greek productions: four feature-length films, ten shorts, and a special out-of-competition program of nine films produced from 1955 to 1960.[23] Despite this modest program, what emerged clearly in the festival's first edition was the strength and engagement of its public. Even short films played to full houses, audiences did not hesitate to drown out films with applause or jeers, and Marios Ploritis, a film critic and member of the jury that year, declared that "the big discovery and the real winner of the festival was the public."[24]

It would take more than three decades for the festival to become the international gathering that Zannas had originally envisioned, but in the intervening years, it would come to attain considerable national significance, becoming the most important film event and institution in the country. Although born of local Thessaloniki initiatives and always closely identified with its namesake city, its status as the country's largest film festival, legislated and funded by the state, made it into a clearinghouse for domestic film production. Throughout its history, it has served as the premier venue for new films produced in the country each year, and sometimes the only major venue, in the case of the many films that do not get picked up for distribution or have short theatrical runs. It has also played a crucial role in the emergence of independent Greek cinema. In its early years, at a time when the Greek film industry was dominated by commercial studios churning out popular melodramas, comedies, and other genre fare, the festival provided visibility and support for smaller films that were more formally innovative or driven by social and political concerns.[25] In particular, it served as a vital platform for what is now referred to as the New Greek Cinema, a "new wave" of independently produced films by directors including world-renowned figures such as Michael Cacoyannis and Theo Angelopoulos, usually dated from the mid-1960s to the early 1980s and generally considered to be one of the most important and artistically fertile periods in Greek film history.[26] The key role of the festival in the development of this cinematic movement was made most clear to me during a talk I attended in Thessaloniki in 2009 by film historian and scholar Eliza-Anna Delveroudi.[27] Her lecture was primarily concerned with modernism in Greek cinema, focusing on the formal qualities of the work of New Greek Cinema directors such as Cacoyannis, Angelopoulos, Nikos Koundouros, Pantelis Voulgaris, Takis Kanellopoulos, and Alexis Damianos.[28] Interestingly, most of her talk was organized around the Thessaloniki festival. In discussing how these filmmakers were experimenting formally, one of the first things she mentioned was how essential the festival had been in providing space for this to happen and promoting these mostly noncommercial films. For each of the filmmakers discussed in her talk, she narrated the development of their work in terms of their relationship to the festival: in which festival editions they had shown which films, and how they were received by critics and the festival public. With the festival serving as the underlying structure of her talk, it was clear that the history of the festival and the history of Greek cinema were closely intertwined.

The festival was not only central to the rise of a Greek film movement in an aesthetic or artistic sense. It also played an important role in the development of a politicized film culture that emerged in tandem with the New Greek Cinema, in which cinema—its institutions, its social spaces, and collective film-going practices—became a vital space for public engagement in national politics. In this regard, many point to 1970 as a watershed year, when the Thessaloniki festival hosted the premiere of Angelopoulos's groundbreaking first feature, *Reconstruction*. In addition to heralding the start of the new wave of independent and formally innovative cinema, the film is widely considered to be a trenchant political response to the military dictatorship in power at the time, "an oppositional way of looking at the new realities that had emerged in a society under political oppression."[29] As I will discuss at further length in chapter three, many festival-goers experienced their attendance of the screenings of such films in those years as a similarly political and oppositional act, one that was also inherently collective. This politicized culture of film-going would continue long after the fall of the dictatorship, expanding outward into a larger social world of film-related gatherings, discussions both formal and informal, and the circulation of published texts, with the festival annually serving as a key anchor of that world.

In addition to contributing to a national cinema and local and national film cultures, the festival has also played a notable role in the national film industry. For many years, it was an important source of funding for independent filmmakers, with festival prizes in many different categories reaching more than a million drachmas. Additionally, it was closely associated with the State Film Awards (*Kratika Kinimatografika Vraveia Poiotitas*), one of the most visible ways in which the state engaged with domestic productions. The awards, publicly funded and administered by the Ministry of Culture, were established in 1998 with the passing of a law outlining the process by which winners and monetary prizes would be decided annually by a committee of fifty, comprising representatives from various film organizations and unions, the Thessaloniki Film Festival, the Ministry of Culture, and the Ministry of Macedonia-Thrace. For a film to be considered for these awards, it had to fulfill basic requirements concerning length, language, and country of origin, and it had to screen as part of the official Greek program during the Thessaloniki festival. Until 2008, when the State Film Awards system was dismantled under pressure from the Filmmakers of Greece boycott, the awards were distributed in a special ceremony that took place at the end of the festival each year.[30] Because of its affiliation with the state and its close ties to members of the film industry in Greece, many of whom often take on jobs working for the organization, the Thessaloniki festival has always functioned as one of the few annual events that gathers diverse members of the Greek film professions together with the film-viewing public, thereby drawing together and giving coherence to this somewhat scattered world.

After the end of the Greek military dictatorship in 1974 and a period of decline and insularity in the 1980s, the festival underwent a complete overhaul in 1992, beginning with the appointment of a new director, Michel Demopoulos, who had lived in Paris during the years of the dictatorship, studying film and launching his career as a critic. While there had often been international components to the festival throughout its history, as well as multiple attempts over the years to make it more international, it was only with the arrival of Demopoulos that Zannas's original vision for a truly international event would be fully realized.[31] To the festival, Demopoulos brought his international experience and contacts, as well as a broad vision for a much more open institution, connected to what was happening in world cinema. Under his directorship, the festival was transformed from a small, national showcase with limited reach beyond the Greek public to the large, cosmopolitan event originally imagined by Zannas, with international premieres, a well-funded international competition, and multiple sidebar programs showcasing films from Greece and around the world. A milestone year for the organization was 1997, when Thessaloniki's tenure as a European Capital of Culture brought a flush of EU funding to support cultural initiatives, institutions, and infrastructure in the city.[32] With the influx of funding it received as part of this program, the festival was able to expand its staff, facilities, and programming, which further raised its international profile. In this way, it functioned as a centerpiece of the city's larger cultural development plan aimed at increased participation in a wider European and even global cultural economy. These developments were in line with a larger trend toward Europeanization that was beginning to emerge at the same time in the Greek film industry, with the establishment of EU funding programs such as MEDIA and Eurimages.[33] Such programs would also become increasingly important sources of funding for the festival, especially after the onset of the sovereign debt crisis, which would cause the Greek Ministry of Culture, the festival's primary funder since the 1980s, to drastically reduce its support.

Throughout the 1990s and 2000s, the festival would continue to grow its presence in the Balkans and the Mediterranean, and cement its position as a node in a transnational cultural-economic network. With the fall of the Iron Curtain and the ensuing instability throughout the Balkans, Greece became more of an economic and political leader among its neighboring countries, and the Thessaloniki festival similarly embraced its increasingly important position, promoting and funding film production and distribution in the region. This was especially the case after a change of government led to the replacement of Demopoulos as festival director with Despina Mouzaki, a film producer who focused her energies on high-profile international programs, costly events with big-ticket foreign guests, and activities designed for the international film industry, in particular the creation of the Industry Center. During this time, the festival came to more closely resemble the major Western European international film festivals on which it was modeled. It is the transnational networks of festivals and film industries that sustain such institutions; they not only participate in these networks but also rely on them for their continued existence. In trafficking in the latest products, forms, and rhetoric of the global film festival network, these festivals demarcate translocal cultural spaces characterized by mobility and cosmopolitanism, in this sense resembling Marc Augé's "non-places" of supermodernity.[34]

As the Thessaloniki festival became more international in its orientation, the institution's traditionally strong identification with Greek cinema, the national film industry, and local and national film cultures started to shift and take a back seat. While the festival maintained programming dedicated to domestic filmmaking, its international programs quickly came to dominate, often provoking complaints from Greek filmmakers that their work was being neglected by the country's most important venue for film exhibition. The criticisms that the festival was facing at the onset of the economic crisis were also connected to this perceived privileging of the international over the national and the local. Many of the people I met who had attended the festival in earlier years shared the opinion that, with its internationalization in 1992, the festival lost the political dimension, as well as the politicized public, that had characterized it through the 1970s and 1980s. A number of people from this generation in Thessaloniki told me that they stopped attending the festival when it became international, precisely because they felt that, while more cosmopolitan and glamorous, it had lost its political relevance and the sense of collective investment that they had so valued; as such, it no longer felt addressed to them as a public. Denunciations of the festival's budget and extravagant spending in 2009 were in part a response to these changes that the organization had undergone in the boom years of the 1990s and 2000s, a result of the influx of EU funding, adjustments to EU cultural policy, and corresponding social and cultural-economic shifts. In a sense, such criticisms could be seen as a condemnation of those larger shifts, with the chastening hindsight afforded by the developing economic crisis. In the context of the larger debates circulating at the time concerning the state, publicness, and civic responsibility, the internationalization and Europeanization of this cultural institution became associated with its becoming less and less a place for the practice of public and collective political life.

Here again, as in my initial encounter with the festival in the dark theater at Anthology Film Archives, we see the intersection of scale and publicness—just the latest iteration of such complex entanglements that have marked the institution throughout its history. Indeed, I would argue that cultural institutions like the Thessaloniki Film Festival merit close critical attention precisely because they allow us to trace the interwoven histories of scales of circulation, significance, and cultural economy, on the one hand, and multiple publics and forms of publicness, on the other hand. In the rest of this book, I move inward from the synoptic view of the festival represented in this chapter to explore more specifically some of the varying and at times conflicting ways that scale and publicness are activated, contested, and put to use in and around the festival and its larger field of cultural production, particularly in the context of the Greek "trouble."

CHAPTER 2

Forms of Publicness

In the inaugural issue of *Public Culture*, Arjun Appadurai and Carol A. Breckenridge sketch the outlines of the journal's namesake concept. Considering a wide range of cultural phenomena, from films and sporting events to packaged tours and "ethnic" restaurants, the authors understand each as a form of public culture or an "arena" in which "emergent cosmopolitan cultural forms . . . shape each other."[1] Thus understood, public culture does not simply comprise various cultural phenomena but more importantly functions as "a *zone* of cultural debate," where different cultural forms—popular, mass, folk, consumer, national, elite, classical, high, low—"are encountering, interrogating and contesting each other in new and unexpected ways."[2] In this sense, the authors see public culture as a "contested terrain," in which a variety of social actors engage in processes of cultural negotiation, the stakes of which are nothing less than the shape of public life itself.

In this chapter, I take this notion of public culture as a starting point for exploring the Thessaloniki International Film Festival as a "zone of cultural debate," an arena in which different discourses and practices of and around cinema come together, collide, and shape one another. My itinerary maps the diverse perspectives and experiences of individuals who gather in this zone, and the publics to which they belong. Hannah Arendt's famous metaphor of the "table" of public life provides a helpful conceptual foundation: "To live together in the world means essentially that a world of things is between those who have it in common, as

FIGURE 3. Sfina's *The Lovers* in Navarinou Square. Credit: Toby Lee.

a table is located between those who sit around it; the world, like every in-between, relates and separates men at the same time. The public realm, as the common world, gathers us together and yet prevents our falling over each other, so to speak."[3]

During my fieldwork, I occupied different positions around this "table"—spectator or festival-goer, volunteer, Thessaloniki resident, industry professional—and this chapter reflects my movement between these positions. As these constituencies meet in the space of the festival, they converge, overlap, or pass by one another, but they can also become entangled in more complex and conflicting ways. Such entanglements are often sites where the interests, identities, and hierarchies of value that structure one public clash or compete with those of another. I examine how these publics variously experience the festival, the different investments they bring to it, how they engage with each other, and some of the resulting social and cultural frictions.

If the festival, as a form of public culture, is a zone of cultural debate, then often what is being debated or contested are not only cultural meanings or practices but, on another level, the very notion of "public." The growing concern for the quality of public life triggered by the onset of Greece's economic troubles also colored public discourse regarding the arts and cultural production, and the state-sponsored Thessaloniki

Film Festival, as one of the country's most important cultural institutions, became a site for debating, enacting, and contesting forms of publicness leading up to its fiftieth-anniversary edition in 2009. In this chapter, I look not only at the various publics gathered in the space of the festival, but also at how those publics and the institution negotiated different ways of being public. My aim is to illuminate what is at stake in these negotiations and to understand the value that different forms of publicness take on in fields of cultural production.

SHADES OF CINEPHILIA

In tracing the species of publicness circulating in and around the festival, I begin with the basic notion of "public" as "a concrete audience, a crowd witnessing itself in visible space, as with a theatrical public . . . bounded by the event or by the shared physical space."[4] Even within this more delimited understanding of "public"—that of festival-goers—a variety of possible positions exist. In an essay on new forms of cinephilia, Marijke de Valck offers a "preliminary taxonomy of cinephiles" at the International Film Festival Rotterdam. Among these, she lists "The Lone List-Makers," the avid and well-informed film buffs who carefully plan their screening schedules well in advance and watch multiple films a day, emerging only for quick snacks or passing conversations with friends; "The Highlight Seekers," who more selectively choose the films that have already been deemed the best of the line-up, either by critics or "lone list-maker" friends; "The Leisure Visitors," who take a more casual approach, opting to watch and often attend whichever screening is available when they get out of work or have a free afternoon; and "The Social Tourists," who think of the festival less as a film-viewing experience than as an opportunity to meet friends for an outing.[5] While all of these festival-goers could be seen as part of the general audience, each represents a different position within this public, with its own set of priorities, desires, and investments. One person can occupy any of these positions at different times, and all of these various shades of the festival public can be represented within one social group, such as the Greek *parea,* or circle of friends.

It was with just such a diverse *parea* that I first attended the Thessaloniki International Film Festival in November 2005. While I had been to screenings in New York organized by the festival, and had visited Thessaloniki before, this was the first time that I traveled to Greece for the festival itself, and I found myself quite disoriented. It is hardly one of the largest international film festivals, especially compared to the top-tier Berlinale or Cannes, but even a festival the size of Thessaloniki's can be overwhelming, with its dozens of venues, screenings, parallel programs, and special events happening simultaneously. Fortunately, this was when I befriended Dimitris, an avid and experienced fan who guided me through the spaces and structures of the festival and helped to orient me in this unfamiliar landscape. Dimitris, in his early thirties, was born and raised in Thessaloniki, where he studied physics at Aristotle University and then took a job there as a researcher. Although his professional interests were far from cinema, he had been a passionate cinephile since he was a teenager and had not missed a single edition in fifteen years. He even went so far as to save his vacation days so that he could take time off work each November and attend the festival without distraction. Dimitris took me under his wing, showing me how to navigate the screening schedule, introducing me to festival staff, and taking me to places around the city that were closely tied to what the festival meant for him: the bar Flou, where he and his friends met at the end of each day to talk about the films they had seen; a quiet café close to the theaters where one could take a break and recharge between films; the best places to get a bite to eat after the last midnight screenings.

In addition to introducing me to the festival, he also introduced me to his *parea:* his sister Evgenia and her friend Myrto, both English literature graduate students at Aristotle University; Myrto's boyfriend Apostolos, a teacher at a high school in the nearby town of Drama and usually in Thessaloniki only on weekends; and Stefanos, a close friend of Dimitris's from the university. In de Valck's taxonomy of festival cinephiles, Dimitris would be a "Lone List-Maker," with his heavily annotated festival catalog and a thick stack of tickets; Evgenia and Myrto would be considered "Highlight Seekers"; Apostolos would be a "Leisure Visitor"; and Stefanos, a decidedly "Social Tourist." Gathered around a table one afternoon in the festival's main café on the *limani,* during one of the first days of the 2005 festival, we flipped through Dimitris's catalog, comparing our programs and trying to decide which films to see together as a group.

Dimitris already had a full week of screenings planned, with four or five films scheduled for each day. His choices reflected his wide-ranging tastes and breadth of knowledge concerning world cinema: multiple films from the special tribute programs to Turkish filmmaker Kutluğ Ataman, Korean director Kim Jee-woon, Taiwanese director Hou Hsiao-hsien, and British director Michael Winterbottom; the most recent film by Danish director Christoffer Boe; crowd-pleasers like Park Chanwook's *Old Boy* and *Sympathy for Lady Vengeance;* plus a handful of films by lesser known directors in the International Competition and Balkan Survey. Dimitris had grown up on the festival; saved the catalogs of each edition he attended; and collected past issues of *Proto Plano,* the daily festival newspaper featuring reviews and interviews with filmmakers and other guests. He followed cinema-related blogs and publications, in Greek and English, and was one of a dwindling group of regulars at the city's few remaining independent and arthouse cinemas. Raised in a family of academics, his tastes in music, cinema, theater, and literature skewed to the international, independent, and alternative; he tended to shun Greek popular culture and often talked to me about how he felt culturally limited living in Thessaloniki, which he felt was conservative, provincial, and nationalistic. For him, attending the festival each year was more than simply watching films; it was an opening of what he saw as the city's usually narrow horizons, and as such it constituted an important part of his cultural identity, which he took quite seriously.

Evgenia and Myrto were less personally invested in the festival. A few years younger than Dimitris, they had become good friends while studying in the same masters program in the United Kingdom. Their attendance at the festival was more casual, entailing one or two films a day, and their choices were largely determined by their Anglophone and Anglophile interests. They asked Dimitris what he thought were the films not to be missed, but in the end, they settled mostly on British and American films. Myrto, who was writing her doctoral dissertation on Irish literature, was thrilled to see that this year's festival had a special section for new Irish films. They were both eager to see Winterbottom's latest feature, *Tristam Shandy: A Cock and Bull Story;* as graduate students, they had studied the eighteenth-century novel on which the film was based, and they wondered how it would be adapted for film.

When I suggested that we all go see *Omiros,* a new film by Greek director Constantine Giannaris, based on a true story about an Albanian immigrant in Greece, the others shrugged with indifference, a sentiment that was common among Greeks at the festival. While some of the films in the Greek program are well attended, the most sought-after tickets are for international films, and particularly those that have played well in other festivals. In the end, Dimitris, Evgenia, Myrto, and I decided to watch a few films together: Winterbottom's *Tristam Shandy;* Fatih Akin's *Crossing the Bridge,* a documentary about music in Istanbul; and later that evening, Miranda July's *Me and You and Everyone*

We Know, that year's American indie favorite and a sure crowd-pleaser. Apostolos didn't provide much input but said that he would see whichever film the rest of the group chose, before heading back to Drama early the next morning. Stefanos, with a wink and an affectionately mocking tone, said that he would not be joining us "*koultouriarides*"—a slang term that roughly translates to the English phrase "culture vultures," referencing "highbrow" culture—for the film that night, but we could meet him afterward at Flou, where he'd be having a drink with some friends who were in town for the festival.

Not that Stefanos wasn't interested in cinema. I knew that he had an extensive and wide-ranging DVD collection, including films by Federico Fellini, Stanley Kubrick, Krzysztof Kieślowski, and Francis Ford Coppola, some of his favorite filmmakers, and in the end, he joined us for a few screenings that year. But he never attended screenings on his own because, for him, the film festival was more of a social than a cinematic event, a distinction that his remark about "*koultouriarides*" served to highlight. What he primarily enjoyed about the festival was that it marked a period of heightened sociality, with old friends returning to the city, and the *parea* getting together multiple times a day. Similarly, Apostolos was not concerned about which film in particular he would see; what was most important was that he would see it with his girlfriend and the rest of the *parea*. For him, the festival was an opportunity to gather with all of his friends on one of the few days that he was back in Thessaloniki. By contrast, Evgenia, Myrto, and Dimitris were more concerned with the actual films, and Dimitris was at the far end of the spectrum, spending entire days in screenings or shuttling between theaters, with friends whenever possible but just as often by himself. That he experienced the festival as less of a social event than did Apostolos or Stefanos does not mean that he was any less part of its public. On the contrary, Dimitris's experience could be characterized as public in multiple ways. In addition to being a part of the festival's public, understood as "a concrete audience . . . bounded by the event," he is also part of a different kind of public, understood as "the space of discursive circulation among strangers as a social entity,"[6] constituted through acts of "indefinite address" and "mere attention."[7] In this sense, Dimitris belongs to several overlapping festival publics, including those of individual films he watches during the Thessaloniki Festival, which is just one stop on their international itineraries; the festival's cinephile public, addressed through publicity materials, programming notes, catalog texts, *Proto Plano* articles, and publications on auteurs or national cinemas; and the larger public of independent world cinema. For Dimitris, his experience of the festival, which is such an important part of his personal identity, is thus multiply public.

The example of this particular *parea* makes clear the extent to which even a relatively bounded and delimited public can contain a wide range of positions, with individual members motivated by varying interests and investments. Moreover, in the figure of Dimitris, we see how the festival brings together not only a number of different publics but also different definitions of "public" itself. On the one hand, Dimitris is a member of the concrete, socially specific, festival-going public; on the other hand, he is part of more abstract publics of varying scale, constituted discursively through the impersonal address of media in circulation. The distinction between these two ways of being (a) public is reminiscent of the distinction that Miriam Hansen makes between two understandings of the film spectator: on the one hand, the concrete "viewer as a member of a plural, social audience," and on the other hand, the "spectator as a textual term, as the hypothetical point of address of filmic discourse."[8] For Hansen, this is a distinction that we see play out both in the disciplinary history of film studies, with film theory's traditional focus on the "spectator as a term of cinematic discourse" and film history's concern for the "empirical moviegoer in his or her demographic contingency," and in the history of early cinema as medium and institution, when the cinematic address shifts from a more concrete, empirically diverse, and active social audience to the more passive spectator of classical Hollywood cinema, a textual or structural position inscribed in cinematic codes and conventions.[9] In the case of Dimitris and his *parea,* we see that the festival as a space of public culture accommodates both types of publics, and multiple positions within each type, which all coexist in relative harmony despite their disparate investments, organizing values, and modes of operation. Within this *parea,* and even for Dimitris as an individual, these publics may come into and fall out of alignment, but they rarely come into direct conflict. Elsewhere in the space of the festival, however, the friction that results from clashing publics, as well as clashing forms of publicness, is more evident.

CONFLICTING PUBLICS

One place where such friction emerges is the Industry Center, which often feels at a remove from the rest of the festival, not only physically but also in its rhythms, in the activities it houses, the participants it gathers, and the publics it addresses. Its facilities, events, and resources are only available to people accredited as industry professionals; at the 2009 festival, this included more than three hundred and fifty directors, producers, sales agents, distributors, programmers, and representatives of film institutes, organizations, and funding bodies, all coming from across Greece, the Mediterranean, Europe, and the United States. The nondescript interiors of the Center's facilities make it feel like a conference or convention running in parallel with the festival, but one that could be anywhere; the fact that all business is conducted in English, variously accented, contributes to the feeling of placelessness. In this sense, the Industry Center is one of the festival spaces that feels most like Marc Augé's "non-place." The particular temporality inside the Center also sets it apart. Most attendees experience the festival as a liminal, celebratory event, a time set aside from workaday rhythms. The opposite applies in the Center, where participants are constantly in meetings, pitch sessions, presentations, and workshops; even lunches and dinners are structured by staff as networking sessions. The average festival-goer does not have the opportunity to venture into this world, and similarly those who attend the festival for the Industry Center usually do not have the time to experience the rest of the festival or much of the city. Most of these Industry Professionals—especially those from other countries and those who come to participate in a particular program such as the Balkan Fund or the Coproduction Forum—fly into Thessaloniki for just a few days, and these days are filled either with work-related activities, social events organized by the Center, or viewing as many films as possible at the Film Market's individual viewing stations.

Claire, a buyer and festivals manager for a French sales company, attended the Thessaloniki festival in 2009 as an industry professional. She later told me that she had little memory of the festival or the city beyond the Industry Center and her hotel room. As both a sales agent for a film showing in that year's Balkan Survey program and a representative of a sales company looking for new titles for potential acquisition, she was working double-time, meeting with prospective distributors as well as hopeful directors and producers trying to sell her their films. She was only there for four days, and the pace was furious; when she was not in one-on-one meetings or watching films in the Market, she was communicating with the office back in Paris or trying to catch up on sleep. Although she left with positive impressions of the Industry Center and found it to be a well-organized, professional work environment, she said that she did not have time to see much of the city, and the

only screening she was able to attend was of the film she was representing. But, she added, this was not unusual; almost all the festivals she
had ever attended in an official work capacity were like this, one blend-
ing into another. Claire was part of a global public of film professionals,
as mobile as the cultural products they make, buy, and sell. It is this
public that the Thessaloniki festival addresses through its Industry
Center, and it occupies a very different position than the public represented by festival-goers like Dimitris and his *parea*.

While the Industry Center may seem self-enclosed relative to the rest
of the festival, it certainly is not internally homogenous. On the contrary, the Industry Center functions as a "zone of cultural debate,"
especially in regard to conflicting regimes of storytelling and constructing cultural meaning and value. This cultural debate was particularly
noticeable in the Balkan Fund Script Development competition, as a
variety of film projects from different countries and cultural contexts in
the Balkans were publicly discussed, debated, and evaluated.[10] Every
year, ten to twelve projects were chosen as finalists from a pool of fifty
to sixty applicants, and their creative teams were invited to participate
in a three-day workshop at the beginning of the November festival,
which included meetings with potential coproducers and funders;
project presentations followed by discussion sessions, where the four-
member jury offered critiques; and an award ceremony during which
three winners were announced, each of whom received €10,000. The
competition was open to feature-length fiction projects in the treatment
or script-development phase, originating from and produced in any of
the Balkan countries, listed as Greece, Cyprus, Turkey, Macedonia, Bulgaria, Romania, Serbia, Croatia, Bosnia and Herzegovina, Albania, and
Slovenia. The call for applications stipulated that each project must be
directly connected to the history and culture of its country of origin and
would be evaluated on its artistic merits, with the stated goal being to
improve the quality of "Balkan cinema" by providing financial support
for the development of film projects from the region at an early stage.

The program also had another purpose, according to the late filmmaker Lucia Rikaki, who was the head coordinator of the Balkan Fund
program until it was discontinued after the 2010 festival. Rikaki had
developed the program in 2003, together with then-festival director
Michel Demopoulos. In a conversation during the 2008 festival, she
explained to me that the idea for the Balkan Fund had come from the
Minister of Culture at the time, Eleftherios Venizelos, who was from
Thessaloniki and wanted to put the city, and Greece more generally, in

a higher-profile leadership position in the Balkans. In developing the new program, Rikaki and Demopoulos turned to their international connections, consulting with Thierry Lenouvel, the founder of the Script Development Fund of the International Film Festival of Amiens, and enlisting the help of Marco Mueller, at the time director of the prestigious Locarno Film Festival, to bring in distinguished participants from abroad and establish the reputation of the new program early on. Through the script competition, the Thessaloniki festival has played an important role in shaping the new international face of Balkan cinema, providing key early support and feedback to projects that would go on to become some of the most celebrated films to come out of the region in recent years, including the Romanian *California Dreamin' (endless)* (dir. Cristian Nemescu, 2007), and the Bosnian films *Snow* (dir. Aida Begić, 2008) and *Grbavica* (dir. Jasmila Žbanić, 2006).

Thus, we see that the Balkan Fund program is characterized by tension between the emphasis on "Balkan cinema," with its implied social and cultural specificity, and the primarily Western European hierarchies of value that dominate the global film festival network, which shaped the program from the beginning and determined the evaluation of the end products' success—a tension that has to do with differences in scale and publics. As a volunteer working with the Balkan Fund staff in 2008, and again as an observer in 2009, I saw this tension come to the surface repeatedly, as it was built into the structure and organization of the program. One of the main criteria for the selection of finalists was the cultural specificity of each project, its "direct connection" to the history and culture of its country of origin, and this was reflected in the projects selected as finalists in 2008 and 2009. Most told stories strongly situated in the social, political, and historical realities of specific Balkan countries over the last few decades— stories of war, displacement, loss, economic hardship, immigration, and rapid social transformations. Yet this historical and cultural specificity tended to get lost during the Balkan Fund workshop, when projects would be discussed in the decontextualized space of the Industry Center by an international jury whose members were chosen as experts precisely for their extensive experience and strong record of achievements in the Western European and British film industries. In front of a silent audience of other finalists, each project's creative team presented their proposal, and these jury members would then evaluate the project primarily in terms of narrative structure, clarity of plot, and character development. Running through these discussions was a concern for "good storytelling," as well as dominant assumptions about what makes a good story and the best way to tell it—assumptions that, while cast as "universal," were often culturally specific.

At the 2008 Balkan Fund workshop, this tension became explicit during the presentation and discussion of *The Last Flirtation of Miss Djukic*, a project proposed by Serbian filmmaker Mladen Kovačević. The film tells the story of two seniors living in a small city in present-day Serbia who go in search of their missing friend, Miss Djukic, only to uncover her secret life as a con artist, the small fortune she had amassed through her schemes, and her conflicted involvement as a young woman with the Communist Youth League. In presenting his project, Mladen described it as "a bittersweet and occasionally phantasmagoric chronicle of Serbian civil society in the past fifty years," a tragicomic film that shows "what happens when senior citizens, frustrated with the prospect of barely financing and enduring the rest of their lives, decide to enjoy a little before they depart." Stylistically, he explained that the film would be a mix of genres, including crime thriller, drama, comedy, romance, and fantasy, and he showed a short clip of roughly shot sample scenes, which combined elements of horror, physical comedy, and black humor. After his presentation, the jurists began their mostly critical discussion of the film; in their opinion, the greatest weakness of the project was its confusing tone and mixing of genres, and they had trouble understanding how the humorous elements of the film fit together with the tragic, as well as with the film's larger social issues. They were also concerned with the film's wider appeal, doubtful that a complicated story about senior citizens in Serbia would attract an audience outside that country. Throughout the discussion, Mladen responded to the questions and comments of jury members, attempting to clarify his vision for the film and explain the wider significance and appeal of the story, all the while visibly becoming more and more frustrated. At the end of the discussion, when it was clear that he had failed to convince the jury, his frustration erupted. Breaking from the usual etiquette of the proceedings, in which criticism only moved in one direction from jury to finalists, he exclaimed, "Only a few of us here come from these countries, and we understand. We that come from ex-communist countries—for us, it's really obvious!" While the jurists' criticisms of the project were articulated primarily in the culturally unmarked language of film form and filmmaking as a craft—narrative coherence, clarity of tone, and genre—Mladen's closing comments had the effect of casting his exchange with the jurists as a case of cultural specificity and misunderstanding, implying that the jurists were not able to appreciate his film because of their inability to understand the culturally specific context and resonances of the story he was trying to tell.

In the end, *Last Flirtation* did not receive an award. When I caught up with Mladen at the Balkan Fund closing party, I asked him what he thought about the whole process, and he replied that he was disappointed but not surprised, explaining, "This is what happens at these sorts of things. People have an idea of what 'Balkan' is, of what a 'Balkan film' should be, and if your film doesn't fit that idea, then they don't like it." In his experience, festivals and the film industry outside the Balkans were not used to comedies from Balkan countries, and they tended to shun films that were not political or social dramas dealing with the challenges and tragedies of postsocialism. Mladen's interpretation of the jury's reaction to his film highlights the Balkan Fund as a "zone of cultural debate." On one level, there was a conflict between the cultural specificity of proposed projects and the Balkan Fund's attempts to be a more international program, aiming at films that have "universal" appeal. On another level, Mladen implied that the "universal" assumptions of the jurists are themselves culturally specific. Ultimately, both the jurists and Mladen were concerned with the film's relationship to different publics; references to the project's "wider appeal," or to its intelligibility to those who "understand," were essentially references to how the film might be received among publics of varying scale, history, and cultural background.

The projects that do well in the Balkan Fund competition are adept at speaking the language of universality. In 2009, one project that was chosen to receive a prize was the film *Romanian Spring,* presented by the Romanian writer-director Anca Miruna Lazarescu. The film is based on historical events: In August 1968, fifty-one Romanian families vacationing in East Germany found themselves unable to return to their homes after the Soviet invasion of Czechoslovakia. After staying for a period in a detention camp, the families were offered 48-hour transit visas through West Germany and free passage across the borders in order to return to Romania. Remarkably, not one of the families chose to use this as an opportunity to defect to the West; all fifty-one families traveled through West Germany and back home. Anca was aware of the story because her own family was involved in this history; her father was one of the young men who chose to return with his family to Romania. The film loosely tells the story of her father and his parents as they are forced to make a decision that will dramatically change the course of their lives. The crux of the story is the decision to return to communist Romania rather than escape to the West, and what is most striking is that every member of all fifty-one families decided to return. The film's unique impact lies in its grounding in this particular historical moment, which is part of a larger twentieth-century global political history.

In Anca's presentation, however, this specific historical and political grounding was relegated to the background, and even erased at times. Anca began her presentation by describing the film as "a tragical comedy that deals with how horrible it can be when finally your biggest dreams are coming true," a statement that casts the film as simultaneously personal and universal, while sidestepping the historical and political import of the film altogether. Early on in the discussion, one of the jurists, Richard Kwietniowski, a British director, screenwriter, and educator, pressed Anca on the historical issue:

RICHARD: Would you agree that the subject of the project is the fact that all 51 families decide to return to Romania? Is that what the film is about?

ANCA: The film is about how fate throws in your way an opportunity you might have dreamt of, and suddenly you get the chance that you always wanted, to change your life. Yes of course, it is a story of people having to decide if they should change completely their lives or not, but most of all it is dealing with the fact of how, in life, you have a certain perspective, that you really badly want to have something, and suddenly you get it, and you have to realize that it was not really what you were dreaming of, it was an illusion.

RICHARD: So, in other words, yes?

This exchange was followed by laughter in the room, as clearly the answer to Richard's question was "no." This foregrounding of the personal-universal story of the main character and his family over the historical-political specificity of the story continued throughout the discussion. While Richard followed his initial question stating that he thinks the "historical quirk" of the fifty-one families returning is wonderful, he also expressed concern for how the film would manage to cover so many characters and so much ground, to which Anca replied, "The story I want is a kind of family story, to try to tell what I want to tell through them." The rest of the discussion centered on individual characters, their personal struggles and desires, and how to best structure the narrative around them. Even Romanian jurist and internationally celebrated screenwriter Razvan Radulescu, who more than any of the other jurors would have understood the historical and political resonances of the film, focused his questions and comments on the main character and the young man's relationship with his girlfriend, wondering about the necessity of the young woman's character in the first place. In response, Anca concluded that the character of the girlfriend might not be necessary after all, as she felt that the story's strength lay within the family itself:

> It should be more about the family, and the relationship between each other, what kind of dreams they have and why they don't fulfill them. So I think in the end, if we are able to make those characters stronger, then we will find that we probably don't need the girlfriend, and we can start at the beginning with just the family. I think it needs to be more about the family traveling, so then we don't need so much the girlfriend, and we don't need so much the other fifty families anymore, because it's a story about this family, how their dreams are fulfilled or not fulfilled, and why these decisions were made.

Astonishingly, the result of the discussion was that the film's writer-director did away altogether with the "historical quirk" of the fifty-one families, one of the most important and compelling elements of the film's specific historical context. The film was transformed into the story of a family's personal journey and its larger "universal"—rather than historically or politically specific—resonances, and it was this personal-universal story that the jurists chose to award. In this "zone of cultural debate," cultural specificity takes a back seat to the rhetoric of "universality" that dominates the global film festival circuit.

The "debate," however, does not end there. There is a moment in the festival when the rhetoric of universality and wider international appeal comes face-to-face with a public that insists on its cultural specificity. This happens at the Balkan Fund awards ceremony, when the jurors announce the winners of the competition, followed by a screening of a new film that was previously a Balkan Fund recipient. Since the film is officially a part of the festival program and the screening is open to the public, this is one of the few moments when the world of the Industry Center comes into direct contact with the general festival-going public, sometimes resulting in tension between the two. In 2009, this tension was expressed primarily as a conflict over language. When Anca went up to the stage to receive her award, she turned to the interpreter, who had translated all of the introductions and speeches from English into Greek, and asked if translation was necessary, as perhaps everyone in the theater spoke English; the interpreter became noticeably upset and indignantly replied that it was not right to expect or to even ask Greeks to speak perfect English. This small moment of friction over language was an echo of a much more pronounced conflict that had taken place the year before, during the 2008 Balkan Fund awards ceremony. That year, the ceremony began with the artistic director of the Balkan Fund, Christina Kallas, welcoming the audience in English with no Greek translation. A portion of the audience responded angrily; a man sitting in the row behind me yelled that not only should her speech be translated into Greek, but that she should *begin* in Greek, rather than English. When the festival president, George Corraface—a French actor of Greek descent—started to address the audience in his somewhat stilted Greek, the audience heckled him, some yelling out, "You should be ashamed!" At that point, the head coordinator Rikaki took the stage and attempted to reason with the audience, shouting over them in Greek, "The whole theater is filled with foreigners! It's completely international!" (*Einai oloi xenoi edw! Einai entelws diethnes!*), but the audience was only placated when Kallas agreed to translate all the English, line by line, into Greek. As the winners were called up to receive their awards, the question of language persisted: Serbian director Javor Gardev made a point of saying, "Thank you," in his belabored Greek; Greek producer Zoe Lisgara gave her long-winded acceptance speech entirely in English, explicitly refusing to speak in Greek and asserting, "I can't stand that kind of thing"; and Turkish director Sirri Süreyya Önder addressed the issue by emphatically delivering his speech in almost comically loud and slow Turkish, which went entirely untranslated. Upon seeing this older, heavily mustachioed Turkish man turn their demand for cultural specificity on its head, the audience burst into laughter and applause.

In this moment of conflict over which language to use, we can see a larger conflict between different festival publics. Through the Balkan Fund program, and the Industry Center more generally, the Thessaloniki festival addresses itself to an international public of film industry professionals and beyond that to the international viewing public of the films that the Center works to develop and promote. This latter public is constituted discursively, as a spectator-position or "textual term," through the address of these films, which are themselves conditioned by the culturally specific assumptions that organize the Center's work. In the case of Mladen's genre-mixing *Last Flirtation,* the jurors' assessment of the project was conditioned by largely Western European assumptions about what kinds of stories are representative of Balkan realities, as well as what would be legible to an audience outside the former Yugoslavia. And the discussion of Anca's *Romanian Spring* took for granted culturally specific notions of fate, family, personal growth, and fulfillment, as well as particular conventions regarding narrative and character development. These unmarked assumptions and conventions are no less particular for their assumed "universality," as they belong to the specific idiom of the international film festival circuit and the world of prestige, independent, and arthouse cinema in which that circuit participates.[11]

The dominance of this idiom in the Industry Center, and throughout the festival more generally, indicates the extent to which the festival privileges the international over the national and the local. This hierarchy of value is common to most international film festivals, and was in fact a defining factor in the emergence and development of festivals, as Vanessa Schwartz demonstrates in relation to the early years of the Cannes festival and its renowned film market:

> Cosmopolitanism was the Festival's driving cultural value. . . . France established its centrality in international film culture by playing host to the world's most important Festival and market. If French national products did not dominate the box office in most parts of the globe, Cannes promoted internationalism and eventually auteurism instead. The Festival contributed to the internationalization of the film industry. . . . The Festival cultivated the idea that such an international film culture existed in the first place and that France could serve as the perfect staging grounds because of the long-term French investment in cultural cosmopolitanism.[12]

In this case, the fact of being—or being perceived as—international is of such value that the national and local are themselves strategically rebranded as international. Just as the Cannes festival functioned to recast France as an inherently international and cosmopolitan nation, so the Balkan Fund and Industry Center were created, as Rikaki explained, to promote Thessaloniki, and Greece by extension, as an international, cosmopolitan center. However, in certain moments, this hierarchy of value comes into conflict with the values and rhetoric of other publics—in the case of the Balkan Fund awards ceremony, with a public that refuses to comply with the privileging of the international and its conflation with universality, instead using language to insist on its own local and national cultural specificity.

The dispute over language at the awards ceremony was the result of friction not only between particular publics—the Greek-speaking local audience vs. English-speaking industry professionals and festival staff—but on another level between different definitions of "public" and different forms of publicness. The enthusiastic applause in response to the Turkish director's unapologetically untranslated acceptance speech suggested that what the audience considered important was not just its own particular local and national specificity, that is, its "Greek-ness," but cultural specificity itself, which was valued over the international, the cosmopolitan, or the universal. Here, one form of "public"—the "concrete," "social," "empirical" audience, temporally and spatially bounded, culturally specific—comes up against not only "foreign" industry professionals in the audience but beyond them a "public"—abstract, "international," presumably "universal"—constituted discursively through the Anglophone address. Furthermore, these different definitions of "public" were enacted in different ways. The local audience was loud, active, insistent, and unruly, in marked contrast to the conventionally passive, quiet, receptive, and well-behaved festival-going public. In the Industry Center, these contrasting ways of being (a) public come into conflict, as those who are invested in one form of publicness confront and grapple with the hierarchies of value that structure other, disparate publics.

OPENING NIGHT: PARACINEMATIC VS. CINEPHILIC

Another instance in which conflicting practices and discourses of publicness encounter one another in the space of the festival is on opening night, when multiple publics tangle with yet other senses of "public" and their moral overtones. The first time I attended the opening ceremony was in 2007, when I worked as a volunteer in the international competition and foreign press office. Arriving at the Olympion, I saw a large crowd amassed at the entrance, straining to get in and spilling out onto the square. As people pushed their way forward, a group of burly guards and young women from the festival's public relations department tried desperately to keep the crowd under control, checking invitations and tickets, letting some in, firmly asking others to step aside. Those allowed in made their way through a gauntlet that had formed in the lobby: on one side, a swarm of photographers, and on the other, festival director Despina Mouzaki, festival president Corraface, and their assistants. Guests, politicians, and celebrities stopped to be photographed, clutching hands with Mouzaki and Corraface against a backdrop printed with sponsors' logos, exchanging greetings and warm wishes in the bright flash of camera lights.

The lobby was a swirl of bodies and movement: film professionals, local politicians, businessmen, and journalists greeting one another and posing for pictures; photographers angling to get the best shot; ordinary festival-goers who somehow managed to find tickets to the opening ceremony; staff members frantically trying to usher people into the main theater and into their designated seats; and the ever-present army of festival volunteers, standing by and awaiting instruction. Inside the theater, a similar chaos unfolded. The aisles were packed as people attempted to find their seats, with the help of young volunteers, many of whom looked lost themselves in the commotion. Seats were taken, disputed, given up, and retaken, while staff members checked and rechecked tickets and seat numbers. Those who managed to make it to their seats soon abandoned them to greet a friend or familiar face. Special guests— celebrities, politicians, and festival sponsors—were quickly ushered to the rows in the front, where a group of photographers and videographers waited. The ceremony was scheduled to start at eight thirty, but it was already well past nine and no one was near ready. As volunteers, we had been prepared by our department heads, who informed us that the same chaos and delay occur each year before the start of the opening and closing ceremonies.

With the theater nearly full and the hour approaching ten, the photographers at the front suddenly rushed toward the center aisle, snapping away, as Mouzaki, Corraface, and a small entourage walked down from the main theater entrance to take their seats in front. As Mouzaki and Corraface approached and began to greet the special guests already seated, photographers surrounded the front row and worked themselves into a frenzy, maneuvering and snapping furiously while their subjects performed a show of warmth and mutual recognition for the cameras. In this moment before the official opening to the ceremony, another kind of ceremony was taking place, a carefully choreographed staging of celebrity, spontaneity, and media activity. The scene had a surreal quality, with those in the front shaking hands, kissing cheeks, and chatting amicably among themselves. On the one hand, they seemed to ignore the frantic activity of media around them, continuing casual conversations even with blinding camera lights in their faces; on the other hand, it was clear that it was precisely for those cameras that these seemingly casual moments were being staged, with the protagonists occasionally stopping and turning to smile as a photograph was taken. As the media ritual at the front of the theater continued, the rest of the audience responded. Some strained in their seats or craned their necks to get a better view, while others rolled their eyes in disdain or glanced impatiently at the time. Yet others flipped indifferently through the festival catalog or checked their cellphones, as oblivious to the commotion as were the festival staff.

As the media frenzy started to die down and everyone took their seats, I found my way to a spot along the theater wall, together with the rest of the staff and volunteers. The opening ceremony primarily consisted of short speeches by public figures, including the festival director, festival president, local politicians, and cultural leaders, punctuated by brief videos and set media pieces. A moment at the end of the ceremony brought into sharp relief the multiplicity of publics present in the audience. After the last speech, the MC returned to the stage to thank the speakers and announce the start of the opening night's film, the much-anticipated new feature by director Wong Kar-wai, *My Blueberry Nights*. With the theater completely full, I resigned myself to standing throughout the film, and as the lights started to dim, I leaned against the wall, trying to get comfortable. To my surprise, however, the audience, rather than quieting down in anticipation of the film, started to shift noisily, as people got up to leave. While I had imagined that some festival staff and special guests would quietly slip out once the official part of the evening was over, I had not expected a mass exodus. Audience members hurriedly pushed their way to the aisles and exits, leaving empty nearly a third of the seats in the previously packed theater. It was impossible that so many people were leaving because they had already seen the film, which, like all opening and closing films at the festival, was shown as a Greek premiere. One of the more experienced volunteers who stayed behind for the film nudged me to one of the empty seats in a nearby row; when I asked her if it was alright for us to sit down, she whispered in reply that this happens every year, and that I should move in as far as possible, as there would be others coming. Indeed, as the audience hushed and the film began, the back doors of the theater opened and a stream of new audience members quietly slipped in, taking the seats that had been left empty.

Watching the movie from the comfort of my newfound seat, I found my mind going back to the madness of the Olympion front door earlier that evening. I realized that many of the people who had been trying frantically to get past the guards and into the theater were motivated not by a desire to see the opening night film but rather by a desire to be a part of the opening-night spectacle. For these people, opening night was not a cinematic event but rather "paracinematic," one of the many happenings—parties, receptions, concerts, exhibits, press conferences, celebrity appearances—that are indirectly connected, if at all, to screening or viewing films, but are nonetheless integral to a film festival and its perceived social and cultural value.[13] The paracinematic ritual is often what Daniel Boorstin refers to as a "pseudo-event," a happening that "is not spontaneous, but comes about because someone has planned, planted, or incited it . . . primarily (not always exclusively) for the immediate purpose of being reported or reproduced," and the success of which is "measured by how widely it is reported."[14] Writing about the Cannes film festival during the 1950s and 1960s, when its symbiotic relationship with photojournalism was first developed, Schwartz describes how festival organizers actively fostered a large press corps to produce a steady stream of "lively and brilliant images" that served as the "primary vehicle of publicity" for the festival.[15] Images of gaiety, lavish parties, and glamorous stars against the backdrop of the sunny French Riviera played a crucial role in the construction of the festival's identity and reputation. More important, the press did not simply document the festival; rather, "its presence also helped to create the Festival's ceremonies," such as celebrities' mounting of the red-carpeted staircase before they enter the Palais.[16] Similarly, the opening-night ceremony at the Thessaloniki festival functions as such a pseudo-event, orchestrated in coordination with the press to generate a particular form of publicness: public*ity*. The driving concern of the paracinematic public is to be a part of that public*ity*, to be present for and even participate in this institutional staging and imaging of celebrity and celebration, and to reap some of the social and cultural capital that the pseudo-event is believed to generate.

As this paracinematic public exited the theater, another entered, one for which the priorities were decidedly more cinematic and cinephilic: not only to see the film, which was likely to find a Greek distributor and have a theatrical run in the country soon, but also to enjoy the privilege of watching it at its Greek premiere in the Olympion. That first night, I was taken by surprise at the audience swap before the opening film, but in subsequent years, I became accustomed to it. I even started to look for that second-wave audience when entering the Olympion for an opening or closing ceremony; unlike the rest of the crowd trying to push its way inside, this group stood calmly to the side, waiting a short distance outside the main doors. One year, I watched as a young man in this group was accidentally caught up in the crowd and roughly told by festival staff to step aside; in response, he rolled his eyes and shot back that he could not care less about the ceremony. Every year, many people like him wait patiently outside the Olympion for the official ceremonies to finish before being allowed in to take the seats of audience members who had left before the start of the film.[17] This second wave had little interest in the spectacle of ceremonies, celebrities, and photographers.

In fact, they were often open about their disdain for this aspect of the festival, which they dismissed as *glamouria,* an English borrowing that disparagingly refers not so much to actual glamour but to attempts at creating or projecting it. However, the fact that the priorities of this second audience are more cinephilic does not necessarily mean that they are somehow more "pure" than those of the paracinematic public. The cinephile's desire to be part of a film's public in a particular way— namely, to be the first to watch a film at its prestigious premiere—is no less a pursuit of social and cultural capital than the paracinematic public's concern for publicity. It just happens to operate within a different hierarchy of value, privileging another form of publicness.

Leading up to the festival's fiftieth-anniversary edition in 2009, the disparity between these publics took on pointed moral overtones. In the larger political and economic turbulence that was breaking out across the country, the cinephilic and the paracinematic publics, with their respective structuring values and investments in disparate forms of publicness, came up against yet another more politicized sense of "public" gaining currency at the time. The growing concern with the quality of public life, state accountability and transparency, and the rights and responsibilities of citizenship had the effect of coloring people's perceptions of the state-sponsored festival, which increasingly came under fire for some of the ways in which it was or was not properly public. The festival was criticized for its large budgets built on public funding, lack of transparency in its finances, and its political connections to the party in power, and these criticisms only intensified upon revelations of the institutions' large budget deficit. In this context, the festival's penchant for *glamouria* became a major focal point. The five years of Mouzaki's directorship had seen a marked rise in red carpets and velvet ropes, parties and concerts, lavish dinners at expensive restaurants, and the ubiquitous presence of photographers and videographers. But in the post–December 2008 climate of austerity and frugality, the same high-profile guests and events that were praised just a few years earlier for bringing cultural prestige and international recognition to the festival and the city were now cast in a different light, and the paracinematic public was derided for buying into the *glamouria* that was now blamed for bringing the festival to the brink of financial ruin.

In an interview for a national newspaper, Dimitris Eipides, who took over as festival director after Mouzaki resigned following the 2009 edition, attributed the festival's considerable debt to what he described as his predecessor's extravagant spending on everything from hair stylists to high-profile guests like Oliver Stone and Takeshi Kitano. He explained that the next festival would be scaled down significantly: "We have a photography exhibit . . . we'll have a concert, we'll have two or three parties. What more could you want? It's a good festival. And it's independent cinema. . . . What's important is that the festival survive."[18] The tension between two different ideas of what a film festival can be was evident in his comments: a spectacular media event vs. a gathering for cinephiles, each privileging a different form of publicness. In the annual switch between publics during opening night, it is clear that each form of publicness also yields a different form of capital; the cinephilic public is no less interested or "purer" than the paracinematic. In the larger politicized climate, however, with the festival being criticized for its paracinematic *glamouria,* the cinephilic became aligned, if not conflated, with the civic and even the political, which, in turn, became its own form of social and cultural capital.

STAGING PUBLICS, PICTURING PUBLICNESS

The festival organizers were certainly not oblivious to these criticisms. Beginning in the summer of 2009, festival staff in Athens and Thessaloniki began work on the special "Street Cinema" sidebar program, which attempted to address some of these criticisms and, in the process, revealed more about the institution's investment in particular kinds of publicness. The Street Cinema program was made up of twenty-seven different public art works that were installed or took place in public spaces throughout the city during the 2009 festival. The line-up included public performances/interventions, installations, projections, music and dance performances, workshops, graffiti/murals, and social practice projects, all by Thessaloniki-based artists, artist collectives, and cultural organizations. All of the projects had a low-budget, DIY sensibility and were supported financially, administratively, and logistically by the Thessaloniki festival. In a publication that accompanied the program, Angelos Frantzis, the artistic director of Street Cinema, states: "This year we wanted to rethink the relationship between the festival and the city, between the cinema and reality and the world of the dream, so we made it our goal to promote the festival in ways that would be original and would transform the city itself into a cinema. Thus, our aim was to take cinema out into the street . . . even in spots where the festival has difficulty reaching."[19] In more strategic language, from the festival's annual report to its board of directors, the aim of the program was "the further strengthening of the relationship of [the festival] with the city of Thessaloniki."[20] The Street Cinema program seemed designed as a response to the criticisms the festival was facing by supporting local artists and organizations and helping them stage low-budget, public art work that in its sensibility stood in marked contrast to many of the other lavish celebrations being planned for the fiftieth edition. In other words, the aim of the program was to counterbalance the *glamouria* with a more democratic and diffuse form of public engagement, or at least the appearance of it.

While the explicit purpose of the program was "to take cinema out into the street," from early in the planning stages it became clear that "cinema" was not quite as important as "the street." Sitting in on an early Street Cinema organizational meeting, I was struck by the emphasis on the publicness of projects rather than their connection to cinema. At the festival's Thessaloniki office, the small organizational committee met to work through the initial responses to the call for proposals, which numbered fifty-five, and select roughly twenty projects for callback interviews. The organizational committee included the artistic director and a festival consultant, both of whom had flown up from Athens for a few days of meetings with Thessaloniki staff, and a few members of the festival production, IT, and public relations staff, all based in Thessaloniki. As we read through and discussed the proposed projects one by one, it became clear that many were not particularly related to cinema. Although the call for proposals had asked Thessaloniki-based artists and groups to respond creatively to the larger theme of the fiftieth edition, "Why Cinema Now?," some proposals described projects that did not refer to cinema at all, while others had only a tenuous connection that existed more in the description than in the project itself, and some seemed to be projects that had already been conceptualized or even executed before, tweaked minimally, if at all, to fit the Street Cinema program. To my surprise, the organizational committee responded to some of these noncinematic proposals with much enthusiasm, particularly those involving a very visible public element or interaction with the general public, while quickly turning down more cinema-oriented proposals that had a weaker public component. For example, a proposal by an experimental filmmaker for a moving-image installation in a gallery setting was unanimously cut, but a proposal submitted by a popular local arts collective, Sfina, to stage a mass public performance of Magritte's painting *The Lovers*—a sort of flash-mob tableau vivant—was immediately put on the short list, despite having no connection to cinema. In evaluating the projects, the committee often used the English term "street cred" to refer to whether a project was or was not public enough. In callback interviews that took place one week later, a representative of Sfina arrived to further discuss its proposal. Although the committee initially brought up its concern that the project lacked cinematic references, the Sfina representative responded that the recreation of iconic images was, in a sense, "cinematic," which was enough to appease the committee members, and they quickly moved on to discuss the logistics of the project—where it would take place and how it would engage the public.

The Lovers performance by Sfina eventually took place on the second day of the festival in Navarinou Square, a busy pedestrian area popular with students, a short walk from Aristotelous Square and the Olympion. About fifty performers, who had gathered at another square a few blocks away to prepare and synchronize their watches, descended on Navarinou at the same time, breaking up into groups of two, draping white pieces of fabric over their heads, and striking variations on the iconic pose from the eponymous Magritte painting. Everyone held their poses for about ten minutes, long enough for them to get the attention of passersby. University students hanging out in the square stared and giggled; younger children playing with a soccer ball peered curiously at the couples and even tried to approach them; some people walking by took out cameras and cellphones to snap pictures in amusement; and one elderly woman, after staring at one of the couples for a few minutes, asked them in a loud voice if they had "lost it," using the end of her cane to try to move the white fabric from their heads. Even shopkeepers from around the square came out to see what was happening. After the designated time had passed, the couples came out of their poses, removed the white sheets, and gathered to talk excitedly about their performance.

I had met the Sfina performers beforehand, walked with them to Navarinou, and found a comfortable spot with a good view onto the square to take in the whole performance and people's reactions. On the one hand, The Lovers was not successful in fulfilling the festival's goal of bringing "cinema into the streets," or even promoting the festival, as there were no tangible connections to either. As I stood watching the couples, I started to chat with the people around me and realized that most of the onlookers had no idea that this was a project connected to the festival, and there was no way for them to know: no signage, posters, flyers, or indication of any kind. A young clerk from a shoe store stood in the doorway of her shop, puzzled but clearly delighted, watching the frozen pairs of Lovers; when I asked if she knew what was going on, she shrugged and laughed that these kinds of strange things happen often in Navarinou and that it was probably some group or other having a little fun. On the other hand, the performance did activate a certain publicness. The gradual awareness of passersby and their varied responses created a palpable sense of a viewing public—in this instance, a group of strangers addressed by and responding to a visual, performative act. It was clear that many of the people in this momentary public had not been aware that such a performance would take place; the sense of surprise and delight at the unexpected, whimsical eruption, especially in the everyday urban environment, brought together passersby into a momentary audience. In this sense, *The Lovers,* like many of the other Street Cinema projects like it, was a successful exercise in publicness.

The Street Cinema program also contributed to the creation of a public in another, more mediated sense. Watching Sfina's performance unfold, I couldn't help but notice the unusually high number of photographers and videographers documenting the event. Apart from passersby taking snapshots more casually, numerous people spread out across the square taking multiple shots of as many couples as they could see with professional still cameras or digital video cameras; among them, I recognized two of the Street Cinema coordinators, some of the festival's own photographers and cameramen, and a couple of amateur photographers who were ubiquitous at festival events. There were so many cameras, and they were so active, that one could almost mistake the performance for a photo shoot, as if it had been staged for the purpose of documentation. In this sense, the Sfina performance, like the opening-night ceremony, functions as a "pseudo-event" designed to generate publi*city*. The next day, pictures of the performance appeared on the festival's website, in its newspaper and newsletters, and on the new Film Festival Television channel (FFTV), playing around the clock on monitors installed throughout the festival's spaces, as well as in local hotels and on demand on the festival's website. The effect of these images—of this publi*city*—is to cultivate the appearance of the festival's publi*cness*. Regardless of whether the performance successfully activated and expanded the festival's public, the documentation of the performance—of this public act, and of the responses of the viewing public that it brought into existence—could be used by the festival to promote an image of itself as public. In this way, the festival *stages* and then *pictures* its own publicness.

The festival's impulse to stage and visualize publics or publicness became clear to me early on in my research, the first year that I worked as a volunteer. Occasionally, the steady activity in the office was punctuated by moments of crisis, such as a guest not arriving on time for a scheduled event, a film print being withdrawn by a filmmaker, or a missing interpreter; in these moments, staff would spring into action, making calls, giving orders to volunteers, or throwing on their coats to go take care of a problem. A few days into the festival, I assumed that such a crisis was behind a phone call that threw Rena, one of the main staff members, into a mild panic. As soon as she answered the phone, her brow wrinkled in concern, and her next move was to call the head of volunteers; when she could not reach her, she cursed anxiously. As I was wondering if something serious had happened—perhaps a volunteer had been hurt, or an important checkpoint left abandoned by the volunteers who were assigned to it—Rena turned to the three of us volunteering in the office that day and told us to take off our badges, put on our coats, and run over to one of the cinemas in another warehouse on the *limani*. As it turned out, the "crisis" was that a master class with two well-known American actors, special guests of the festival that year, was scheduled to begin in just a few minutes, but the theater was still more than half empty. The master class staff was frantically asking all the festival departments to send their volunteers to fill empty seats; of course, we had to take off our badges, so that we would not appear as festival workers. When we arrived at the master class, I noted that the attendance was not that bad; looking more closely at the audience, however, I soon recognized the faces of many young festival volunteers, *sans* badges. A festival staff photographer paced at the front of the theater, snapping pictures of the actors and the increasingly large audience as the master class began. This was not the only instance in which the festival's sizable army of volunteers would be called upon to fill seats; in fact, it happened regularly enough that soon we were able to tell whenever Rena would receive such a call, and before she had hung up, we would be ready to head to the next under-attended master class, lecture, or panel discussion.

It is not hard to understand why festival staff would be concerned about the appearance of a meager audience, especially at an event involving stars or other distinguished guests. But the festival's impulse to picture its public runs even deeper than a fear of bad optics, something that was captured eloquently in a moment toward the end of the opening ceremony of the fiftieth-anniversary edition. After all of the introductions, speeches, greetings, and performances, the MC for the evening, a popular Greek actor named Christos Loulis, concluded the opening ceremony with a gimmick: a live-feed video of himself, projected large on the Olympion screen, tracking him as he left the theater. Sitting in the audience, I felt momentarily disoriented as Loulis, the man, jumped off the stage and was replaced by the face of Loulis, the screen image, who walked up the central aisle, crossed the lobby, and went out into Aristotelous Square, all while continuing to address us, the audience, still seated in the theater. Once outside, the camera turned 180 degrees, to show us the front of the Olympion building, which was suddenly aglow and shifting, lit up by a massive animated sequence projected onto it. The animation was a playful activation of the Olympion's surface, a full-size simulacrum of the building's facade layered onto the building itself, using trompe-l'œil effects to create fantastical simulations of the building rippling, crumbling, or gathered up like a piece of fabric, with figures of different sizes and scales swinging from one of the building's balconies to another, or peering out from inside, massive fingers poking out through windows. This large-scale 3D projection was especially commissioned by the festival to be one of the highlights of the fiftieth-anniversary celebrations, so it was no surprise that the festival would take pains to include it in the opening ceremony. But what came next was surprising: the camera panned over to a group of onlookers, clearly organized and placed there by the festival production team, staring up at the projection. As the camera lingered over the faces of this staged public outside, the public seated inside the Olympion was made to watch them watching, caught up in a loop of publics, orchestrated by the festival itself. In this moment, the festival's insistence on the appearance of its own publicness was keenly palpable, as it chose to end its fiftieth-anniversary opening ceremony by picturing itself as public to its public.[21]

What became clear to me as I sat in the Olympion that evening was the extent to which the festival's interest in publicness lies in the *image* of publicness. Unfolding on the screen before us was an image of a public watching a simulacrum of a building, a simulacrum that outshines the real building on which it is based and onto which it is superimposed. I read this scene as an evocative reflection of what those of us inside the building were ourselves experiencing: looking up at the faces of the staged public outside, we were actually watching a simulacrum of a public, an appearance of publicness that, for the festival that orchestrated it, might be more important than publicness itself. This doubled scene of simulation brought into sharp relief the festival's deep investment in the appearance of publicness.

Just as "public" and "publicness" have a variety of interrelated meanings, so do the terms "appearance" and "to appear." On the one hand, one appears in the sense that one is or becomes visible to others. On the other, one can appear in the sense of seeming, that is, giving the impression or semblance of being something. And yet a third meaning—"to make (something) appear"—while neither an official definition nor in common usage, can nevertheless be inferred backwards from the more commonly used transitive of "to disappear," that is, "to make disappear." In the Sfina performance, and in the festival's mobilization of its volunteer seat-warmers, I see these different definitions of "appearance" coming together with varying notions of "public" and "publicness" in multiple configurations. In the Street Cinema program, we see an attempt on the part of the festival to appear—to give the impression of being—more public, in the sense of democratic, open, and accessible. The performance of *The Lovers* does "make appear" a viewing public in Navarinou Square, but the excessive photographing and video documentation indicate that the appearance or image of a public, and the subsequent use of that image for the purposes of public-*ity*, are just as, if not more, important than the gathering itself. The festival's privileging of the image or semblance of a public is even more apparent in its "appearing" of volunteers-cum-audience members at under-attended events, and in the loop of publics orchestrated by Loulis's opening ceremony gimmick.

One configuration of "appearance" and "publicness" that is not evident in these examples, and is missing from the festival more generally, is what Arendt describes in her discussion of the public realm. For Arendt, the public realm, or the world common to a people, is constituted through appearance, which she defines as "being seen and heard by others as well as by ourselves," and without which a sense of a shared reality would not be possible: "The presence of others who see what we see and hear what we hear assures us of the reality of the world and ourselves."[22] The reason for such copresence is not simply to "appear public," to give a semblance of collectivity, openness, popularity, or democracy. In other words, for Arendt, publicness originates in appearance, but it does not end there. Rather, mutual appearance and the public realm that it brings into being provide the necessary conditions for the greater goal of collective, political life. Arendt understands political life to be impossible outside of collectivity, to the extent that she even defines "politics as the space of appearance" itself.[23] In this configuration, appearance, publicness, and political life are mutually constitutive.

What is key about Arendt's formulation is that the publicness born of copresence and mutual appearance does not ensure unity or consensus, and a public's shared reality is not monolithic or even coherent.

Rather, the public realm as she understands it is necessarily characterized by irresolvable difference:

> The reality of the public realm relies on the simultaneous presence of innu-
> merable perspectives and aspects in which the common world presents itself
> and for which no common measurement or denominator can ever be devised.
> For though the common world is the common meeting ground of all, those
> who are present have different locations in it, and the location of one can no
> more coincide with the location of another than the location of two objects.
> Being seen and being heard by others derive their significance from the fact
> that everybody sees and hears from a different position. This is the meaning
> of public life.[24]

Because public life is predicated on difference "for which no common
measurement or denominator can ever be devised," political life is also
not a matter of coming to agreement or consensus, but rather is necessarily agonistic and incomplete. As Bonnie Honig points out, Arendt
insists on multiplicity as the condition of collective and political life,
and in this framework, the public realm functions as a space of contestation, where politics are practiced as an agonistic "action in concert
that is also always a site of struggle ... with *and* against one's peers
because it takes place in a world marked and riven by difference and
plurality" rather than by identity or sameness.[25]

For the most part, this sense of publicness as discordant, agonistic
collectivity is absent from the social space of the film festival, which as
an institution is concerned with more harmonious forms of publicness
that it can orchestrate, stage, and control. This impulse is most clearly
exemplified in the festival's Just Talking program, which began with the
2006 edition of the festival, not long after Mouzaki began as director,
and ran for five years. The program consisted of a series of structured
conversations taking place nearly every day of the festival. At a quiet
point in the afternoon before the prime-time evening screenings, a group
of five to ten filmmakers whose work was being shown gathered to have
an informal discussion about their films. The discussion was moderated
by a staff member and open to the public. In 2009, these sessions took
place in a beautiful old building on the *limani,* in a warm, inviting, light-
filled space with comfortable chairs, wine and snacks, and a breathtak-
ing view of the harbor. Microphones were set up both for the filmmakers
and the audience members, while at the front of the room sat a large flat-
screen monitor, on which the moderator could call up trailers from the
films of each participating filmmaker, as well as film clips especially
selected for the program. The entire space had been carefully designed

and equipped not just for an audience but also for a public: a coming together of individuals engaged in informed critical discussion and debate. The ideal audience member was someone who had watched the films, read reviews and interviews in the *Proto Plano* newspaper, formed questions and opinions about the work, and was ready to pick up the microphone and participate in a polite, moderated exchange of opinions. In this sense, Just Talking attempts to enact the Habermasian model of the ideal bourgeois public sphere, with its emphasis on reason, rational communication, and collective deliberation.

As is the case with film studies in general, the notion of publicness commonly taken up in the subfield of film *festival* studies can usually be traced genealogically back to this seminal formulation of the bourgeois public sphere. Representative of this tendency is Cindy Wong's extended discussion of "Festivals as Public Spheres," in which Wong surveys a wide range of festivals, reading them as instantiations of the classic Habermasian model, or seeing in them examples of Nancy Fraser's and Michael Warner's later formulations of alternative or counterpublics.[26] Accordingly, Wong places great emphasis on discussion, communication, and the circulation of discourse, describing festivals as "spaces where different kinds of ideas can be represented and where discussions may ripple beyond immediate events or settings . . . a public sphere where voices from private global citizens are addressed. And the films, in turn, become not only texts but also springboards, creators of discussion in panels or question-and-answer times that follow."[27] The question-and-answer session is often held up as a prime example of the way in which film festivals create "social fora in and around screenings in which film-makers and activists gather to exchange ideas and discuss," and festivals are understood as "place[s] of discussion," where "talking and meeting is a central feature," and "a film can only be successful if it communicates with the audience."[28] From Wong's language, it is clear that her understanding of festivals rests on the assumption that publicness is synonymous with communication, exchange, and dialogue—a model of publicness that leaves little room for the disruption, incoherence, and noise that can characterize more agonistic models of collectivity.

There are a number of reasons why this formulation of the festival as public sphere is flawed or incomplete. First of all, it takes at face value forms of publicness such as question-and-answer sessions, discussion fora, and audience gatherings, assuming that they constitute or contribute to the functioning of a true public sphere. However, as I have shown in the ethnographic material presented in this chapter, such "public" moments are often staged by the festival to *simulate* publicness or create an *appearance* of being public, usually for the purposes of generating images that then circulate as publi*city*. This is true even in the case of the Just Talking program. Regardless of how well or sparsely attended a session may have been, the festival's staff photographers and videographers were ever present, capturing the staged discussion in images and sound bites that would reenter the stream of the festival's discursive output, particularly in the daily *Proto Plano* and on the FFTV channel. This publicity material fosters a sense of the festival as a space not just of publicness but also of a particular *kind* of publicness: a model of public interaction as communicative, deliberative, ordered, and coherent. Furthermore, its effectiveness *as* publicity relies on the obscuring of its own staging or construction, and on the elision of other forms of publicness that might rupture or threaten that model. These dynamics become more apparent after close and sustained ethnographic engagement, but they are easier to miss for someone like Wong, whose understanding of how publicness operates within a film festival is based primarily on more surface-level attendance of festival screenings and on the analysis of discursive output, either from the festival itself in the form of catalogs, brochures, and newsletters, or from other entities such as popular press that operate in the same cultural economies and have similar investments in publicness-as-capital.

For the same reason, Wong is unable to discern how this model of the bourgeois public sphere, the appearance of which is so actively cultivated by the festival, gets enacted—or not—in practice. Assuming a straightforward enactment of the model of publicness as communication and dialogue, Wong focuses on the content of that communication rather than its variably successful performance. In this limited sense, she is able to consider a kind of agonism, in the sense of disagreement, argument, or contention, for example, in her discussion of festivals as a platform for protest against the Iranian government, or of LGBTQ festivals as constituting a counterpublic sphere. But she only considers such oppositionality in terms of its content—issues, agendas, identity politics—thereby missing Warner's crucial point that counterpublics are "counter" not only because of the issues or identities on which they are centered, but more importantly because of their unassimilable form.[29] In the audience outburst at the Balkan Fund awards ceremony, we can see an instance of such (counter)publicness, where the deliberative model of the public sphere is, in practice, disrupted by the refusal of communication altogether. In chapter three, I will explore in greater detail this question of counterpublic and agonistic *form,* through an examination of the Greek filmmakers' boycott, the most significant "disruption" faced by the festival in its fiftieth year.

If the film festival as an institution of public culture is a "zone of cultural debate," then what is being debated in that zone is not just cinema, or cultural products, or even cultural meaning but the public itself, different kinds of publics, and varying discourses and practices of publicness. In the context of the larger civic discourse developing in Greece around the time of the festival's fiftieth edition, there was much at stake in claiming forms of publicness such as transparency, openness, collectivity, and accessibility, which can confer onto their claimants social, political, and cultural capital. Perhaps, in the case of the festival, such publicness could also translate into economic capital, as it would justify continued public funding of an institution that has never turned a profit and does not earn nearly enough in sales to support itself. But in the troubled climate of 2009, when political action and resistance quickly took on renewed social and cultural significance in Greece, other forms of publicness, truly agonistic or "counter," came to the forefront of collective life. In this context, the passive publicness that the festival was so intent on staging and "appearing"—a receptive, discursively conditioned public, one that quietly watches and opines, but never resists or disrupts—seemed profoundly out of step, especially for an institution of the festival's visibility and reach. The criticisms and protests that the festival faced in its fiftieth-anniversary year were in part a response to this incongruity, a demand that the institution engage in a substantive way with the country's larger troubles, their concomitant ruptures, and agonistic forms of public life. In the next chapter, I take a closer look at some of the ways these ruptures were variably addressed, navigated, suppressed, and otherwise managed during the 2009 film festival, particularly through the mobilization of history.

CHAPTER 3

Histories of Conflict and Collectivity

The theme chosen for the fiftieth-anniversary edition of the Thessaloniki International Film Festival was the open-ended question, "Why Cinema Now?"[1] In promotional materials, newspaper and magazine articles, television interviews, and the festival's own publications, organizers explained the meaning of the motto time and again by referencing a Jean Renoir quote as the inspiration for the theme: "Deep down . . . the problem is that everyone, every cinematographer, every worker, every set painter, every carpenter, every production designer, every actor would have to reinvent everything from the beginning in order to keep cinema alive."[2] In the festival's annual report to its board of directors, this Renoir quote is interpreted as a call "to see cinema all over again from the beginning, as something constantly new," and the question "Why Cinema Now?" was similarly meant as a challenge to reconsider the relevance and significance of film today.[3] Referring to the fiftieth-anniversary theme, festival director Despina Mouzaki gestured to the present economic and political situation: "In an era of a global crisis . . . this becomes an urgent question. Today more than ever we need to rethink everything, starting from the beginning."[4]

In a television interview before the festival, Mouzaki described how they had arrived at the motto, repeating the Renoir quote and explaining, "We thought that, for the fiftieth anniversary, there's no point in looking to the past, but in order to look towards the future we ourselves have to raise questions concerning the nature and essence of cinema."[5] What was

FIGURE 4. "The junta didn't end in '73!" Credit: Toby Lee.

most odd about her statement was that she was giving an interview for a five-part television series dedicated precisely to the *history* of the Thessaloniki Film Festival, and in this context, her outright dismissal of the past seemed out of place, or untimely. Similarly, the choice of the theme for the festival, and the insistent institutional call to "rethink everything from the beginning," lent a strange temporality to the 2009 edition. Given the larger economic, political, and social "trouble" that was starting to boil over that year, the question "Why Cinema Now?" could have been understood as a timely response to that historical moment, addressing questions circulating in public discourse about the value and necessity of the arts and public culture in such trying times. However, the "now" referenced in the motto ultimately turned out to be a more timeless rather than a historically specific one. A commemorative publication presenting past distinguished festival guests answering the question "Why Cinema Now?" features a largely ahistorical rhetoric, dominated by references to the timeless "power of cinema" and the generic "need for stories."[6]

This untimely timelessness was in marked contrast to the sense of historical awareness that was intensifying in public discourse in Greece at the same time. The "trouble" that was starting to dominate public life in 2009 had the effect of turning people's attention to earlier periods of civil unrest and state violence in modern Greek history, specifically the turbulent years around the fall of the military dictatorship in 1974. Beginning as early as December 2008 and continuing into the years of austerity and recession, references to the dictatorship figured prominently in political graffiti, banners, and slogans shouted at protests. The phrase "The junta didn't end in 1973," for example, drew a parallel between the current government and the past authoritarian regime. As Kostis Kornetis argues in discussions about the December 2008 "uprising," the resonances between these past periods of conflict and the present "trouble" were multiple, complex, and contested, with both participants in and commentators on the unrest variably claiming and disavowing connections to the activism and resistance movements of the 1970s.[7] These claims and disavowals were part of a larger heightened public preoccupation with this recent history that characterized the early years of the Greek "crisis," framing the present in terms of what anthropologist Evthymios Papataxiarchis once described to me as the "moyenne durée." Evocations of, or engagements with, this enframing history—a history of conflict, dissent, and an agonistic public life—were not neutral but rather strategic mobilizations of the past serving to fortify, invalidate, or reinscribe political positions in the present.

In this context, the festival's ahistorical rhetoric was all the more conspicuous, as was a general lack of historical consciousness that, apart from a few telling exceptions, characterized the 2009 festival. While a landmark anniversary such as the fiftieth would seem to be a natural occasion for the festival to look back and consider its institutional history, or its place in larger national and cultural histories, in actuality major historical exhibitions or screening series were noticeably absent. That the festival chose not to showcase this history does not mean that it is not significant; on the contrary, conversations with subjects in the field and my own research made it clear to me that the history of the festival is significant both on the level of national cultural politics and that of people's memories and experiences. Against the untimely sense of timelessness that characterized the 2009 festival in general, a few episodes stood out for their historical or historiographical focus. Among these were an honorary awards ceremony and screening, the publication of a special volume on the history of the festival, and the public presentation of that retrospective volume. In this chapter, I analyze these historiographical moments to understand how overlapping social, cultural, and political histories—histories of cinema and publicness, as well as of conflict, rupture, and agonistic political collectivity—were put to use in the present and to what ends.

COMMEMORATING HISTORY

Midway through the 2009 festival, a special event was held honoring key figures from the festival's past. Titled "From 1 to 50: The Fiftieth Thessaloniki Film Festival meets the First Week of Greek Cinema," the event comprised a ceremony in which important figures from each period of the festival's history were given honorary awards, followed by the screening of a restored print of the film *The River* by celebrated Greek director Nikos Koundouros, which played in the inaugural festival in 1960 and won that year's top prize for best director. From the title alone it is clear that the aim of the evening was to stitch together a coherent institutional history of the fifty years of the festival, a move that was reinforced by the decision to present it in the main screening hall of the Olympion, where the first edition was held. This deliberate attempt to produce a continuous and carefully constructed historical narrative was not only a commemoration of the past but also, and more importantly, a strategic use of that past to address present concerns: a mobilization of history that throws into sharp relief some of the challenges that the festival was facing at the time, as well as the principles or values governing its response to those challenges.

In many ways, the event constitutes what Pierre Nora refers to as the quintessential *lieu de mémoire:* a site of memory, not only where the past is remembered, commemorated, or celebrated, but also where we can see memory itself being thematized, where the act of remembering is rehearsed in an attempt to recover one's relationship to the past, even if temporarily. *Lieux de mémoire* include archives, museums, and monuments, but also less materially defined experiences or concepts such as anniversaries, reunions, a historical generation, or even commemorative moments of silence. For Nora, such *lieux de mémoire* are symptomatic of a society that is losing its memory or its capacity to experience the past as a lived part of the present. In such a society, one's relation to the past is mediated through history, understood as "the reconstruction, always problematic and incomplete, of what is no longer"; this history, rather than memory, "is how our hopelessly forgetful modern societies, propelled by change, organize the past."[8] According to Nancy Wood, Nora takes the severance of the past from the lived experience of the present to be characteristic of all modern societies, which "have separated memory off from the customs, rituals and traditions which it quietly inhabited in the premodern world, and by insisting that memory declare its presence through external signs, they have weakened memory's endogenous grip on collective life. Nora's *'lieux de mémoire'* are themselves the impoverished substitutes of the *'milieux de mémoire,'* 'environments of memory,' which have all but disappeared. By treating memory primarily as an arena of cultural display, modern societies have ensured its compartmentalization as an experience."[9] With "true memory" no longer accessible, we "deliberately create archives, maintain anniversaries, organize celebrations, pronounce eulogies, and notarize bills" as practices of "commemorative vigilance," experiencing the past through the enshrinement of its reconstructions.[10]

Nora broadly attributes the rise of *lieux de mémoire* to the changing temporality and increased mediation of life in modern societies, which he argues causes a disconnection from the past. In the case of the festival's fiftieth anniversary, however, there was an even more specific sense in which the past had been severed from the present. For much of its history, the festival had been closely identified with Greek cinema, but in 2009, this national identification, which had started to weaken with the festival's internationalization in 1992, faced its most serious threat in the form of the boycott by the Filmmakers of Greece (FOG). As will be discussed in further detail in the following chapter, the FOG boycott originally began as a protest against corruption and lack of transparency in the distribution of the annual State Film Awards. As part of their protest, the filmmakers vowed not to participate in the 2009 State Film Awards and to withhold their films from the festival until new regulations were passed. By threatening to keep Greek films from the jubilee edition of the country's main film festival, the FOG members hoped to spur the government to action; in time, their demands grew to include an overhaul of film legislation, state funding structures, and the Thessaloniki festival itself. Specifically, they argued that the state funds poured into the festival each year should be used to support film production instead. Calling for an end to the State Film Awards system and even the festival's annual Greek program, they demanded a smaller festival, primarily international in character, and the creation of a Greek film academy that would give its own annual awards, in Athens. In the end, the filmmakers' demands were not met, and many of the most important Greek filmmakers were absent, together with their films, from the 2009 festival. Thus, a festival that began as the "Week of Greek Cinema" was celebrating its fiftieth anniversary with few Greek films, which was especially troubling in what was widely considered to be a breakout year for young, new Greek filmmakers, almost all of whom were members of FOG and whose films found success at major international festivals abroad. In this sense, the 2009 festival marked a break from its past identification with a national cinema and a potential unraveling of the traditionally intertwined histories of the festival, Greek cinema, and national cultural production.

It is not surprising, then, that the commemorative awards ceremony and screening shone a light directly onto that past, very deliberately highlighting and celebrating it. Sitting in a packed audience of local cinephiles, film scholars, historians, critics, students, and professionals from the Greek film world, I watched as the evening began with the MC, festival programmer Konstantinos Kontovrakis, welcoming us to what would be "a journey (*poreia*) through the fifty years of the festival's history." He then narrated a brief history of the festival from its first edition, highlighting important events and people at each stage, beginning with March 1960, when Pavlos Zannas and the Techni Arts Society first proposed the idea of the film festival; in September 1960, four films were shown in the competitive section of the First Week of Greek Cinema, in the Olympion, the very same hall in which we were seated. Kontovrakis's narrative then abruptly jumped twenty-six years to 1986, the next stop on this "journey through history," when director Manos Zacharias and Melina Mercouri, then the Minister of Culture, introduced a new legal framework for the festival that brought the institution from under the supervision of the Ministry of Industry to the Ministry of Culture. The MC then jumped another six years to 1992, when the festival changed radically in structure and character, becoming a full-fledged international film festival resembling the major ones of Western Europe, a definitive break from the festival's identity up to that point. After another jump of five years to 1997, when film critic and historian Giannis Bakogiannopoulos, then working in the Ministry of Culture, introduced yet another new legal framework for the festival, Kontovrakis fast-forwarded to the present, to the hall in the Olympion, where, he declared, a number of "protagonists" from this fifty-year story would be given honorary awards. Next, he called up these "protagonists," one by one, to give speeches and receive their awards: Mina Zanna, widow of Pavlos Zannas; Athanasia Tsatsakou, the current president of Techni, receiving an award on behalf of the Society; Zacharias; Bakogiannopoulos, together with two other film critics who had written about the festival from its very first edition; cast and crew members from films that had participated in the 1960 festival; and finally, Koundouros himself, whose recently restored film *The River* was shown to close the evening.

Victor Turner, in his work on the anthropology of performance and celebration, states that one of the main functions of a ceremony is the celebration of the social entity. He writes that "when a social group . . . celebrates a particular event or occasion, it also celebrates itself. In other words, it attempts to manifest, in symbolic form, what it conceives to be its essential life, at once the distillation and typification of its corporate existence."[11] Turner also maintains, however, that there is another side to the celebration, arguing that "celebrations have their perilous side, for they expose the chaos and indeterminacy" in social life.[12] Similarly, anthropologist Ronald Grimes describes the public celebration as "a rope bridge of knotted symbols strung across an abyss."[13] In this view, social celebrations are public performances of collective identity or cohesion that attempt to keep crisis at bay—to contain disorder, deal with indeterminacy, or suture a schism. When faced with an abyss, or a crisis, the public celebration is a way to make sure that we get across to the other side. The honorary awards ceremony and screening was clearly an attempt at just such a celebration, trying to bridge the break between past and present that was opened up by the FOG boycott. Not only was the ceremony presented as a "journey" back into the past, revisiting significant moments in the festival's history as a national institution, but it also tried to draw a direct connection to the present by calling forth important figures from that national history and awarding them in person. In this way, the ceremony functioned as a *lieu de mémoire,* a site on and through which history might be recuperated, by bringing together the past and present in the same time and space.

What became clear during the ceremony, however, was that this history was discontinuous. The sense of historical break or rupture during the 2009 edition was not unusual or exceptional, but rather had characterized the development of the festival throughout its history. Returning to the MC's narrative "journey," we see that it is no smooth ride. Rather than gliding through a continuous timeline from 1960 to 2009, we are taken on a lurching tour that jumps from one moment of profound institutional change to another, moments that represent rupture rather than continuity in the festival's history and identity. Despite having gone through periods of relative institutional stability, the festival has repeatedly experienced moments of sudden transformation, usually accompanying changes in directorship, government, or cultural politics—three things that are closely linked. As I listened to the MC, I was reminded of a conversation I had earlier with a local Thessaloniki filmmaker who insisted, "We can't talk about *one* festival. There is no *one* festival. Over the past fifty years, it's been many different festivals." The ceremony illustrated his point: the festival's institutional history is fragmented, and its institutional identity has never been fluid or continuous over time, with frequent changes in character, staff, structure, and overall direction.

Given that this history is marked by rupture and discontinuity, attempting to bridge the rupture between past and present by revisiting that history would seem a self-defeating exercise. If the very history that we are trying to recuperate and reclaim is fragmented and incoherent, then how can the *lieu de mémoire* function to reconcile us to that past? To answer this question, perhaps it is helpful to shift focus from *mémoire* to *lieu,* that is, to focus not on the act of remembrance but rather on the site. In his critique of Nora, Reinhard Bernbeck calls for such a shift in focus, arguing that, "in Nora's rhetoric, the spatial metaphor 'site' clearly plays a more important role than the term 'memory' itself. The site functions as a means of memory and is the mooring for the diachronic narratives. The reason is easy to find. Stasis, a resting point, is directly related to a collective identity that is anchored in a site. Since time and diachrony produce change, 'identity' and staying the same despite changes requires endurance . . . an account of sameness that dominates and minimizes change."[14] In the quiet moment between the end of the awards ceremony and the start of the screening, I looked around me at the Olympion's stately interior, located right in Aristotelous Square, and realized that while the commemorative event was about the festival's *history,* implicitly and more importantly, it was about its *place.* The honorary award ceremony was held not just in the same city but in the same space: the same hall in the Olympion where the first festival took place in 1960, where *The River* was first screened, and where Koundouros first received his award. Tying together all the "jumps" and "stops" in the discontinuous "journey" through the festival's history was not the MC's narration; rather, what stitched together these disparate periods was the radical specificity of location—the city of Thessaloniki, and even the Olympion itself—and the continuity of place over time.

In the Olympion, the ceremony addressed a crisis of history, but it also addressed a public that had a particular investment in place. The FOG boycott presented a potential rupture not only in the festival's institutional history but also for the local festival public. In Thessaloniki, public reactions to the FOG boycott were colored by the suspicion that the protesting filmmakers wanted to undermine the city and its institutions. The filmmakers argued that Athens, as the capital of Greece, was the rightful home of a national cinema, its showcases, and its awards, while locals accused the filmmakers of trying to take the spotlight away from Thessaloniki. A January 2010 article on the front page of *Exostis,* a weekly Thessaloniki publication focusing on local arts and culture, was indicative of how many locals felt. The author claimed that the FOG members "decided to sabotage the fiftieth-anniversary film festival by abstaining from it," and that their focus on Athens as the center of Greek cinema would eventually lead to the dismantling of the Thessaloniki festival, as more and more state funds would be directed to the capital.[15] For the local festival public, what was at stake in the FOG boycott was how Thessaloniki as a city was to be defined. The festival, one of the country's largest and most high-profile cultural events, annually transforms the city into a place with national standing. The possibility of losing that standing was seen as a threat to the city's cultural position and capital. In this instance, even the prestige and glamour of the international festival was not enough; it is clear that there was an investment in being identified as a place with national significance.

This concern was made palpable early on in the ceremony when Mina Zanna was called on stage to receive an award on behalf of her late husband. In her acceptance speech, Zanna recounted some of her memories of the festival, in particular from 1986, when her husband had reacted furiously to a proposal by Mercouri and Zacharias to move the festival to Athens. At first, I took little notice of this story, as it was one I had heard before, but I was struck later in the ceremony when Zacharias, on stage to receive his own award, picked up this storyline. Stepping to the microphone with his award in hand, he declared emphatically that he and Mercouri never wanted to take the festival to Athens, and it had never been a real proposal but rather a passing idea of no importance. With no preamble and none of the usual acknowledgments or expressions of gratitude, Zacharias instead used all of his time onstage to address Zanna's story, saying little else and quickly walking off. I was surprised by his abrupt speech; it seemed odd that someone of Zacharias's stature and historical importance would choose to focus, so insistently and exclusively, on what appeared to be a matter of little historical significance. Clearly, something was at stake in the story of the festival's potential, and ultimately unrealized, move to another city. Zacharias's outburst, an odd moment in the otherwise carefully choreographed ceremony, pointed to the sensitivity of the local public concerning place, triggered by the "threat" of the FOG boycott.

The awards ceremony can be seen as an attempt to address and contain this "threat." In the very form of the event—an awards ceremony— the festival enacts the very thing that the local public was afraid was going to be taken away from them, namely, the State Film Awards and the national prestige that comes with them. Furthermore, the awards were given to individuals, such as Zacharias, Koundouros, and Bakogiannopoulos, who brought together the local and the national in that they were important to the history of the festival as an institution but were also figures of national significance, culturally and even politically. In this way, the award ceremony inscribes the local as national, restoring the position of Thessaloniki in the larger national cultural narrative and thus smoothing over the threat raised by the FOG members' demands. And in this context, Zacharias's abrupt acceptance speech makes sense: Zanna, in telling the story of a previous threat to the relationship between the festival and its host city, herself threatens the "rope bridge" that the award ceremony represents, and Zacharias is quick to respond, defusing her story.

Thus, the honorary ceremony and screening constituted the festival's attempt to address two interrelated crises—the festival's relationship to its history and the festival public's sense of place—brought on by the country's larger troubles and their reverberations in the film world. In its response to these crises, the festival privileged continuity over rupture, harmony over conflict. By staging this return to the past in the historically significant space of the Olympion, the festival used space to try to hold together history, while using history to reinforce a sense of place and its connection to its local public, in this way attempting to smooth over conflict, avert rupture, and avoid offense. In this sense, the commemorative event evinces the underlying conservatism not only of *lieux de mémoire* but of Nora himself and his larger project. Critics of Nora have rightly noted that although the stated aim of his *lieux de mémoire* project is to deconstruct these sites of remembrance, "an undercurrent of sentimentalism and nostalgia within the project ultimately bolsters many of these sites."[16] The object of this nostalgia is the nation, conceived as unitary, which serves as "the basic unit for memory cultures" in Nora's theory.[17] This framework of the homogenous nation and an idealized past has the effect of leaving little room for plurality, heterogeneity, and difference, both in the operation of *lieux de mémoire* and in Nora's understanding of history and collective memory.

Similarly, the restorative impulse of the honorary ceremony aims precisely at suturing any breaks or conflicts that might threaten the appearance of an unbroken relationship between the festival, a national cinema, and a local public.

PUBLISHING THE PAST

This concern for controlling the historical narrative and, more specifically, for writing conflict out of that history becomes even more apparent in two other interconnected *lieux de mémoire* from the 2009 edition of the festival: first, the publication of a retrospective volume, *1960–2009: 50 Years of the Thessaloniki Film Festival (1960–2009: 50 Chronia Festival Kinimatografou Thessalonikis)*, and second, the public presentation of the book that took place in the closing days of the fiftieth-anniversary festival. The commemorative publication represents the festival's main attempt at writing and monumentalizing its institutional history. When work on the publication began in January 2009, I was invited by Athina, head of festival publications, to be a part of the research team. Attending editorial meetings and working together with the small group of researchers and editors over the following months, I observed how the festival constructed its own history, while during the book presentation, I saw how this history was then taken up by the public and used to reflect on the present.

The main issues that emerged in the process of working on the publication were questions of the authorship, as well as the publics, of history: by whom and for whom history is produced. When Athina first described to me the idea for the publication, she referred to the book using the word *lefkoma,* which translates in English to "scrapbook" or "album" in the sense of a collection of clippings, and from the first organizational meeting, this was the word used in the group to refer to the publication. The model of a scrapbook complicates the idea of authorship because, unlike a written history or memoir, it functions more as a collection of traces of the past than as an overarching historical narrative, and each trace might have its own complicated history of authorship. At the same time that the scrapbook represents a highly subjective, curatorial act, it also allows its creator or compiler to claim a certain objectivity, deferring the responsibility of authorship to the multiple writers, cited or not, of its constituent elements.

As the research and editorial team, or the authors of this particular history, we occupied a number of positions. There was Anna, a key staff member in the production department who had worked for the festival for more than a decade and was in charge of the small festival archive housed in the Thessaloniki office. For these reasons, Anna was a logical choice for the team. Lina, an adjunct lecturer in film history at the Aristotle University film department, was considered the group's resident expert in Greek film history, in which she had a PhD. Another group member was Thomas, erstwhile film critic and longtime employee of the festival, who was involved in programming and publications. In addition to his experience working for the festival, Thomas was a sort of historical figure within the institution: a member of the older generation who had attended the festival as a teenager in the 1970s and had written about it as a journalist and film critic in the 1980s, before being hired by the festival in the early 1990s. He had seen the festival through most of its development firsthand, and in addition to his experience as a writer and editor, he could bring to the project his own memories and knowledge of the institution. The head editor was Ifigenia, whose professional background and extensive experience in arts administration, public relations, and cultural policy made her inclusion a politically strategic choice as well as a practical one; not only could she deftly take on the duties of editor and general coordinator, but as someone well connected in the arts in Thessaloniki and well versed in its micro- and macro-politics, she could also help to navigate the potential pitfalls of writing the history of such a politically embedded cultural institution. Overseeing the whole project was Athina, whom I had gotten to know well in my first few months in the field; herself an academic, with a recent PhD in film studies, Athina had taken an interest in my work and asked me to join the project team as a researcher.[18]

In a conference room at the festival's Thessaloniki offices, our first meeting began with a general discussion concerning the publication, its shape, and function, during which everyone quickly agreed that the *lefkoma* would have to be as thorough and objective as possible. For Athina and Lina, both film scholars, it was a question of scholarship; they emphasized that they wanted the publication to be not only a commemorative book, appropriate for a gift and the coffee table, but also a volume that could serve as a resource and reference for other scholars. Ifigenia felt that anything perceived as subjective or editorializing would have political implications. The concern for objectivity was illustrated most clearly in the debate over the publication's introductory text. We were shown examples of commemorative, retrospective publications from other festivals and cultural organizations. Flipping through them, we noticed that they all contained a long opening text, either synthesizing the history of the organization or offering an analysis or interpretation of that history, followed by timelines, data points, photographs, and other forms of documentation. We considered who would be the best person to write such an introductory text for the *lefkoma;* someone suggested Mouzaki, the current director of the festival, while others proposed Michel Demopoulos, the previous director, since he had led it for nearly fifteen years and was responsible for transforming it into the institution as it exists today. But ultimately, both were deemed inappropriate: too polarizing due to the acrimonious changeover in directorship and the party politics behind it, namely, the victory of New Democracy over PASOK in the 2004 national elections. Someone suggested established film critics and historians, such as Bakogiannopoulos and Giannis Soldatos, but even these choices were not considered "neutral" enough. It was argued that anyone with the authority and experience required to write the introductory text would have a particular point of view or would at least be accused of having one, and the team did not want anyone to accuse the festival or the editorial team of pursuing a larger agenda or ulterior motive with the book. In the end, the decision was made to have no such text at all; apart from the formalities (*typika*) of opening remarks by the director and a short text describing methodology, structure, and abbreviations, only photographs and information about each festival edition in the form of data points would be published. In the quest for absolute objectivity, or at least the appearance of it, the group went so far as to attempt to erase authorship completely.

Despite this concern for "objectivity," it was also clear from our first meetings that the very nature of the group's work was interpretive. Even in simply deciding what information to present, and in what form, the group would be determining how the history of the festival was structured, and how, through that version of its history, the institution would be perceived and understood. Meeting periodically for a few weeks, the group discussed for hours how the different editions of the festival should be presented; if the festival's chronology should be divided into "eras," by decade, by festival director, or at all; if anecdotes and "unofficial" stories should be included, or only the bare facts about each year's programming, and which facts; if equal attention should be given to side-bar events, exhibitions, master classes, and Industry Center activities; and which members of the festival programming and organizational staff from each edition should be included. A great deal of deliberation was conducted over how to deal with various elements of the festival structure beyond the annual event. Since the early 1990s, the festival has grown into a large organization that includes year-round film screenings and educational programs at the Olympion; an annual documentary festival in Thessaloniki; other smaller thematic festivals and screening series, such as the VideoDance festival and the Panorama of Gay and Lesbian Films; and a number of programs focusing on national or regional cinemas and the work of individual filmmakers. Should all of these be mentioned year by year, in a separate section, or not at all? There was also the tricky question of how to deal with the State Film Awards, a point of contention among the festival public and especially that year, given the filmmakers' protest of the awards system. In debating which elements to include in the book, and how, the editorial team was debating how to define the festival and how to write its history. For example, their decision to relegate the history of the State Film Awards to a short appendix at the end of the publication reflects a particular point of view concerning the relationship between the festival and the awards, and had the effect of putting distance between the festival and the Ministry of Culture just as Greek filmmakers were boycotting the festival for its state affiliations.[19]

Thus, even in these early stages of conceptualization, tension existed between the ideal of objectivity and the necessary subjectivity of the editorial process. This tension centered on the question of authorship, the particular positions from which this history was written, and how these positionalities determined the shape of that history. These questions also emerged in the research process and in discussions of how the material we gathered would be presented. The materials for this "scrapbook" were taken from a few sources: the small archive of old catalogs, programs, publications, and photographs at the festival offices in Thessaloniki; archives of old newspapers in the Thessaloniki public library; and the somewhat meager collection of festival-related materials at the HELEXPO archives. Much of the *lefkoma,* at least concerning the first three decades of the festival, draws heavily from an earlier publication that commemorated the thirtieth anniversary of the festival in 1989. In an early organizational meeting, all members of the research team were given a copy of that publication as a primary source for our research. This earlier publication details, year by year, the films screened, prizes given, and members of the organizational committee and various juries; each entry also includes a narrative text, often extensive, with anecdotes, gossip, and descriptions of some of the major events, controversies, and reactions of the press and public. As a research team, much of our work entailed cross-checking the information from this publication with materials we found in archives and information online. The more anecdotal "At a Glance (*Me mia matia*)" sections in the *lefkoma* were often taken, sometimes nearly word for word, from the narrative sections of the thirtieth-anniversary publication. These were supplemented with stories from old newspaper articles or personal recollections of the team members and individuals such as Soldatos, Bakogiannopoulos, and others. In general, research on the festival's earlier years was made difficult by the often fragmentary and sometimes chaotic condition of the archives in which we worked, as well as the unresponsiveness of some of the individuals contacted for input and commentary. The last twenty years of the festival were easier to research than the first thirty for a number of reasons, including the festival's increasing discursive output after Demopoulos became director in the early 1990s; improving archival practices in the last two decades, especially with the introduction of digital technologies; and the firsthand experiences and personal memories of the research and editorial team. The idea of authorship was complicated by the variety of sources from which all of this material was drawn, the many people who "authored" this diverse material, and in some cases the difficulty of identifying these authors, particularly when it came to anecdotal information.

A further complication is the problematic authorship of the thirtieth-anniversary publication, which is usually attributed to film critic Babis Aktsoglou, who is listed in a small introductory note as the editor. Apart from the introduction, however, there are no other references to Aktsoglou and the editorial team. In addition, the book contains no citations or bibliographical information. While the factual information Aktsoglou provides—lists of films, jury members, prizes given—can be cross-checked with old festival catalogs and the press, his narrative passages and the anecdotal information they contain are harder to verify. Although this publication is as much of a scrapbook as the fiftieth-anniversary *lefkoma*, presenting a patchwork of stories and historical information, its multivocality is left unmarked. Through the lack of citations, the third-person narration, and near erasure of the writing team's hand, the history constructed in the publication is presented as authoritative yet authorless. Not surprisingly, this sense of authorless authority is repeated in the fiftieth-anniversary publication, which, like the earlier one, lacks citations and bibliography. While it contains more information about its sources and the editorial process than its predecessor, this information is still limited to two introductory pages in a volume of three hundred and seventy, including a brief listing of the editors and researchers, the names of a handful of individuals who contributed stories and materials, and a general description of some of the archives and publications accessed.[20] Although it chronicles the history of the festival in exhaustive detail, the *lefkoma* largely erases its own genealogy, doing away with intertextual references and bibliographical information. In this way, the messy multivocality of the scrapbook—the fragmentary, chaotic yields of the research process—is streamlined, through the editorial process, into uniform lists and carefully designed layouts that both efface authorship and claim a universal authority.

While authorship is effaced in the volume, its intended readership is easier to detect. One way in which the editorial team delineated the volume's intended public was through its treatment of the language question: whether the publication should be bilingual, appearing in both Greek and English. Ever since 2005, when the decision was made to publish all festival catalogs, monographs, and other printed material in both languages, its bilingual editions have been a point of pride for the institution, a symbol of its increased internationalization and integration into the global film festival circuit. With the *lefkoma,* however, the group decided early on, and without much deliberation, that the book should only appear in Greek. The reason had to do with size: everyone agreed that the book would already be quite large as a single-language publication, and that a bilingual volume would be unwieldy. But the implications of the decision went far beyond the book's materiality, effectively eliminating its international public. That the decision was taken rather quickly, without much debate, indicates a shared understanding among members of the group that the book's main public would be Greek. This was illustrated even more clearly at a later meeting, when the question of language came up again in a slightly different form, this time concerning how to translate or transliterate the titles of foreign films and names of foreign filmmakers and festival guests. Various options were discussed: listing all foreign titles and names in their English versions, or retaining foreign titles and names in their original languages while providing English or Greek transliterations. Finally, Ifigenia suggested the model to which everyone would eventually agree: the titles of foreign films would be listed only in their Greek translations; foreign names that existed originally in Latin letters would remain unchanged; and Greek transliterations would be used for any names not originally in Latin letters, for example, those in Arabic, Russian, Mandarin, or Japanese. Again, the effect of this decision was to make the book largely inaccessible to anyone unfamiliar with the Greek alphabet. This approach contrasts with the one taken in the other commemorative volume published by the festival the same year, "Why Cinema Now?," where the responses of past festival guests, Greek and foreign, to the question are presented in both Greek and English, divided into two columns on the same page.

In their decisions concerning language, translation, and transliteration, the editorial team had in mind a primarily Greek public. But there was yet another sense in which a particular public was being envisioned in this process, related to the team's original concerns about the book's perceived politics. In October 2009, after all the research and most of the editorial work was completed, I caught up with Athina to discuss the status of the project. She said that the book was almost ready to print; the only task remaining was a final, detailed examination, particularly of photographs and anecdotal information, to make sure that everything was in order politically. When I asked her what exactly they would be looking for in the material, she specified names that should not be mentioned and some that should, people who should not appear next to each other in photograph arrangements, stories that should be omitted. For this, she would be flying to Thessaloniki to spend a few days working with Ifigenia. Both Ifigenia and Athina were known for their acute sense of political dynamics and were highly attuned to micropolitics, on the one hand, and larger party and cultural politics, on the other. Combing through the *lefkoma* material in this way, they were adjusting it to a very particular public, one familiar with and sensitive to moments of controversy or conflict in the festival's history, with an eye to how this version of its past would navigate the political dynamics of the present. In this respect, the editorial approaches to authorship and to the public converged; in both cases, the goal was to craft a historical narrative while avoiding offense and conflict.

MEMORIES OF CONFLICT AND COLLECTIVITY

At the public presentation of the book, one *lieu de mémoire*—the retrospective publication—served as the starting point for another. For the official book launch, on the penultimate day of the 2009 festival, a group of "experts" gathered in front of an audience to present and discuss the volume. Among the packed audience was the usual army of journalists, photographers, and videographers, while on the panel sat notable public figures and intellectuals such as Zacharias; Bakogiannopoulos; Ilias Kanellis, journalist and cofounder of the *Athens Review of Books;* and Antonis Liakos, a well-known historian and public intellectual. Rounding out the panel of speakers were Athina, festival director Mouzaki, and festival president George Corraface. At first glance, the event seemed to be like any book launch, a staging of public endorsement by distinguished figures designed for optimum publicity. But the conversation that emerged around the retrospective publication ended up constituting a site of memory in its own right, a space in which history was actively being revisited and reconsidered, and memory itself foregrounded. However, where the publication carefully smoothed over historical conflicts and contention, the book presentation conversely took up and made space for conflict and rupture, both past and present. As such, it pushes back against the conservatism in Nora's formulation of *lieux de mémoire,* offering an alternative understanding of the relationship between conflict and collectivity.

Mouzaki kicked off the book presentation with opening remarks, which were read directly from her short prologue at the beginning of the volume:

> The research for this volume and its execution were carried out according to methodological and scientific criteria which correspond to the need to create a useful tool for whomever is interested in the history and the evolution of the festival. In addition, however, to the recording of the institution's history, this volume constitutes a basis for the development of future histories of the festival, providing the elements which will allow other scholars to synthesize their own readings of events. And besides all of this, we hope that this publication will be for its reader, who is also a spectator of the festival, not only another archive, but an impetus to awaken memories, to bring to mind once again images and sounds from films and people, from personal moments, from all that each of us has lived all these years in Thessaloniki. . . . This publication is a duty and responsibility to the important history of the festival. But also something beyond this: a way for us to live once again the wonderful moments that the Thessaloniki film festival has given us, to live once again the experience, which constitutes the heart of the institution, in the present tense, without the weight of nostalgia, but as if everything is happening again and again, in the exact same moment that we're reading about it.

Mouzaki's speech describes precisely how a *lieu de mémoire* functions: not only a place or site where history is represented, but also where that history is taken up and pulled into the present, in an attempt to revive memory and reconnect past and present. Her emphasis on the importance of historiography, using proper "methodological and scientific criteria," is outweighed only by her insistence on the "memories" and "personal moments" that such histories can awaken, the past experienced "in the present tense." Following Mouzaki, the panelists took turns discussing different aspects of the publication and the festival's history. Most addressed the historiographical merits of the volume, praising its "objectivity" and thoroughness, and underlining the need for such historical work. For example, Bakogiannopoulos, bemoaning what he saw as the generally sad state of historiography and archives in Greece, especially concerning film history, praised the publication as a step in the right direction; in particular, he pointed to the "At a Glance" sections for each year and, reading one aloud, commended the "lack of subjectivity of an editor or critic." In his closing comments, he called for the collection of oral histories, before people of the older generation passed away. Similarly, Kanellis began his discussion of the book praising it as "the one and only record of facts and events having to do with the festival, in a country where professional historians and researchers have trouble gaining access to archives. The fact that the festival, by its own initiative, decided to make its archive public in this way is very important for historical research." Liakos, like Bakogiannopoulos, described the volume as a good start, but one that needed to be supplemented with the oral testimonies of those who were involved with the festival as well as members of the public. He then went even further, arguing that all of these testimonies, together with any remaining posters and print materials, should be entered into a special archive, and turning to address Mouzaki directly, he proposed that the festival soon host a conference on the history of cinema in Greece.

Considering the professional interests of these panel speakers and the fact that they were making their comments in the context of a book launch for a historical publication, it is not surprising that they chose to reflect on historiography and emphasize the importance of "proper" historical work. But another common thread that emerged in their comments was less expected: namely, a focus on conflict as an important part of the festival's history, and perhaps even *the* most important part. For example, after Kanellis discussed the historiographical significance of the commemorative publication, he went on to praise its "At a Glance" sections, stating that what interested him most were not descriptions of major cinematic events or their larger social and political contexts, but rather "the secondary events, apart from cinema: the heckling, the protests, the complaints." He then read entries from the "At a Glance" section of a few festival editions, most of which had to do with moments of conflict: the public's vocal disapproval of particular films or jury decisions; filmmakers refusing to accept prizes for political reasons; complaints about the festival's lack of organization; rumors of the festival being moved to Athens; and even the establishment of the first "anti-festival" as early as 1961, when two directors whose films were not chosen by the preselection committee organized screenings of their films in Thessaloniki at the same time as the festival. Kanellis was careful to point out that he considered these moments of conflict as "important not just for the study of film history, but for the study of the social history of our country over the last fifty years."

Zacharias also chose to focus on conflict, describing the "bad state, the state of decay" in which he found the festival when he started working with Mercouri, in the early 1980s, on national film policy and film institutions in Greece. He explained that "it was with the new filmmakers of that period, after the regime change (*metapolitefsi*), who showed up and started demanding a better situation, that things started to change. And that's how the need for a new legal framework arose." Zacharias referred to the fall of the military dictatorship in 1974 and the subsequent transition period. The social and political resistance that was building for several years under the junta exploded upon the fall of the regime, followed by a period marked by great civil unrest, political activism, and the intense politicization of many aspects of everyday life. The festival, at the time still under the control of the Ministry of Industry, was also affected by this climate of unrest. In 1977, many filmmakers resisted the Ministry of Industry's attempts at reorganizing the festival's administrative structure, which they felt shut them out of important organizational committees and juries, by refusing to participate in the official festival and organizing their own "anti-festival."[21] This was the start of a series of negotiations that eventually led to the new legal framework mentioned by Zacharias, which addressed the filmmakers' demands by moving the festival from the control of the Ministry of Industry to the Ministry of Culture and overhauling the institutional structure not only of the festival but also of the Greek Film Center. After describing how he worked with Mercouri, Pavlos Zannas, and others to build and implement this new legal framework, he concluded by referring to the FOG boycott:

> Why am I saying this? Because thirty years have passed, and obviously there have been important changes, there are urgent needs, and again a new movement has emerged, from new filmmakers, who again are demanding the strengthening of opportunities for their creative work with a new legal framework. And here I want to emphasize two things that, in my opinion,

are most important. With all these disputes, which are signs of life and vitality, we need to protect our two basic institutions: the Greek Film Center and
the film festival. In the midst of all these controversies, fights, debates, oppositions, objections, we need to leave our two institutions untouched.

Most striking was Zacharias's focus on a period of the festival's history
marked by dissent and intense conflict, and his representation of that
conflict as instrumental to the renewal of the institution and improvement of film infrastructure in Greece at the time. Moreover, he brought
that historical perspective to bear on the present trouble, insisting again
on the "disputes . . . controversies, fights, debates, oppositions, objections" as positive signs of vitality.

Similarly, Liakos's discussion of the festival's history also centered on
notions of conflict, agonistic collectivity, and resistance. He began by
talking about the festival as part of a larger "education" that his generation received through cinema: "The film festival, the films, the cinema
clubs, the journals—it was all a learning context, which shaped a whole
generation, beyond the stereotypes of school, the bureaucratic way of
transferring knowledge at that time." For Liakos, the history of the festival was intertwined with the larger social history of Greece:

> One could say that the festival follows and is a counterpart to the history of
> Modern Greek society. First of all, starting from the '60s, it's been a field of
> communication, of mutual recognition, of socialization, a field which con-
> nects the '60s, the sudden opening of that period, with later the period of the
> dictatorship, the rise of the public, its autonomous role, the role of the "sec-
> ond mezzanine"—all of these elements that bring together the festival-as-
> institution with the festival-as-public. And it's also a point of resistance; it
> prepared the way for the climate that would develop later, the climate of
> resistance. The relationship between the festival and the resistance during
> the years of the dictatorship is a very important part of the history of this
> festival. At the same time, the relationship between filmmakers and the festi-
> val is also very important. In a way, the festival resembles a kind of Roman
> democracy, in which the public (*demos*) engages in discussion with the patri-
> cians, the plebeians with the patricians, the filmmakers with the Ministry of
> Industry, the juries with the film critics. And to tell you the truth, I'm glad
> that this dynamism manifested itself this year as well, with this separate fes-
> tival of the FOG filmmakers in Athens. I'm glad in the sense that these
> moments of opposition show that the festival is still alive.

Like Zacharias, Liakos presented the history of the festival as a history of
collective action, public conflict, debate, and resistance. With the "second
mezzanine" (*defteros exostis*), he was referring to the practice of festival-
goers in the second balcony of the cinema who vocally, and sometimes

violently, let their opinions be known. The practice of the second mezzanine first arose in the early 1970s under the junta, when ticket prices for festival screenings varied according to the category of seating, and the second balcony was usually filled with youth and students who could only afford the cheapest tickets. The second mezzanine was famous for interrupting screenings, and sometimes even stopping them altogether, with jeers, heckles, or ironic applause. In the 1970s, during and immediately following the dictatorship, the second mezzanine's reactions were often politically motivated: thunderous applause and, in later years, audience awards for films that were considered progressive, and loud disapproval for films thought to be supported by the state or deemed too commercial, even leading to physical violence and police intervention. In the 1980s, the second mezzanine reached a fever pitch, even devolving into a kind of hooliganism, according to some, and the practice died down entirely by the early 1990s. But for many people of Liakos's generation, and even younger generations who were too young to have experienced it directly but are familiar with the lore, the second mezzanine is a well known and fondly remembered part of the festival experience, representing a level of audience engagement and critical interaction that many feel no longer exists among the festival public. By referring to the second mezzanine, Liakos evoked this particular history of the festival, which he then elaborated with references to resistance under the junta, the "Roman democracy," and the actions of the filmmakers protesting the Ministry of Industry in the 1970s. This was a history of the festival centered on agonism, collective dissent, and an unruly public, and he extended it to the present moment, to encompass the actions of the FOG members who organized a special week of screenings to show their films in Athens, just a few days before the start of the Thessaloniki festival they were boycotting. For Liakos, as for Zacharias, this conflict was not to be avoided but rather a positive sign of "dynamism" and vitality, an indication that the festival was still a space for social and political action, resistance, and protest.

These memories of the second mezzanine, and of the festival as a space of agonistic public engagement and political resistance, were shared by many people I met in the field who had attended the festival during the 1970s and 1980s. In a series of interviews, Theodoros, a long-time, dedicated festival-goer, described to me the atmosphere when he first attended as a teenager in the 1970s:

I had a group of friends, there in the second mezzanine. We used to come here early in the morning to get tickets. At the theater of the Society for Macedonian Studies, where the festival used to be then, we would come at four thirty in the morning to get in line for tickets. We stayed out at bars very late, in 1974 or 1975, and afterwards we would come here at four thirty in the morning to wait for the box office to open. For some movies, there were lines beginning the night before—students, youth, etc. It was part of this climate, kind of revolutionary.

When I asked him in what sense the climate was revolutionary, he explained:

At the festival, they played some films that would not have played in the cinemas, and there was a politicized environment. In other words, to stand in line to go and watch *The Traveling Players* [1975, dir. Theo Angelopoulos] was important, because it was the first film that talked openly about the civil war, about issues that were taboo already before the dictatorship. . . . Some films which had an intense political character, just to go and to applaud was revolutionary. This was apart from the fact that cinema was still a form of ideological opposition, resistance. . . . So going to the cinema, which had not yet entered that "lifestyle" stage, was an act of resistance, opposition, struggle.

For Theodoros, this aspect of cinema-going, as a collective political act, was connected to a larger radical shift in public life after the fall of the junta:

The city was very lovely then . . . because everyone was out in the streets, everyone was talking and discussing and fighting, what to do and what not to do, after the dictatorship. On a social level, personal, in relationships—it was an unbelievable climate, which was a kind of euphoria of the spirit, to go out and to talk about things, to meet up with others, and to fight with each other, and to love each other. It was a really wonderful climate, in which of course the university and the students played a big role. You can imagine that, because cultural things were still not so many or so well organized, like concerts etc., cinema was at the top of the cultural world, and it was crazy. Discussions in the bars, staying up all night after being at the festival, at Dore [a local restaurant popular with filmmakers and festival-goers], until the morning, looking for directors.

The festival in the 1970s and 1980s represented for him a way of being and acting collectively, which he felt was now lost, in the festival and in social life, more generally:

There was the climate of the *parea*, we went out together even though each person was different, did different things—it was something that we don't have anymore now, not just in cinema, but anywhere. . . . Because the period of collectivity has passed, in other words to do things together, to get together, to be a *parea*. . . . I'm not nostalgic, I don't like to be nostalgic. Nostalgia is a very bad thing, in my opinion. But it's something, inside me.

I miss it, I miss this feeling of *pareas,* of fighting, of provocations, differences—but there was a communication, which unfortunately is lost, and that's what we're paying for now, in my opinion.

What is important to note in Theodoros's reflections is his characterization of the *parea* not as a homogenous unit in which everyone shares the same opinion and identity, but rather as a space of "provocations, differences," and even fighting. While attending a screening and being part of the public for a particular film was a collective political act, that collectivity entailed disagreements, tensions, and conflicts. For Theodoros, agonism was an integral part of how this kind of collectivity functioned.

In the fiftieth-anniversary retrospective publication, moments of conflict from the festival's history were not avoided; in fact, it was clear from Kanellis's reading of excerpts from the book that it included many such moments, and there are references to the second mezzanine, the various anti-festivals, and tensions between filmmakers and the state. But in the book, these moments of conflict are described "objectively," listed in the volume's uniform bullet-point lists, and thus neutralized, subsumed by a larger flow of facts and data. In contrast, Kanellis, Zacharias, and Liakos highlighted this sense of conflict, presenting it as the defining characteristic of the festival's history. While the volume's editorial team actively tried to avoid potential conflicts, stressing "objectivity" and even authorlessness, and attempted to weed out anything that was too contentious, these panelists saw contention as not just necessary but even desirable. They were not idealizing conflict simply for the sake of conflict; rather, in conflict they saw a lively, dynamic, and vital form of public life. Debates, fights, oppositions, and controversies were an integral part of the festival's social, political, and cultural significance. Throughout its history, the film festival provided the occasion for this kind of gathering—an unruly, agonistic, and critical collectivity—and the book launch served as a site for remembering and reclaiming that history, and connecting it to the present.

In this sense, the book launch sheds light on and critically qualifies the notion of the *lieu de mémoire.* For Nora, the function of the site of memory is to reinforce notions of identity and patrimony through the recuperation of an ever-distant history. He writes that *lieux de mémoire* are a response to the disappearance of *milieux de mémoire,* or "real environments of memory," which have come to be replaced by an obsession with history: "This conquest and eradication of memory by history has had the effect of a revelation, as if an ancient bond of identity had been broken and something had ended that we had experienced as self-evident—the equation of memory and history."[22] According to Nora, the breaking of this "bond of identity" is experienced as a loss, and it "has required every social group to redefine its identity through the revitalization of its own history" in and through the *lieu de mémoire*.[23] As Nancy Wood explains in her discussion of the relationship between identity and collective mobilizations of the past: "In 'identity,' the singularity and permanence of the self (or group) are asserted and repeatedly rehearsed; in 'memory,' the repertoire of representations of an individual or collective past is embraced as the distinctive repository and resource of a present consciousness; in the patrimonial, a specific heritage is claimed as a precious possession which constitutes the founding proof of one's singular identity."[24] In Greece, the three elements of memory, identity, and patrimony are usually believed to come together in the classic *lieux de mémoire* of archaeological sites, particularly in symbolically laden ones such as the Acropolis, which are often used to tie national identity to particular versions of cultural heritage.[25]

In the book launch, however, we see a site of memory functioning in a different way. At this site, memory practices are aimed at constructing and reinforcing not a particular collective identity but rather collectivity itself: an agonistic public; critical social engagement; and the dynamism of a disagreeing, dissenting, and disorderly community. This collectivity is not defined as such by a shared identity or interests, but rather by agonism, multivocality, and contestation. In the honorary awards ceremony and the fiftieth-anniversary *lefkoma*, we see the construction of a cultural and institutional history that absorbs past moments of rupture and conflict, suturing them into a coherent narrative that serves the "restorative nostalgia" that underlies Nora's understanding of *lieux de memoire*.[26] Furthermore, this history, particularly as it is constructed in the honorary ceremony, is articulated with a particular understanding of publics and publicness as critical, cultivated, and "well tempered."[27] In contrast, what emerged from the book launch was a remembrance of the festival as a space of agonistic collectivity, where the members of a critical and unruly public gather to dispute, contest, and resist—one another as much as the state, the dictatorship, commercial interests, or social norms. In the context of the turbulence taking hold of the country in 2009, and the subsequent troubling of the usual discourses and practices of publicness and public life, the evocation of this agonistic past was not mere nostalgia. In returning to and even idealizing a past moment when the festival, and cinema more broadly as a field of cultural production, functioned as a space of dissensus, the participants in the book launch were intervening in the present, reintroducing agonism as a valued term into the emerging civic discourse—perhaps even as an organizing term, naming a form of publicness and collectivity appropriate to those troubled times.

CHAPTER 4

Dissensus and Its Limits

Many of the mobilizations and suppressions of history that took place during the 2009 festival dealt with histories of agonism, conflict, and (counter)publicness, and were either direct or indirect responses to the boycott of the festival by the Filmmakers of Greece (FOG).[1] The festival administration worked hard to smooth over the disruption caused by the filmmakers' protest, and the impact of the boycott registered minimally in the international film festival circuit, the international press, and the festival's foreign public. Speaking with international guests and participants at the Industry Center, I found that many were not aware of the boycott, and those who were knew only general information or vague details about it, which did not greatly alter their experiences of the festival. Locally, however, major newspapers and the popular press closely followed the protest movement, and among members of the Greek public, its effects were much more pronounced. During the festival, friends often complained about the quantity and quality of the Greek films shown. With most of the country's active filmmakers abstaining in protest, only a handful of Greek films were submitted to the festival by a few who disagreed with the FOG, and most of these films were considered to be of middling quality, at best. Others felt that, despite all the parties and celebrations organized for the fiftieth anniversary, the festival lacked its characteristic buzz and energy, due to the absence of the Greek filmmaking community and their entourages. Yet others were irked by those very parties and celebrations, which they considered unacceptable given the

FIGURE 5. FOG posters in Athens. Credit: Toby Lee.

festival's precarious financial situation and the spotlight the FOG boycott shone on the issue of how public funds were spent.

As this last sentiment makes clear, the absence of FOG members cast
a shadow not only on the films that were shown and the general atmosphere, but specifically on how the festival was understood in the context
of the social, political, and economic trouble overwhelming the country
at the time. In this heightened climate, the FOG boycott had the effect
of repoliticizing the festival, highlighting its relationship to the state and
enfolding it in the larger debates over civic rights and state responsibilities that were coming to dominate public discourse. In this chapter, I
take a close look at the development of the FOG protest movement to
illuminate the forms of publicness that were being articulated and mobilized in the filmmakers' collective rhetoric and actions, and to understand the relationship between citizen, state, and cultural production
that was being configured in the process.

CHANGING THE CONVERSATION

From its beginnings as a small gathering of filmmaker friends, the FOG
movement was steeped in the intensely politicized atmosphere, civil

unrest, and agonistic spirit that spread quickly across the country after the violence of December 2008. Over coffee one day in early 2010, Stelios, one of the group's founding members, described to me how the movement had started with a conversation between him and a few other Greek directors, when they first considered boycotting the State Film Awards. He explained that the idea arose from a need to respond, both to what they saw as a perennially broken institution and to the larger wave of protests that followed the police shooting of Alexis Grigoropoulos: "This came about as a consequence of December 2008. In December, different things happened as a result of the murder—people went out into the streets, people destroyed and burned things, these things always happen. But at the same time, many people got together, as if some walls were broken down, and some people looked at each other and said, we have to stand together, to do things together. Our lives changed that December. The people we met, all sorts of things. It all started from then." Stelios described an especially inspiring episode on December 16, 2008, when a group of young protesters broke into the newsroom of New Hellenic Television (NET)—a branch of the Hellenic Broadcasting Corporation, the public broadcaster in Greece—and interrupted a newscast. The fifteen or so protesters forced the crew to fade from a video of then-prime minister Kostas Karamanlis delivering a fiery speech to his New Democracy parliament members to a live image of themselves standing in the newsroom and holding up banners declaring "STOP WATCHING. EVERYONE OUT INTO THE STREETS" (*STAMATISTE NA KOITATE. VGEITE OLOI STOUS DROMOUS*), "IMMEDIATE RELEASE OF ALL THOSE ARRESTED" (*AMESI APOFYLAKISI OLON TON SYLLIFTHENTON*), and "FREEDOM FOR US ALL" (*ELEFTHERIA SE OLOUS MAS*).[2] Stelios had been part of this protesting group, and it was clear from our conversation more than a year later that the experience still affected him. Pausing to take a deep breath, he acknowledged, "Now that I'm thinking about it, I'm getting moved all over again, because it was a real attempt to do something."

People watching the broadcast must have been startled by what they saw. A familiar image of Karamanlis, at the speaker's podium in the parliamentary assembly, was replaced, after a few seconds of superimposition, with the live studio feed of the protesters holding up their banners. For nearly thirty seconds, their image overlapped with the voices of Karamanlis and the announcer summarizing the prime minister's address; then the sound faded, leaving only the silent image of the protesters for more than forty seconds, practically an eternity in live broadcasting, especially for one of the country's major channels. What was most striking about this act was that it managed to undermine and eventually silence the discourse of the state, literally by interrupting the broadcast of the prime minister's speech, but also figuratively, in the sense that NET and the major media networks, including the privately owned companies, are widely believed to operate in collusion with the state.[3] Coincidentally, the protesters interrupted Karamanlis's address about the government's illegal land-swap deals with the Greek Orthodox Vatopedi monastery, a major scandal that, together with the shooting of Grigoropoulos, had sparked the mass "uprisings" in the first place. As first image and then sound faded out, the customary political rhetoric, expertly performed by Karamanlis—"We will not allow truth to be distorted! We will not be caught up in petty machinations that aim at the criminalization of the political life of this land!"—was silently undermined by the image of the protesters. Neither the image nor the protesters' own rhetoric, as painted across their banners, constituted the thrust of the protest, as NET often broadcast such images in its coverage of street marches, sit-ins, and occupations. But on a television channel that, like most, fills every available second with sound, what was most powerful was the forty seconds of dead air. The protesters' act of breaking into the newsroom to deliver that willful silence can be understood as a pointed act of refusal: entering an arena of (supposedly) public discourse precisely to refuse participation in it, and by so doing undermine the discourse itself. The protesters did not lack their own discursive output; in addition to banners, they also brought copies of a text they distributed afterwards, which denounced mainstream media for their "criminalizing," "simplifying," and "distorted" coverage of the mass protests, and calling on the public to gather and organize in public spaces. But the performative power of their action lay in their initial act of "refusal," their public and insistent silence.

This moment of protest can be seen as an example of what Jacques Rancière refers to as political dissensus: disrupting the given distribution of the sensible, or what is visible, audible, legible—what "makes sense"—in any social or political order. For Rancière, the dissensus at the core of any truly political act is not simply the opposite of consensus or "a confrontation between interests or opinions," but rather a deeper disruption of the conditions under which such a confrontation might take place, a more fundamental challenge to a given order of things.[4] The interruption of the NET newscast functions as this deeper rupture, introducing into the known audiovisual order of the state news channel a startlingly unfamiliar silence: an unassimilable break that does not make sense according to the norms of state news television, or broadcast television more generally, and therefore serves to momentarily scramble those norms. Such a disruption aims not (only) to communicate a message but more importantly demand new conditions of possibility for communication in the first place—new speaking positions, new modes of address, new terms: "Political argumentation is at one and the same time the demonstration of a possible world in which the argument could count as an argument, one that is addressed by a subject qualified to argue, over an identified object, to an addressee who is required to see the object and to hear the argument that he 'normally' has no reason either to see or to hear. It is the construction of a paradoxical world that puts together two separate worlds."[5] The larger goal of such a refusal is to reconstitute the scene of discussion as well as the participants in it, to constitute the speakers otherwise and thus to make possible a different discussion, a different distribution of the sensible, a different order.

The logic of refusal and oppositional spirit that drove the NET protest inspired Stelios and a small group of filmmakers to meet and discuss their next steps. This group included Vardis Marinakis *(Black Field)*, Angelos Frantzis *(In the Woods)*, Margarita Manta *(Gold Dust)*, Stella Theodoraki *(Ricordi Mi)*, Antonis Kafetzopoulos *(Plato's Academy)*, Filippos Tsitos *(Plato's Academy)*, Panos Koutras *(Strella)*, and Giorgos Lanthimos *(Dogtooth)*. Whether as directors or producers, they all had films premiering that year and therefore were eligible for the State Film Awards, which they all opposed. These filmmakers shared the opinion that the awards voting process, which was supposed to be anonymous, was corrupted by alliances, bribery, and vote-fixing by entrenched members of the Greek film industry's old guard; as evidence, they pointed to the 2008 State Film Awards, in which two films produced by the same person won nearly all the awards. To Stelios and his colleagues, the State Film Awards were just one symptom of much larger problems: a failed national film policy badly in need of an overhaul; a Ministry of Culture staffed with indifferent career politicians who for years had promised but failed to deliver a new film law; and, more broadly, a state crippled by corruption and unable to enforce its own laws. In an act of protest, the filmmakers decided that they would not submit their films for awards consideration, essentially refusing to participate in the process. Stelios explained their decision: "We thought that, simply, if the filmmakers don't take their films to the state awards, the state awards won't ever happen. A show that happens based on us—if we don't go, then this thing won't take place." Like the protest that interrupted the NET news broadcast, the filmmakers' boycott was a refusal to engage with the state on the terms given.

This act was followed by intense organizing, strategizing, and discursive output. What started as about twenty filmmakers abstaining from the State Film Awards process soon grew into a larger movement. In the first two weeks, the group grew to nearly seventy, and in the month following, there were more than one hundred members, according to Antonis Kafetzopoulos, a well-known actor, producer, and director, and one of the group's original members. Chatting with me before a special FOG screening in Thessaloniki in early 2010, Kafetzopoulos explained that new members first came to the group primarily through word-of-mouth and personal connections. During this heady time, Kafetzopoulos came up with their name: *Kinimatografistes stin Omichli*, which translates to "Filmmakers in the Mist." Kafetzopoulos said the name was a reference to the film *Gorillas in the Mist*, because he felt that independent Greek filmmakers were, in their own way, an endangered species; with private funding difficult to come by and the state support structure increasingly dysfunctional, independent filmmakers were finding it harder and harder to work. The gorilla was chosen as the group's mascot, and the English name "Filmmakers of Greece" was chosen in part for its acronym (FOG), which conveniently referred to the "mist" of the original Greek name. Over the summer and into early fall, as the group continued to grow and began to build a public image, the title and mascot lent themselves to clever branding. The group built a website, where they published texts in Greek and English detailing their opinions and demands; held press conferences to publicize their positions; organized screenings, which were advertised with carefully designed posters and magazine advertisements featuring the gorilla mascot; and even made a short animated trailer, a video calling card that was widely disseminated, with the gorilla mascot emerging from a foggy background.

This increasingly strategic public presentation was part of a larger systematization and even professionalization of FOG, which started to replace the more informal quality that characterized the group's beginnings. Members organized themselves into committees overseeing different areas of interest, including film education, documentary filmmaking, and the establishment of a new film academy, and their demands were expanded, elaborated, and codified into a set of policies. What began as a protest of the State Film Awards quickly became a movement, the goals of which were much larger in scope, reflecting the varied interests and professions of the group's rapidly increasing membership.

According to Stelios, the focus of their demands increasingly shifted onto the need for legislative and financial reform, owing to the influence of new members, more established independent producers who had been pushing for a change to the film law for a few years already. In addition, members who worked as teachers, in private film schools and in the Aristotle University film department, pushed the group to take more of an interest in film education. By the time FOG launched its website in October 2009, it had an official position, with five basic demands, which it publicized in all its activities and print materials:

All of us—directors, screenwriters, and producers of Greek cinema—who constitute the movement "Filmmakers in the Mist" abstain from the State Film Awards and the Thessaloniki Festival, as a protest against the indifference of the state in regards to issues concerning our field. We seek the passage of a modern and practicable law based on the following principles:

1. An increase in the total amount of public funding set aside for film production. Apart from how this could happen (direct state funding, tax incentives for private investors, the return to producers of the special tax levied on movie tickets, implementation of the law that requires television channels to put 1.5 percent of their profits towards film production, cutting bureaucratic expenses, restructuring of funds including a decrease in the cost of the Festival and other activities, the taxing of new media, etc.), what interests us most is that the total amount available for film production be increased, so that it may approach the level appropriate for a dignified national cinema, as in other European countries.

2. The distribution of funds in such a way as to ensure support for all types of domestic cinema, in the most objective way possible. In order for this to happen, it is imperative that all advisory and funding bodies be staffed with widely approved individuals of recognized authority. The balance between commercial and artistic cinema must be ensured through the equal support of, on the one hand, film entrepreneurs, and on the other hand, the Greek Film Center or other agencies that will support creative, auteur-driven, and polyphonic cinema.

3. Assured distribution and exhibition of Greek films. Distributors and theater owners should be rewarded, through state support measures, to the degree that they comply. The more Greek films they show in the period between October and April, the more they will be rewarded. However, there will have to be a measure put in place to ensure that all types of films are shown, so as to avoid an oligopolistic situation.

4. Re-organization and optimization of the Thessaloniki Festival and the State Film Awards. We consider of utmost importance the presence of Greek films in the Thessaloniki International Film Festival, which we call upon to contribute to the promotion of Greek films abroad. We seek the separation of the so-called State Awards from the Festival, and the renaming of the awards to the "Annual Film Awards," which will be given out every March in Athens. The organization and administration of these awards can be handled by creative professionals within the Greek film world, who by way of a Film Academy will deal with all relevant matters.

5. Systematization and upgrading of film education, in the form of a comprehensive film school, which will be based on a curriculum according to select international models and will aim at the promotion of film theory and practice.[6]

FOG members refused to participate in any state-sponsored events or activities, including the festival, its various Industry Center programs, and the Thessaloniki Documentary Festival in March, until the government replaced the existing film law with a comprehensive new law addressing their five main points.[7]

At first, the filmmakers took pains to emphasize in their public statements that their boycott was not a protest against the festival itself. FOG members interviewed for an article in a local Thessaloniki newspaper in August 2009 maintained, "We don't have anything against the festival," and "We're not in opposition to the festival." In the same article, director Lagia Giourgou asserts, referring to a week of "FOG Films" screenings to take place in Athens in early November, "It's not an anti-festival, we're not giving awards, we're simply screening our films."[8] Stelios explained that the festival was chosen as the target of the boycott primarily because "it was the best possible way to protest"; as the most high-profile state-supported film event in the country, it was the most public and visible site to draw attention to their demands. But as time passed, it became clear that their criticisms were also aimed, in part, at the festival itself, particularly because of its budget and the structure of its relationship to the State Film Awards, which had the effect of ghettoizing Greek films into a nonselective program that was always overshadowed by the festival's international competition. FOG's stance toward the festival became especially critical after the Film Division of the Ministry of Culture published figures detailing the amount of support it gave to different agencies and organizations from 2005 to 2009.[9] According to these figures, the Greek Film Center and the Thessaloniki Festival received about the same amount over the five-year period; considering that only about half the annual budget of the Greek Film Center goes to funding film production, this meant that the festival annually received nearly twice the amount of public funding as film production.[10] With the specter of the state's potential bankruptcy, and amid rumors of the festival's staggering debt, which some estimated at close to €10 million, nearly as much as its entire budget for 2009, the FOG filmmakers began to refer to the festival as part of the larger problem—yet another misguided, dysfunctional, and even corrupt state activity. Although technically the festival is a legally autonomous private entity, the filmmakers' criticisms of the institution had the effect of highlighting the close relationship between the festival and the state, thus bringing the institution into the larger conversation about the failures of the state.

The FOG movement faced criticism from a variety of sources, including some among the festival's local public in Thessaloniki who thought the group was trying to undermine the city and its main cultural institution; the major film industry unions, which felt that the independent movement threatened their authority and political position in the Greek film industry; and members of an older generation of filmmakers, film critics, arts administrators, and cultural bureaucrats who were concerned that the FOG filmmakers would dismantle structures of state support that they had fought to build only a few decades earlier. Even among filmmakers who agreed with the movement's goals, there was disagreement over their chosen methods. For example, my friend Nicoletta, who joked about leaving Greece as a "cultural immigrant" because of her exasperation with state funding structures, said that she was against the FOG boycott. Although she agreed with their demands, and was equally frustrated with the situation, she thought it ridiculous to give up the opportunity to meet potential coproducers, talk to possible funders, and pitch her projects to members of the international film industry. She also argued that it was important for Greek films to be a part of the festival because of its long history of showcasing Greek cinema, and she pointed to the honorary awards ceremony and screening of *The River* as proof of that history's significance. Other dissenting filmmakers, including the few who ended up showing their films in the 2009 festival, gave similar arguments. Director Stavros Ioannou asked, "Should we sacrifice our films for this law to happen? . . . I owe €200,000 on this film, and I need €30,000 just to make copies of it. Should I leave them in the can? Let's press for the law, yes, but not with our films ready to be screened." Kyriakos Katzourakis found it "pointless and unfair, this initiative to not participate in the state awards and in the Thessaloniki Film Festival, the only organization that supports and promotes Greek cinema internationally."[11] Underlying these arguments were particular understandings of the nature of the festival: in one case, a market or place of business, and in another, a home for a national cinema. In contrast, the FOG members had a different understanding. In their initial choice of the festival as the "site" of their boycott, it was already clear that they saw it as an arena in which they could address and engage with the state. As time passed, and they became more critical of the festival, it became less a neutral arena and more a space *of* the state. Indeed, through their public criticisms of the festival, they were actively (re)inscribing it as such. In this sense, their boycott was a refusal to engage with the institution on the given terms as it was traditionally defined. As with Rancière's notion of political dissensus, the FOG protest constituted more than simply a dissenting opinion. Rather, it attempted to redefine the institution, reconfigure their own relationship to it, and thus reconstitute the field of engagement.

Although FOG members did not explicitly reference any historical precedents for their movement, their actions echoed the "anti-festivals" and public protests of the more politicized period of the festival's history, in the 1970s and early 1980s, as Antonis Liakos and Manos Zacharias pointed out at the commemorative book launch. In addition, there are ways in which their movement recalls the French filmmakers' protest of the Cannes film festival in May 1968. Spearheaded by leading directors, including Louis Malle, Jean-Luc Godard, and François Truffaut, the 1968 protest arose in solidarity with the students' and workers' movements in Paris, and it was part of a larger movement, represented by the sprawling new organization "The Estates General of French Cinema," that sought whole-scale, bottom-up reform of French national film policy and cinema institutions. The 1968 protest was successful in turning the glamorous festival into a political battleground and then shutting it down completely, a remarkable feat considering its size and international importance.[12] Similarly, the FOG members were initially inspired by the climate of protest sparked by the events of December 2008, and their actions were meant to pressure the state to produce a new film law and overhaul the institutional structures of film production and film education in Greece. In negotiations with festival leadership early in the fall of 2009, the filmmakers attempted to transform the festival into a more politicized event and, more specifically, to position it in opposition to the state. Stelios, together with a few other FOG members, met with festival director Despina Mouzaki and said that they would end their boycott and participate in the festival only if it would be held not as a celebration but protest:

> We proposed to them that, if the festival were to change and didn't celebrate its 50th anniversary and instead opened up the issue of Greek cinema as the basic element of the festival, with discussions here and there, and if it were to cut all receptions and such in half—we proposed a lot of things. . . . But they didn't do anything. The only thing they said was that they would organize one discussion, on one day, with the theme of Greek cinema, which took place without us anyway. . . . The point was for them to take a dynamic position, to make clear to us that the festival was taking a position, putting itself out, risking itself a little bit, to say that it was with us. At the moment when they should have taken a political position, a critical position, they didn't. They could have even said, "We're not taking any Greek films for the

festival this year." But instead they tried to cover the whole thing up, to hide what was happening under a rug.

The FOG members aimed for changes not only in the festival's programming but more importantly in the underlying meaning of the event and in the institution's political positioning. In other words, they wanted to transform the festival from a space of public celebration to one of public protest and, in so doing, change the terms in which the festival was understood, shifting the definition of "public" from "of the state" or "state-related" to the more Arendtian sense of agonistic collectivity. When it became clear that the festival would not agree to such a wholesale transformation, the filmmakers viewed the festival's reluctance to accommodate their demands as a sign that it was, in fact, allied with the state. Stelios explained his understanding of what happened:

> There wasn't a person in there who had the political will . . . the vision and the grit to say, "Yes, I am an employee of the Ministry of Culture, but I'll protest what's going on." Because the film festival, they're employees. It's an agency which is governed by the Ministry of Culture; thus they're paid by the Ministry, they're defined by the Ministry. So there was the argument that I can't raise my head against that to which I belong. Some people say that if the state subsidizes art, then art is enslaved to the state. Here's an example of that, what happened with the festival.

As talks with the festival organization broke down, the filmmakers became resolute in their refusal to participate in the 2009 edition. While their attempt to transform the festival itself was unsuccessful, their refusal had the effect of transforming the event's discursive context. At a time when the festival was attempting to focus public attention onto its impending anniversary celebrations, the FOG boycott cast it instead as a space of the state, thus shifting the terms of public discourse around the festival.

PERFORMING THE COUNTERPUBLIC

This transformative effect of the FOG movement was not limited to the festival but rather took hold around the Greek film world more generally. The extent to which it changed the terms of discourse in this wider field of cultural production was evident at a public debate in September 2009 as part of the Opening Nights Athens International Film Festival, the main annual film festival in the capital city. The debate, on the topic of Greek cinema and its future, was organized specifically to address the turmoil in the Greek film world brought on by the FOG boycott and its demands for a new national film policy. On the second floor of the flagship Ianos bookstore in the center of Athens, in a large open space often used for book presentations and press conferences, a crowd gathered: representatives from the major film unions and Greek Film Center, and members of FOG, among others. Seated behind a long, narrow table on a slightly elevated stage were representatives from the six major political parties that were to be on the ballot in the emergency national elections, which had just been announced at the beginning of September and were to take place in early October, adding political urgency to the debate. In addition to representatives from the center-left PASOK, the far-left SYRIZA, the communist KKE, the far-right LAOS, and the Green Ecologists, the Secretary General of the Ministry of Culture was there to represent the party in government, the center-right New Democracy. Seated at a table facing them were four journalists known for writing about film, and arts and culture more generally, for major Greek newspapers (*Kathimerini, To Vima, Eleftherotypia,* and *To Ethnos*). The presence of representatives of the political parties contributed to the tense and serious atmosphere. That someone with the stature of PASOK representative Maria Damanaki, who many believed would be the next Minister of Culture, had agreed to participate indicated that the political stakes for the event were high.

The moderator of the debate was Orestis Andreadakis, then director of the Opening Nights festival. As he opened the event describing the rules of the "debate," it became clear that it was less a debate than a kind of public interview to clarify and evaluate the positions of the politicians on the stage. Andreadakis explained that the journalists would pose questions to the politicians, or "candidates" (*ypopsifioi*), each of whom would respond in turn. At the end there would be time for audience responses: one from a representative of the Inter-union Committee overseeing the various film industry unions and guilds (*Diasomatiaki Epitropi ton Kinimatografikon Foreon*), one from the members of FOG, and a few from the general audience. Andreadakis' use of the word "candidates," presumably for the position of Minister of Culture, to refer to the participants on stage unmistakably set the tone of the debate, marking it as an interrogation of the politicians. Indeed, as the journalists posed their questions, the debate took on the tone of a vetting session, with the "candidates" being asked to articulate specific policy proposals that they would pursue should they win the upcoming elections. And as each of the politicians answered in turn, it became clear that the debate also functioned as a campaigning opportunity for the various parties to present their cultural policy platforms in the best light possible.

For example, the first question asked, by To Vima journalist Giannis Zouboulakis, referred to a statistic at the heart of the FOG members' complaints, namely, that only five percent of the annual state budget for cinema actually went to support the production of films, while the rest was used for "peripheral" activities such as festivals, institutional administration, and bureaucrats' salaries. Zouboulakis asked, what would each candidate do to address this situation? Theodoris Dravillas, the representative from the ruling New Democracy party, answered by shifting responsibility from the Ministry of Culture, which he argued simply distributed funds to the two main institutions, the Greek Film Center and the Thessaloniki Film Festival: "Each of these institutions has its own administration, its own general assembly, its own board of directors, and they alone determine how their money is used. The Ministry of Culture is merely a distributor of the original funds, and we have never intervened or had a say in how that money then gets used by those institutions." In her response, PASOK's Damanaki took aim at Dravillas's words, asserting that "the Ministry of Culture does in fact have the power to dictate a redistribution of funds" and promising that the PASOK ministry would redirect more funds to production. She also pointed to the provision in the existing national film policy that dictated that a percentage of the tax revenue from movie theater tickets be returned to film production, stating that one of the main goals of the new Ministry of Culture would be to make sure that this erratically enforced provision be fully implemented. In response, the Communist Party's Eva Mela added the need to enforce another provision of the same law that called for one and a half percent of profits from television channels to be set aside for supporting film production, as well as the need to democratize the structure by which state funds are distributed. Rigas Axelos, of SYRIZA, agreed with Damanaki and Mela, but also stressed the need for the government to put into place economic incentives for private investment in film. He also refuted Dravillas's earlier claim that the country's largest film institutions are autonomous from the state: "Regardless of what has been said earlier, the truth is that these supposedly 'autonomous' institutions are actually very closely tied to the Ministry, since the lists of candidates for the board of directors and general assembly are circulated for months in the offices of the Ministry, so that the Ministry can comb through the candidates and weed out the ones they don't want."

Underlying all these responses was a larger question about the "proper" role of the state in processes of cultural production and the shaping of public culture. While Dravillas claimed that the government was not responsible for the distribution of funds, implying that the state should not be meddling in the decision-making processes of funding bodies, Damanaki contended that the state not only had the ability to affect funding decisions, but that it should. Axelos, however, argued that the state did, in fact, meddle improperly, interfering in the hiring of personnel for political purposes, while Mela joined Damanaki and Axelos in calling for the state to enforce existing laws designed to support film production. Although Dravillas's position seemed far from those of the other candidates, they were all based on the values of objectivity, transparency, and accountability. Dravillas's assertion that the Ministry was not involved in the affairs of the various institutions it funded was an attempt to present the state as neutral, distance the Ministry from what was seen as an improper distribution of funds, and show that the government had nothing to hide. Axelos's denunciation of the Ministry's political scheming was based on the same privileging of objectivity and transparency. The three nonincumbents promised a government that could be held accountable to enforce laws, whether those laws aim to increase public or private funding.

As discussed in greater detail elsewhere in this book, these terms—accountability, transparency, objectivity—were very much in circulation during the period leading up to the emergency parliamentary elections of October 2009. Along with these values, which represented characteristics of an ideally functioning state, an ideal of the active, engaged citizen was also in circulation. This idealized notion of the citizen and her relationship with the state was captured in a campaign commercial for PASOK that played heavily in the months before the elections, in which PASOK emerged victorious. It opens with a shot of large white letters spelling "*KRATOS*" (STATE) towering over a group of people. The letters, resembling large sculptures, are dirty and in disarray, some fallen and others leaning precariously, all surrounded by a high sectioned fence marked with a red sign barring entrance. The crowd—men and women in plain clothes, teenagers, workers in construction hats, policemen, and men in suits—approaches the letters; removes the fence; and begins to clean, repaint, and place the letters upright. As the group diligently works together to fix the "state," a man's voice declares over music, "We won't change anything in our country if we don't change the state. We need a state that's friendly to the citizen. That functions with transparency." The narrator then lists a number of proposed measures, including the online publication of all laws and governmental decisions, expansion of the online Center for Citizen Services, cleaning up the electoral system to rid it of bribery, and increased regulation of the hiring of civil servants. In the last shot, the narrator delivers the final lines: "The time has come for us to build a state that functions with transparency and that effectively serves the citizen. The citizen comes first." Meanwhile, the "citizens" who helped repair "the state" hang out happily in front of the bright, restored letters as though in a public square: an older couple walk hand in hand, a young man and woman chat on a park bench, a woman pushes a stroller, and two boys play with a ball. Echoing much of the anti-corruption rhetoric that dominated public discourse in the months before the 2009 elections, this commercial promises a transparent, accountable, and honest state. Beyond this, it also makes the promise of democracy, even direct democracy, but it is only able to do so through an odd slippage. Despite what we see in the commercial—citizens taking direct action, "cleaning up" the state themselves—none of the specific "measures" narrated in the voiceover can be taken by citizens; rather, they are all actions and initiatives that must be carried out by the government. Although what we see (citizens actively fixing the state) is not the same as what we hear (government measures to fix the state), the juxtaposition of the two in this punchy commercial has the effect of conflating citizen with government and, by extension, voting in the elections with direct democracy. The commercial argues that voting for PASOK to fix the state is equivalent to fixing it oneself, which results in a happy, healthy public.

This ideal of direct democracy—that is, of citizens participating directly in the affairs of the state—was a talking point that came up repeatedly from the politicians present at the debate, most notably after a question posed by Robby Eksiel, film writer for *To Ethnos*. In his question, Eksiel referenced the FOG's demand for an overhaul of the annual State Film Awards. The protesting filmmakers, who viewed the existing annual awards system as corrupted by both money and political maneuvering, wanted the system to be taken out of state hands completely and turned over to a new National Film Academy, comprising active members of the Greek film industry. To the various party representatives, Eksiel asked, "Is there parliamentary will, apart from the new law, for a ministerial decision to change the system which is perceived as corrupt?" New Democracy representative Dravillas began by raising the issue of trust: "It's a shame that there's a system that people don't trust, a shame when those who are being evaluated cannot trust those who are evaluating." His specific proposal was to expand the voting body in the awards system to "seventy-five, a hundred, even thousands"; he then continued, jokingly, "Maybe all the people of the country (*olos o laos*) should vote for the awards in a referendum, to make it truly democratic!" In pushing his logic to an admittedly absurd extreme, he connects the possibility of trust with the model of direct democracy, and it set the tone for the rest of the politicians, whose answers all reflected some aspect of Dravillas's response. Noting that the question of the State Film Awards system "is a good example of the need for dignity and transparency in how the state deals with cinema, and also the need to not have the whole system hijacked by the interests of a few groups," Damanaki stated that "the number of voting members should be larger to avoid the possibility of small interests," and rules should be put in place to limit the power of any particular cultural minister; her answer pits clientelism, nepotism, and the interests of the few against more democratic interests and processes. Axelos followed by arguing that the problem was not how many people vote but rather how they vote in a system that accommodates or even encourages behind-the-scenes conspiring, and he proposed that filmmakers themselves be allowed to come up with a new system, with "no state and no agency from above" dictating how they are to be evaluated. While Axelos takes a slightly different angle from Dravillas and Damanaki, his response still draws on the power of the democratic ideal of people actively deciding for themselves the structure of the system in which they are to operate. Nikos Mylonas of the Green Ecologists took a more blunt approach to the question, declaring unequivocally but vaguely, "We support democracy, the inclusion of as many citizens and institutions as possible. We want the widening of voting members, as well as the creation of as clear a voting system as possible in order to decrease the possibility of scheming and to create something as objective as possible."

All this talk of democracy—of transparency, accountability, objectivity, meritocracy—would perhaps be out of place in other debates centering on a national cinema, but in this case it was an indication of the degree to which the FOG movement had succeeded in politicizing the public discourse on cinema in Greece, so that the structuring terms of that discourse were now the responsibilities of the state and the rights of the citizen. Like the PASOK campaign commercial, such a discourse posits a relationship of trust, service, and direct interaction between state and citizen: a two-way relationship in which citizens have the power to change and shape the state that governs them, and the state responds to the needs and desires of its citizens. More importantly, not only did the event insist *discursively* on notions of accountability and direct engagement between state and citizen, but the actual "debate" was an attempt to perform or enact that very relationship and those very values. In its form and organization, it was clearly designed to enact the ideal of democratic dialogue, providing a structure in which political candidates were brought face-to-face with members of the public and made to engage with them directly in a rational-critical dialogue. This concern was evident in the moderator's frequent reminders to all the participants about the proper debate process: when each person is allowed to speak, for how long, and the proper way for each person to make an address. Andreadakis's nearly obsessive insistence on the proper forms of interaction and engagement highlights the performative dimension of the debate, as an enactment of a particular form of publicness and of public interaction with the state.

This performance was suddenly disrupted when, after the journalists finished posing their questions to the panel of candidates, it came time for FOG to respond. Rather than following the "rules" of the prescribed process as laid out by Andreadakis, the FOG members responded with a refusal to participate on the given terms. Instead of asking a question about policy proposals or the new film law, as was expected, they used their turn as an opportunity to comment critically on the debate and make a number of their own public statements. As a representative of FOG, producer Konstantinos Moriatis began cynically: "We don't have a question, because we really don't think that the new law is going to be hammered out here." Despite Andreadakis's loud immediate objections to this "breach of process," Moriatis continued, albeit half-seriously, "So what we're asking for now, since we're practical people, is that we're going to organize a Week of Greek Cinema to show the films we've made this year, which means we need about €10,000. We've asked the leadership of the Thessaloniki festival for it, but they haven't given us an answer yet." With Moriatis's statement, the FOG was essentially opting out of the particular form of public interaction—the performance of an ideal of direct democracy and of direct engagement between state and citizen—that the debate was trying to enact and, in so doing, calling into question its very purpose. Their refusal to participate opened up a rupture in that discursive space, into which they inserted their own discourse. After Moriatis spoke, director Elisabeth Chronopoulou read an official statement, written collectively by the FOG, denouncing what they considered to be an attempt by the Greek Directors' Guild (GDG) and other film industry unions, together with the Thessaloniki Film Festival and Ministry of Culture, to undermine Giorgos Papalios, the president of the Greek Film Center (GFC), by conspiring to orchestrate a vote of no-confidence at the last GFC general assembly. The statement went on to express support for Papalios, describing him as someone who supports new talent and works to help struggling filmmakers, thus threatening "those who are indifferent to the advancement of Greek cinema and care only for their narrow individual or corporate interests." Next, Vardis Marinakis read a statement addressed to the Directors' Guild, its president, and board of directors accusing them of playing politics and pursuing personal gain rather than fostering filmmakers and filmmaking in Greece. Last, director Konstantina Voulgaris read the names of the sixty-four filmmakers who had signed the statement, some of whom were members of the GDG and were resigning from the guild. The filmmakers' statements set off an explosion of reactions. Some in the audience erupted in applause and vocal approval, while some shouted that they wanted to add their names to the list of signatures. Andreadakis yelled into his microphone, declaring that all of this was out of line and breaking the rules of the debate, while the president of the Greek Directors' Guild, Haris Papadopoulos, visibly upset, shot out of his seat and demanded to be given a chance to respond. What ensued was a shouting match between Papadopoulos and Papalios, also present for the debate, with each aggressively accusing the other of improper conduct. As Papalios yelled that Papadopoulos was, "as the Americans say, a 'loser,'" the entire room devolved into chaos, with the politicians making a quick dash for the door, journalists and audience members standing up and shouting at each other, and Andreadakis imploring everyone to settle down and return to their seats. At that point, however, it was already obvious that the "debate" was over, and the room eventually started to clear.

In its spirit of refusal and disruption of discourse as usual, the FOG's intervention was reminiscent of the protesters' interruption of the NET newscast. As with the latter, what was most striking about the FOG statements was not *what* was being advocated or communicated, but rather *how* the message was delivered. In fact, the content of the FOG declarations did not depart much from the underlying rhetoric of the rest of the debate. The same references to corruption, clientelistic politics, transparency, and objectivity that dominated the politicians' statements also served as the rhetorical basis for the FOG's positions; their accusations just happened to be aimed at others. Thus, the real impact of their intervention came from the *form* that it took: rejecting the format of the debate as performance of democratic dialogue, casting the effectiveness of that performance into doubt, and in its place enacting a different form of public address. In this sense, they were acting as a counterpublic as defined by Michael Warner, who insists on the performative, or "poetic-expressive," character of counterpublic discourse: "A counterpublic maintains at some level, conscious or not, an awareness of its subordinate status. The cultural horizon against which it marks itself off is not just a general or wider public but a dominant one. And the conflict extends not just to ideas or policy questions but to the speech genres and modes of address that constitute the public or to the hierarchy among media. The discourse that constitutes it is not merely a different or alternative idiom but one that in other contexts would be regarded with hostility or with a sense of indecorousness."[13] In other words, what distinguishes a counterpublic is not just the oppositionality of *what* it says or claims, but rather the "political dissensus" of the discursive act itself, that is, the oppositionality of its *form* and the disruption it introduces into a larger discursive context dominated by more conventional modes of public address.

In the case of the Opening Nights debate, the dominant form of publicness, built into the organization and the rules of the event, was that of deliberative democracy: reasoned, orderly, communicative. It is the same sense of publicness as communication and dialogue that, as discussed earlier in this book, the Thessaloniki Festival was so invested in cultivating—or, perhaps more precisely, cultivating the *appearance of*. In her critique of deliberative democracy, Chantal Mouffe criticizes its assumption of "the possibility of grounding authority and legitimacy on some forms of public reasoning" and its belief in "a form of rationality which is not merely instrumental but has a normative dimension: the 'reasonable' for [John] Rawls, 'communicative rationality' for [Jürgen] Habermas."[14] Proponents of this liberal model, such as Rawls and Habermas, insist on notions of "rational consensus," "communicative action," and "free public reason" as the key to an orderly, well-functioning collective life. Pointing to what she calls "the limits of consensus," Mouffe argues that "this model of democratic politics is unable to acknowledge the dimension of antagonism that the pluralism of values entails and its ineradicable character."[15] Like Hannah Arendt and Bonnie Honig, Mouffe starts from the premise that multiplicity, plurality, and irresolvable difference are unavoidable characteristics of public life, and conflict and contestation necessarily follow. The model of "agonistic pluralism" that she proposes, similar in many ways to the agonistic collectivity that Honig describes, does not aim to eliminate such conflict through "deliberation and rational discussion": "Indeed, given the ineradicable pluralism of value, there is no rational resolution of the conflict, hence its antagonistic dimension. . . . One of the keys to the thesis of agonistic pluralism is that, far from jeopardizing democracy, agonistic confrontation is in fact its very condition of existence. Modern democracy's specificity lies in the recognition and legitimation of conflict and the refusal to suppress it by imposing an authoritarian order."[16] Here, truly public life is made possible through contestation, through the "vibrant clash of democratic political positions," through the mobilization of affect to support those positions, and in the continuous tangle that constitutes the political.[17] And for this reason, the forms of collective life and the configurations of power that result from these contestations and clashes are always provisional and partial.

It is this agonistic sense of publicness that the FOG's disruption introduced into the debate and its performance of orderly, democratic dialogue. In an event carefully orchestrated to stage a reasoned, well-behaved public interaction between state and citizen, the filmmakers' rejection of the prescribed process constituted a refusal to engage with the state on the given terms. Most important, their counterpublic act had the larger effect of dissolving the order of the event altogether, causing the debate to erupt into chaos and end prematurely. Where they failed with the festival—to transform it from a space of celebration into a space of protest—they succeeded with the Opening Nights debate, transforming the orderly scene of public dialogue into an unruly scene of conflict and contestation, marking this field of cultural production with the agonistic collectivity that was taking over public life more broadly.

SCALES OF CITIZENSHIP

The filmmakers' refusal to participate in the debate was not, however, a refusal to engage with the state. On the contrary, the main purpose of the group's public statements and actions was precisely to address and renegotiate their relationship with the state, and FOG members consistently positioned themselves primarily as citizens. Although they did identify as a group of filmmakers, artists, and cultural producers, this identification was not foregrounded through an insistence on any particular aesthetic movement or agenda; instead, their public rhetoric always emphasized the responsibility of the state to provide the necessary conditions for a healthy film industry.[18] Thus, the filmmakers' rejection of the citizen-state engagement staged by the Opening Nights debate was not a rejection of the citizen-state relation itself but rather of the specific way in which it was being formulated in the structure of the debate: as an orderly dialogue, but with the public only able to pose questions and, like in the PASOK campaign commercial, with citizens taking on a passive role, limited to registering their will only through the act of voting, and with the capacity for action granted only to the state. In contrast, the FOG's actions proposed and performed a different model of citizenship, one whose relation to the state was unruly, non-compliant, agonistic, and complicated by multiple scales of collectivity, from the local to the transnational.

The degree to which the FOG members were perceived as citizens standing up to the state was made clear to me one evening after an open discussion during a week of "FOG Films" in Thessaloniki in January 2010. The filmmakers had organized the screenings as a way to finally show their work in Thessaloniki after withholding their films from the 2009 festival; together with the screenings, a series of open discussions was held so that the filmmakers could talk with members of the local public about issues such as the new film law and film education reform. A similar week of screenings and discussions had taken place in Athens in early November 2009, right before the start of the Thessaloniki festival; while the discussions in Athens had been packed, full of FOG members and FOG sympathizers, in Thessaloniki the discussions were less well-attended, and there was tension between the FOG and many people in the audience. The open discussion on film education reform was particularly tense. In the main theater in the Olympion—the festival building where, somewhat ironically, FOG had rented the cinema for their week of screenings—an audience of local filmmakers, teachers, and students from the Aristotle University film department listened as Antonietta Angelidi and Rea Walden, representatives of the FOG committee on film education, outlined the group's positions. Their statements remained general, as with most FOG position statements. Rather than giving specific or concrete suggestions for what might be changed or improved, they outlined broad shifts that they wanted to see, including state support for film education to be incorporated into elementary and secondary school curricula, improvement of the ailing Aristotle University film department through administrative reorganization and the allotment of more resources, and the creation of a new state film school in Athens that would foster "innovative" work. Their positions were articulated in terms of citizenship and the state; in their closing remarks, they asserted, "For all of this, we need the support of the state, as much political will as economic support, because film belongs to all of us. As art, it expresses and renews our culture. As education, it improves the developmental level of the country and shapes better citizens."

In an audience of people with enough interest in cinema to attend such a discussion, I did not expect these general, and generally reasonable, positions to face much resistance. However, much of the response was antagonistic. While some expressed agreement with the filmmakers' positions, a number of people complained that FOG was downplaying the importance of the film department in Thessaloniki, which in their eyes was an existing state film school badly in need of more support, and they expressed concern that a new state film school in Athens would divert resources and attention away from their own department. Thanasis, a local journalist and film critic, asked if the FOG film education committee had been in touch with other organizations or institutions, noting that the Thessaloniki Film Festival had a long history of organizing educational programs. A group of students stated dismissively that they had already been discussing these issues for years, as an organized group and on their own dedicated website. Complaining that they had never had the help or interest of the professional Greek film world, they asked where FOG had been all this time. At one point, a fight nearly broke out between FOG members and another small group of students who had started to record the discussion with a video camera for a documentary they wanted to make on film education in Greece; the FOG members responded negatively, claiming that as organizers of the event, only they had a right to record the event, and as the argument heated up, one filmmaker even tried to snatch the camera out of the student's hands. The sense of antagonism was palpable, and it continued after the discussion ended, as I sat down for a coffee with some of the event's attendees, including Thanasis; Penny, an adjunct lecturer at the film department; and some of her students. One student, Kalliroi, had been working as an usher during the discussion, and she was a staunch supporter of FOG. She became noticeably upset and tried to interject as Thanasis spoke disdainfully of the filmmakers, arguing that they should have come to represent themselves during the festival in November, and that it was out of line for them to come now, bringing with them ideas and plans that he felt were disconnected from the local public. Penny agreed, complaining that no one from the FOG film education committee had even contacted anyone at the Aristotle film department to notify them of the open discussion, let alone to ask for their input. At one point, however, Kalliroi interrupted to defend the

FOG members: "You can't blame them—it's not like the festival was going to pay for them to come up to Thessaloniki and stay in hotels. And besides, we can't keep talking about what's past—we have to think about the present, what to do now and in the future. At least they're doing something! They're not a big organization or an agency. They're just people, just normal people who have a right to work. They're workers (*ergazomenoi*)! They're citizens (*polites*)!" In response, everyone at the table grew quiet and nodded in agreement. I was surprised to see that even Penny and Thanasis, who just minutes before had been discussing FOG in such critical terms, seemed to agree with Kalliroi, and Thanasis added pensively, "You're right—it's a citizens' movement (*kinisi politon*)." It seemed that, regardless of varying public perceptions of the FOG movement, the filmmakers had succeeded in presenting an image of themselves as citizens—not simply as a highly specialized group of cultural producers looking to better their lot, but as a group of cultural workers claiming their rights as subjects of the Greek state. Even in an unsympathetic crowd, this image of citizens addressing the state ultimately trumped other perceptions.

What is foregrounded in this identification of FOG as a "citizens' movement" is the filmmakers' position as *national* subjects, and in this sense, their boycott offers a counterpoint to Thomas Elsaesser's characterization of film festivals as "post-national" phenomena, that is, "another way of transcending the national for European films" as they address foreign publics, circulate in foreign markets, and become transnational cultural products.[19] While film festivals may have had their beginnings in the organizational logic of nations, he writes, the nation now exists in film festivals only as a "second-order concept"—a discursive construct, strategic rhetoric, or self-conscious category.[20] In an article on film festival programming, Liz Czach suggests that even this is no longer the case, as the relevance of the category of national cinema is now called into question: "Its future in an era dominated by so-called post-nationalism seems uncertain. When co-productions and co-ventures as funding models are gaining popularity, the ability to easily define and delineate a national cinema becomes increasingly more difficult."[21] For Czach, the category of the national in the context of film festivals is becoming less relevant in a world characterized more and more by transnational processes and products. In the case of the FOG boycott, however, we can see how the category of the national is just as relevant as ever. As the filmmakers insisted, they chose the festival as the site of their protest because it was the one public arena in which their actions would be most visible and effective. What is important to note here is that their protest was effective precisely because of their identification as Greek filmmakers. As a small group of professionals working in a subsidized industry, they had neither the political nor economic clout to effect change; however, what they did have was their visibility as Greek filmmakers, an important asset during a year in which the state-sponsored festival was eager to present its fiftieth-anniversary edition as a celebration of Greek cinema, new and old. By refusing to participate in the festival, the filmmakers were activating their national identification, putting it to use in negotiating their relationship to the state. In addition, it is important to remember that the ultimate goal of the protest was to effect real change in national film policy. While the filmmakers used the rhetoric of citizens' rights, they did so to engage the state; address and make demands of their government; and change the conditions under which they, as citizens of the Greek state, produce and exhibit films. In this sense, the nation is not simply a "second-order concept." To be a Greek filmmaker, working in Greece, means to be subject to a very real complex of conditions, laws, and policies that regulate all aspects of filmmaking, from fundraising, permits, and production to distribution and exhibition. As Janet Harbord argues, the discourse of the "post-national" elides some of the ways in which cinema and nation are still closely connected, not just discursively or symbolically but also structurally and materially, through the work of national film centers and institutions; the film industry's contributions to the national economy; and tax exemptions, subsidies, and other government measures and regulations.[22] For the protesters, it was this practical and material relationship to the state that was at stake in their boycott, and it is in this way that we see the nation still very present in the Thessaloniki festival.

But the resistance with which the FOG was met during the open discussion in Thessaloniki indicates that this sympathetic perception of the protest as a national "citizens' movement" was not uncontested. Rather, a number of different scales—local, national, European—were activated, both in the boycott and the reactions it provoked. In Thessaloniki, public reaction to the protesting filmmakers focused on the local rather than the national. A dominant opinion in local press and conversations with festival-goers was that the FOG was undermining Thessaloniki and its institutions, and all of its actions were seen in this light; the boycott was seen as an attempt to sabotage one of the city's most important cultural institutions on the occasion of its jubilee, and the plans for a film academy in Athens were viewed as an attempt to take from Thessaloniki its traditional (and mostly symbolic) status as the film capital of Greece. In particular, critics of FOG pointed to the filmmakers' insistence that the Thessaloniki festival and its Greek program no longer serve as the clearinghouse for new Greek films, and that the State Film Awards be dismantled entirely and replaced with national film academy awards given out in a ceremony in Athens. In the open discussion on film education reform, many of the criticisms of FOG's positions were based on the perception that the local film department and the festival's educational initiatives were being overlooked, snubbed, or even threatened. While there was sympathy for the FOG members, who were regarded as citizens negotiating with the state, this perspective competed with the predominant view that the boycott was the work of a group of Athenian filmmakers uninterested in Thessaloniki, its public, and its filmmaking community and whose actions posed a threat to the city. While in public FOG members never spoke ill of the Thessaloniki public, always choosing to present their movement as nationally relevant, in private they expressed frustration with the Thessaloniki filmmakers and public, whom they considered to be provincial and narrow-minded. These tensions came to a head during the FOG screenings in Thessaloniki when, on the fourth day, an open discussion entitled "Thessaloniki and Greek Cinema" culminated in a row between representatives of FOG and local Thessaloniki filmmakers.

In presenting their case to the public, the FOG members identified themselves as citizens and cast the stakes of their protest as national, while the Thessaloniki public responded by insisting on their own local identity as a public, the specific identity of the protesting filmmakers as Athenians, and the festival as a local institution. But upon closer inspection, we see that these categories of local and national are mutually implicated. For example, filmmakers and the cinema public in Thessaloniki saw the FOG and its boycott as a threat to their locality precisely because they felt that something very important was being taken from them, namely, national status. When faced with the possibility of the State Film Awards and the official Greek program moving from Thessaloniki, they responded furiously; not content with the prestige of the international festival, they made it clear that there was a great deal at stake in being identified as a nationally significant place. As the site of the Greek film festival and the Greek State Film Awards, the city of Thessaloniki had national dimensions and a national presence for at least ten days of the year; it was a place that was defined, understood, and experienced as a national one. The possibility of losing that status was seen as a definitive threat.

Similarly, the FOG's insistence on the national was not uncompli-cated. Because the group started unofficially, growing primarily through word of mouth between friends, most of its members were indeed film-makers based in Athens, and relatively little effort was made to reach out to filmmakers beyond this group or in other parts of the country. Thus, FOG cannot truly be said to be representative of the national filmmaking community. In addition, their goal to bring the national film awards to the capital city of Athens, a seemingly logical move, hides a less obvious but equally powerful insistence on the local: another kind of "provincialism" that lies at the heart of Greece's perpetual prob-lem of centralization. In this case, it is the particular locality of Athens, always defined as national and central, that we see at play.

Finally, all of the filmmakers' actions unfolded within a larger Euro-pean and international context. For example, the group's claims had more traction precisely because of some of its members' successes abroad that year. Had films like *Dogtooth, Strella,* and *Plato's Academy* not garnered international attention and prizes at festivals like Cannes, Locarno, and the Berlinale, then the FOG members would have had much less leverage in threatening to keep their films from the Thessalo-niki festival, and their boycott would have received much less domestic attention. The international context was also an important factor for some of the protesting filmmakers in calculating the stakes of the boy-cott. As Stelios explained to me, the protest "wasn't just a condemna-tion. It was an action, with real costs. For some of the others, the stakes weren't so high; their films had already premiered at other big festivals. But for me, this was my first film, and it hadn't been chosen for any other festivals. This was going to be its premiere at an international film festival, with foreign distributors. So [our boycott] has cost me." For the many FOG members who were in a similar situation, their decision to boycott the festival as a means of pursuing changes within their country meant that they were sacrificing the opportunity to promote their films beyond it. And in making their claims, the protesting film-makers, many of whom had studied and/or worked abroad, justified their demands by pointing to the vast disparity between the conditions of film production in Greece and the resources and state support avail-able to filmmakers in other European countries. Among the many texts that circulated among FOG members, some of the most discussed and most often referenced were documents outlining public funding for film production, distribution, and exhibition in France, Germany, Denmark, and the United Kingdom. In this sense, the protesters attempted to engage the state as European citizens, demanding rights and privileges comparable to those enjoyed by filmmakers elsewhere in Europe.

In the filmmakers' boycott, we see an agonistic model of citizenship practiced across multiple scales of collectivity. The notion of citizenship at work in the boycott, as well as in reactions to it, was complicated by the intersection of different and sometimes conflicting identifications, interests, and investments across the local, national, and transnational. A closer look at how the FOG movement conceived of this state-citizen relation—and particularly how it conceived of *cultural* citizenship, or the relation between state, citizen, and cultural production—reveals an underlying logic, as well as another slippage or conflation between state and citizen, that may explain the movement's end.

HOMO ŒCONOMICUS AND THE PATRON-STATE

Although FOG defined itself primarily as a "citizens' movement," in opposition to a dysfunctional state, there were many ways in which the distinction between the group and the state, in its various representatives and agencies, was blurred. At the most obvious level, numerous FOG members were themselves employees or representatives of state agencies or state-supported organizations. For example, a founding member of the movement, Angelos Frantzis, was also the artistic director of the 2009 Thessaloniki festival's opening and closing ceremonies, as well as of the Street Cinema program. At the same time that he boycotted the festival by keeping his new film from playing in that year's Greek program, he was also busy preparing for the festival's fiftieth-anniversary celebrations and, of course, as an employee of the festival with a relatively high position, he was in attendance for the 2009 edition. Lucia Rikaki, another active and enthusiastic member of the FOG movement, also served as the long-time head coordinator of the Balkan Fund program and as such attended the festival. Marcos Holevas, who took on somewhat of a leadership position among the protesting filmmakers, was also head of the Greek Film Commission, another state agency.

But on another level, the group's relationship to the Greek Film Center was a point of ambiguity. The GFC is the main state agency to which Greek directors and producers can apply for public funding. At the end of the Opening Nights debate on Greek cinema, FOG members unequivocally expressed their support for Papalios, president of the GFC. Papalios, who started his career in the early 1970s as a producer for some of Theo Angelopoulos's first films, is a well-respected figure in the Greek film world, and the FOG members felt that he was their ally because of the increased support that younger directors and producers had received primarily through his work at the Film Center. As a FOG member explained to me, for a long time there was the sense that public funding for film production was granted according to seniority, not merit, and many FOG members felt that Papalios was actively fighting that system by ensuring that younger filmmakers were granted production funds. In so doing, Papalios was at odds with many film industry unions, which placed a high value on seniority; according to FOG, however, these unions had grown over the years into a stagnant holding pen for film professionals who were no longer actively making films, and therefore acted as a drain on state funds.[23] In their statement at the end of the Opening Nights debate, FOG directors denounced the Greek Directors' Guild, from which they withdrew their membership, in solidarity with Papalios. Despite their support for Papalios, many in FOG had complaints about the Greek Film Center, primarily because they believed that it did not devote enough of its annual budget to supporting film production, and many state fund awardees continued to await their money, some for several years. Their frustration became evident at one of their meetings, in early March 2010, where those present were asked to say if they were owed money by the Center and, if so, how much. As directors and producers around the room started detailing how much they were owed and how long they had been waiting, one of the filmmakers exclaimed in frustration, "Everyone has been saying over the past few years that these directors are the 'children' of the Greek Film Center. Well, maybe the kids don't have a father anymore!"

At this meeting, it was decided that the group needed to stage another public event, a dramatic intervention to keep the movement in the public eye. The filmmakers opted for a symbolic occupation of a state agency building that would double as a press conference, where they would reiterate their demands for a new film law. Everyone agreed that the intervention should take place either in the main building of the Ministry of Culture and Tourism or in the Film Center building, for symbolic reasons, as each represented the state. The Ministry was quickly ruled out because it was tucked away on a quiet side street, and the invisibility of the intervention would render it useless, while the Film Center occupied a building along a pedestrian plaza one block from the new Acropolis Museum, a much better location for a public intervention. At this point, however, the filmmakers' ambiguous relationship to the Greek Film Center proved problematic. Some objected to occupying the Film Center building, because their main target was the Ministry of Culture, not the Center. Others argued that an occupation of the Film Center would be pointless. One producer asserted that it would be ridiculous to stage an occupation of an organization that is not only sympathetic to their movement but would welcome their intervention; another director agreed, saying that because they were already identified with Papalios, and because they would be welcomed by Film Center staff, their intervention would face no resistance and the very meaning of "occupation" would be negated. Yet others argued that the GFC should, in fact, be the target, and that the FOG movement should make an effort to distance itself from the Center. These deliberations point to the ambiguous relationship between the members of FOG, who were trying to position themselves publicly in opposition to the state, and the state agency with which they shared a close but conflicted connection. In the end, the group decided to go ahead with the symbolic occupation-cum-press conference of the Film Center two weeks later. As they anticipated, they were warmly welcomed by Center staff, who learned of their action ahead of time and had even cleared space, rearranging furniture and opening up dividers between conference rooms to better accommodate the "occupiers." As Film Center staff members met the crowd with greetings of "Come on in!" "Welcome!" and "Bravo!," I sensed that the politicized intention of the filmmakers was neutralized, and the rest of the intervention unfolded as though it were a regular FOG press conference, ironically hosted by a state agency.

This conflicted relationship between the protesting filmmakers and the Greek Film Center, simultaneously a representative of the negligent patron-state and an ally or "father," was a symptom of a deeper ambiguity in the FOG's relationship to the state. In my conversations with people on all sides of the FOG debate, a word that often came up in describing Greek cinema was *kratikodiaitos,* which in its meaning and connotations reveals a great deal about this ambiguous relationship. In its literal translation, *kratikodiaitos*—a combination of the two words *kratos,* meaning "the state," and *diaita,* meaning "diet"—means "fed by the state," and it is used, often disparagingly, to describe any entity that relies primarily on state funding for its continued existence. In Greece, most fields of cultural production can be characterized as *kratikodiaitos,* as sales and ticket revenue are often not enough to support sustained activity, not to mention large cultural institutions. When used to describe particular works such as films, the term often carries negative connotations about the quality of the work. For example, during a meeting at the Greek Film Center, then vice president of the Center Dimitris Sofianopoulos explained to me that in his opinion, Greek cinema was not state-supported because it was commercially unviable, but rather that the opposite was true. In other words, it was commercially unviable because it was *kratikodiaitos:* "Basically, filmmakers get money from the state with no strings attached. You don't have to pay it back, and you don't have to answer to anyone, and so you have directors running off with the money and making movies that don't take anyone into account, not the funders and not the audience." For him, the solution was not to stop public funding for film production but rather to make productions more accountable for the funds they did receive and give the Center more control in determining the quality of films produced. FOG filmmakers had differing opinions on independent Greek cinema's "state diet." One basic argument was that cinema *should* be fully supported by the state rather than relying on private investors or commercial success, the idea being that only when cinema is free of commercial obligations can it achieve artistic freedom of expression. In a strange twist, the state, which in Greece is usually associated with bureaucracy, sluggishness, and lack of creativity, here comes to be associated with innovation, artistic freedom, and experimentation, while the free market is seen as constraining and limiting.

Some members of FOG argued that despite the usual characterizations, Greek cinema was not, in fact, *kratikodiaitos,* precisely because so little public funding was available or, when promised, actually received. In other words, according to these filmmakers, the "state diet" was actually a "starvation diet." And yet others felt that if the existing film laws were actually implemented, Greek cinema would not be *kratikodiaitos* at all but rather *aftotrofodotoumenos,* "self-fed" or self-supporting. This argument was detailed in an early public statement made by FOG and disseminated online, where they claim:

> Every year, the Greek state receives about 10 million euros in income from the special tax on movie tickets. Note: this money does not come out of the larger state budget, but rather is a direct tax on those who go to the movies. This tax was created (based on the French law) explicitly and exclusively IN ORDER TO FUND GREEK CINEMA. . . . Last year, Greek films sold 2.5 million tickets, which represents twenty percent of all movie tickets sold in the country, and Greek cinema created jobs for a large number of workers in all areas of film production and distribution. In other words, these films created a work economy that surpasses 25 million euros. . . . In addition, from these jobs, the state collects at least 5 million euros a year in income tax.[24]

The statement goes on to explain that only a small percentage of this tax income generated by the film industry gets reinvested into film production through the Greek Film Center's annual budget, while the rest goes to support peripheral or unrelated activities. The filmmakers maintain that if the state were to implement its own laws, much more of this tax income would be returned directly to producers to support film production. In the current situation, however, with the film industry generating more money in tax revenue than it receives through state funding, the industry is "making a profit for the state and contributing to its annual budget!" Following this logic, one filmmaker even went so far to as to declare in a FOG meeting, "The state is robbing us!"

Whether the filmmakers were correct in their interpretation of the law, this statement is significant for the way it articulates the relationship between filmmakers and the state. By focusing on the film industry as the source of public funding, through the tax revenue that it generates, the filmmakers position themselves rather than the state at the head of this funding stream. Reversing the usual relationship implied by the term *kratikodiaitos,* FOG portrays the film industry as patronizing the state. Pushing this interpretation further, I would argue that this portrayal of the relationship between the film industry and the state even blurs the distinction between the two, as the filmmakers imply that state or public money is, in fact, rightfully "their money." In the overlapping of two of their basic claims, that the state should support the film industry and that it should do so through funds that the film industry itself provides to the state, we also see an overlapping of the state and the filmmakers. In the argument that state funding belongs to the public because it comes from the public, two senses of the term "public" converge: "public" as in *the* public, and "public" as in "of the state." Although the FOG movement defined itself in opposition to the state, underlying the movement is a close relationship, and even identification, with the state.

Most importantly, this relationship is conceived as fundamentally economic, with the state and citizen made equivalent via a mechanism by which each is converted into the common currency of economic value. In FOG's justification of public funding for film production, the filmmaker-citizen and the various state agencies involved are all understood in terms of the economic value that they can generate, absorb, regulate, or disseminate. With this quantification of the citizen-state relationship, citizenship and publicness itself come to be understood in economic terms. This totalizing economic perspective is an example of what Michel Foucault describes as the neoliberal drive "to apply economic analysis to a series of objects, to domains of behavior or conduct which were not market forms of behavior or conduct . . . to apply the grid, the schema, and the model of *homo œconomicus* to not only every economic actor, but to every social actor in general."[25] Building on Foucault, Wendy Brown argues that this neoliberal market rationality "normatively constructs and interpellates individuals as entrepreneurial actors in every sphere of life . . . configuring morality entirely as a matter of rational deliberation about costs, benefits, and consequences."[26] What results from this economizing logic is a gutting of the citizen as political subject: "The model neoliberal citizen is one who strategizes for her- or himself among various social, political, and economic options, not one who strives with others to alter or organize those options. A fully realized neoliberal citizenry would be the opposite of public-minded; indeed it would barely exist as a public."[27] Here we arrive at the central contradiction of the FOG movement. Although the group positioned itself as an oppositional movement aligned with the larger "uprisings" unfolding across the country in 2009, which were deeply political and concerned in large part with the decline of public life, it articulated its relationship to the state in fundamentally economic terms, thus embracing the logic of *homo œconomicus,* which, in effect, vacates the political. The goal of the FOG may have been to draw attention to the responsibilities of the state toward its citizens by demonstrating to what degree two senses of "public"—"the public" and "of the state"—are mutually constitutive, but the market rationality that it mobilized to make its argument had the effect of negating a third sense of "public," the Arendtian sense of political collectivity. Moreover, it is the same neoliberal rationality driving the state policies that created the conditions that the filmmakers were protesting in the first place. By buying into the logic of *homo œconomicus,* the FOG movement conflated state and citizen in a way that ultimately went against its stated political interests.

The confusion resulting from such conflation and blurring of the citizen-state relation was also reflected in the group's demands for and reactions to the new film law. The FOG members wanted the state to have a smaller presence, which was made clear in their demand for the dissolution of the State Film Awards, as well as their insistence on a tax incentive for private investors, the only legal provision for the funding of film production that would not involve state money in any way. Indeed, when the new law was finally proposed in the fall of 2010 and passed in December of the same year, it was praised by members of FOG as an exciting new film policy that fostered development in the industry by cutting down on bureaucracy and outdated state structures.[28] The law did away with the State Film Awards, established an independent Film Academy, and instated the tax incentive for private investors. It also drastically reduced bureaucratic bulk by shrinking the size of hiring committees, selection committees, and boards of directors for the various state film agencies and organizations, including the Greek Film Center and the Thessaloniki Festival; doing away entirely with the large general assemblies that used to constitute an important part of these organizations' administrative structures; and streamlining hiring and selection processes. A close look at the new law, however, reveals that the authority of the state is as strong and wide-reaching as ever. Cutting down on bureaucracy meant that processes that would have normally gone through large general assemblies, committees, or boards were now determined quickly by the Minister of Culture and Tourism, including the appointment of directors and new board members; in this way, power was concentrated in the hands of government officials. In addition, new private investment tax incentives were legislated in such a way as to route all such investments through the state. The law stipulated that all private funds for a film must first be registered with the Ministry of Culture and Tourism, deposited into an account at the Greek Film Center, and then dispersed through the GFC to the producers of the film, which must also be registered with the Ministry. Within a system designed to make the film industry more independent from the state, the state continues to play a central role. On top of these contradictions and tensions was the larger irony of the FOG members, so critical of the state, yet turning back to it and demanding more legislation. As cultural producers, they were unable to think themselves outside of the state.

In the end, the passage of the new law did not have the effect that the filmmakers had hoped it would. In the summer of 2012, I ran into a couple of FOG members at a screening. It had been a year and a half since parliament had passed the new film law, and I asked them if things were any better now. Was it getting easier to fund projects? No, they both responded, with an air of resignation. The new law had come right on the heels of the country's first bailout by the troika of the European Union, European Central Bank, and International Monetary Fund, and since then there had been further bailouts, a government resignation, a caretaker government, and an ever-worsening economy, all of which made the implementation of the new law nearly impossible. With the recent announcement that the Ministry of Culture would be subsumed within a consolidated Ministry of Education, Religion, Culture, and Sports, the filmmakers were convinced that all public funding for film production would be frozen. Their tone of weary acceptance reflected a sentiment I encountered often at that time, one of the darkest periods of the recession: Amid crisis and austerity, when even schools and hospitals struggled to stay open, how could anyone continue to insist on public funding for the arts and cultural production?

The effective failure of the new law, and the filmmakers' resignation to that failure, was not just one of any number of possible outcomes. Rather, it was the logical conclusion of FOG's embrace of market rationality in its confrontation with the state. While other forms of publicness were at work in their movement—in particular, the agonistic counterpublicness enacted through their strategy of refusal—ultimately, the filmmakers argued for the public value of cinema in economic terms. In doing so, they configured state, citizen, and cultural production in relation to one another via the logic of *homo œconomicus,* which evaluates everything according to potential profitability and "a calculus of utility, benefit, or satisfaction against a micro-economic grid of scarcity, supply and demand, and moral value-neutrality."[29] Having bought into this logic, the filmmakers had no choice but to concede when, as the crisis escalated and resources became increasingly scarce, this economizing rationale dictated that public funding for filmmaking was no longer affordable. According to this hierarchy of value, when belts begin to tighten around what is considered necessary or essential, cultural production is left outside that designation and instead deemed a "luxury," leaving little room for alternative understandings of the public value of the arts, and indeed of public life itself.

CHAPTER 5

The Value of Mereness

The sense of resignation that settled over the film world by 2012 can be seen as one potential answer to this book's opening question, "Is culture a luxury?" This question, at the heart of public debate over the relationship between the state and cultural production, entered into urgent circulation in Greece early in the economic crisis. After the center-left PASOK victory in the 2009 emergency national elections, amid the chaotic shuffling of government positions and speculation about who would be chosen for prime cabinet spots, it was announced that the Ministry for Touristic Development would be merged with the Ministry of Culture to form the new Ministry of Culture and Tourism. At a time when the dire condition of many state-sponsored cultural institutions and initiatives had led to heightened public criticism over the state's handling of cultural matters, this coupling of "culture" (*politismos*) and "tourism" triggered a fresh round of commentary and reflection. In a series of op-ed pieces published in *Kathimerini* immediately following the elections, Antonis Karkagiannis wondered, "Really, what is the deeper relationship between Culture and Tourism that would drive prime minister George Papandreou to consolidate the two?"[1] Arguing that "Culture"—identified as "dance, music, sculpture, painting, architecture, theater, poetry . . . and cinema"—serves to "uplift us" and "make us better [people]," and that "Tourism" is a purely commercial endeavor, Karkagiannis charged that the decision to join the two under the same Ministry was misguided, a consequence of the fact that "we're

a film by
christina phoebe

can a film
be like a nest?

amygdaliá

FIGURE 6. Poster for *Amygdaliá*. Credit: Christina Phoebe Thomopoulos.

always trying to find that [culture] has some 'practical purpose,' some usefulness so that we might be able to understand, finally, what is culture (*politismos*) and what is the job of the Ministry of Culture." He concluded his piece by asking, "What indeed is the work of the Ministry of Culture . . . which is considered (from every point of view but especially the economic) the unwanted stepchild of every government?"[2]

Karkagiannis's concluding question was a variation on a more general query circulating in public discourse at the time, and which has continued to be a point of contention: When the state is faced with what is, in effect, bankruptcy, both economic and political, why do we need state support for the arts? When there are so many basic social needs that are not being adequately met—health care, employment, education, social security— why should the state be concerned with fields of cultural production? In other words, what is the public value of the arts and cultural production? At the Thessaloniki Film Festival, the pressure of this question could be felt as soon as the fiftieth-anniversary edition came to a close. Facing deep cuts in funding from the Ministry of Culture, the new festival director and his staff embraced and projected an attitude of austerity and thrift, as well as a marked sensitivity to the economic crisis and its effects. The opening ceremony of the 2010 festival was pointedly parsimonious, including little more than a few short speeches, while the program of screenings, exhibitions, parties, and other events was significantly leaner than in previous years. In the film world, there was a feeling of general resignation. Explaining why the Balkan Fund program was eliminated after the 2010 edition, one of the program's former coordinators asked me, "How could we justify spending so much money on a script competition, when the situation out there is so bad?"[3] And as we saw at the end of the previous chapter, the worsening economic crisis had caused even members of the FOG, whose movement started on the basic premise that the state should fully support cultural production, to simply accept that the state was unable to do so. Their acceptance was a concession that culture is indeed a luxury, and public funding for the arts an unnecessary expense amid recession and austerity.

Despite the filmmakers' resignation, there were and still are many who continue to insist on the necessity of state support for cultural production. The arguments most often mobilized in support of this position tend to fall along one of two main lines of reasoning, one of which is exemplified in the second op-ed in Karkagiannis's series, entitled "The Absolute Value of Culture." Not unproblematically taking the example of "the Antiquities" as the cultural field par excellence in which the state has been heavily involved, he contends:

> Many maintain that the Antiquities are in some way the conclusive DNA of our "race," which traverses and cuts through our over three thousand year old persistent and permanent presence in this corner of Europe. . . . One thing is certain: if, along with the Antiquities, we take into account the Byzantine and more modern relics, then we have a people who, despite invasions and admixtures, remains clinging to the same piece of rock for centuries, next to the sea, speaking basically the same language and opening its soul to the world in the same way. As many doubts have been expressed concerning the organic continuity of those periods of historical presence, the identification of a people in space and time with its Culture suffices as the starting point for self-knowledge and constitutes that people's particular presence in the modern world. The question is not if we are the blood-heirs [of the past civilization], but rather if, in the modern world, we are its continuers, in a way that is creative. The management of Culture as the management of education is both understandable and worthy of special state concern, and only as such does it find its "useful purpose."[4]

Karkagiannis's understanding of the "Antiquities" and their significance is a prime example of what Eleana Yalouri describes as the experience of archaeological sites in Greece as *lieux de mémoire,* attempts to reconstruct or fabricate bonds of identity with an idea of an ancient culture.[5] Karkagiannis's justification for state-supported "Culture" is based on profoundly essentialist and even biological notions of collective cultural identity and historical continuity; in his opinion, this vaunted cultural heritage is what defines the Greek "people" and their place in the world today, and for this reason the state is obligated to support, preserve, and protect this "Culture." His deeply conservative stance is representative of a nationalist cultural essentialism in Greece that has persisted since before Greek independence and continues today, serving different political interests and social needs at different historical moments. Despite having been extensively deconstructed by anthropologists, historians, and cultural critics, among many others, this essentialist ideology is still offered up by many people today, explicitly or as an underlying assumption, as the justification for state support for cultural fields.

The second line of reasoning in support of public funding for the arts follows the logic of what I call "cultural capitalism."[6] With this term, I am referring to the way in which forms of cultural production are used primarily to accrue cultural and symbolic capital, which can eventually be translated into economic or political profit in a transnational cultural economy. My use of this term builds on Pierre Bourdieu's theory of fields of cultural production, in which these cultural fields are seen as the sites of struggle over symbolic capital. In Bourdieu's formulation, even those fields of cultural production that are marked as most "autonomous," that is, relatively independent from the values and priorities ruling the economic and political fields, are still articulated in economic, quantitative terms and in terms of accrual. This is evident in the way Bourdieu writes about "pure art," characterized as a field founded on "the obligatory recognition of the values of disinterestedness and on the denegation of the 'economy' (of the 'commercial') and of 'economic' profit."[7] Even so, he still describes it as an economy—albeit an "anti-'economic'" one—that "is oriented to the accumulation of symbolic capital, a kind of 'economic' capital denied but recognized, and hence legitimate—a veritable credit, and capable of assuring, under certain conditions and in the long term, 'economic' profits."[8] For Bourdieu, any field of cultural production, regardless of how "autonomous" it might be, "continues to be affected by the laws of the field [of power] which encompasses it, those of economic and political profit."[9] In this system of "cultural capitalism," all forms of cultural production are understood quantitatively, in terms of how much capital they can generate, and are used strategically to maximize profit, whether symbolic, economic, or political.

In Greece, the politically and economically expedient use of ancient and classical cultural heritage has long been a strategic practice, used by individuals, groups, organizations, and the state. In the early 1980s, however, as Greece shook off the shadows of the military dictatorship and began in earnest its bid for entry into the European Community, the strategic use of public culture by the state took on a new tone, exemplified by the slogan embraced by Melina Mercouri as early as 1981, her first year as Minister of Culture: "Culture *(politismos)* is the heavy industry of Greece."[10] While the most famous of Mercouri's many initiatives as Minister of Culture was her campaign for the return of the Parthenon marbles and the building of a new Acropolis Museum, for the purposes of this study, I find more revealing her work within the European Union to establish the program that is today known as "The European Capital of Culture." Each year, the European Union designates two European cities to serve as "Capitals of Culture," receiving significant EU funding to organize a year-long program of cultural events and initiatives, and create or support existing cultural institutions and infrastructure within the city. Initially conceived by Mercouri as the "European City of Culture" program in 1983, and inaugurated in 1985 with Athens as the very first City of Culture, the program's stated primary goals are rather lofty: "to highlight the richness and diversity of cultures in Europe, celebrate the cultural features Europeans share, increase European citizens' sense of belonging to a common cultural area."[11] But the program's more practical purposes, widely acknowledged as the real reason for its continued existence and success, are economic: urban regeneration, development, and promotion of tourism, which raises cities' international visibility and profile. Over the years, the program has increasingly been seen as an economic boon for cities chosen to participate, resulting in fierce competition to be selected as the next Capital of Culture, with elaborate campaigns started years in advance. The renaming of the program in 1999, from "European City of Culture" to "European Capital of Culture," can be seen as reflecting this emphasis on the economic.[12]

In this sense, the Capital of Culture program is part of a larger cultural economy, comprising what Regan Rhyne describes as "a new breed of cultural industries that are shaped by global economic shifts in the transnational circulation of cultural products . . . . a new economy of public/private subsidies for the arts toward the production of post–Cold War global citizens."[13] In the "cultural capitalism" of this late twentieth- and early twenty-first-century economy of creative industries, state policies aim at using the arts and forms of cultural production to accrue symbolic, political, and economic capital, as much within the country as internationally.[14] Thessaloniki's tenure as Capital of Culture in 1997 was similarly conceived as an opportunity for the city—and by extension the country—to better its position in this European cultural economy. The international film festival circuit plays an increasingly important role in this economy, and the Thessaloniki Film Festival was a central element in the city's overall cultural program, especially after its strategic transformation in 1992 to more closely resemble the large international film festivals in Western Europe. In 1997, funds from the European Capital of Culture program were used to renovate the Olympion building, which was then gifted to the festival organization, and construct the screening spaces and other facilities in warehouses on the old port. In the following years, the festival continued to distinguish itself in the international festival circuit, and until the onset of austerity in 2010, the state steadily increased its support for this cultural institution, considered to be an important link to the larger European and even global cultural economy. Public funding for the festival could thus be seen as part of a larger state cultural-capitalist project.

Although these two interrelated justifications—one cultural-essentialist, the other cultural-economic—are the most commonly given in support of public funding for the arts, both are deeply suspect. The problems with the first line of reasoning are obvious, with its extreme conservatism and ethnocultural nationalism. According to this rationale, the "public" of public culture is understood in nationalist and essentialist terms, and it is particularly dangerous in the Greek context, where it too easily aligns with the interests of the far-right and fascist social and political movements that have seen marked growth over the last ten years. The second line of reasoning is equally problematic, aligning as it does with the logic of *homo œconomicus* and the neoliberal economizing of public life, according to which anything can be deemed a "luxury," especially under conditions of increasing precarity. As we saw with the FOG movement in the previous chapter, when we calculate the public value of the arts and cultural production in such cultural-capitalist terms, we vacate them of their political potential and leave them vulnerable to devaluation as "merely a luxury."

CINEMA AS A PUBLIC THING

In contrast to these two predominant lines of reasoning, I offer a third way of understanding the public value of the arts—what Wendy Brown would call a "counterrationality," organized according to "an alternative table of values" less determined by nationalist and capitalist agendas.[15] In formulating this alternative valuation of cultural production, I take Bonnie Honig's notion of "public things" as a starting point. In her book *Public Things: Democracy in Disrepair,* Honig brings Hannah Arendt's concept of the "world-stabilizing power" of durable things into conversation with D. W. Winnicott's psychoanalytic theory of objects as holding environments to foster attachment, integration, and adhesion. Using this vocabulary, Honig proposes that we think of "public things" such as infrastructure, natural resources, public institutions, and public spaces as part of the "holding environment" for a robust, democratic public life. She argues that "at their best, public things gather people together, materially and symbolically, and in relation to them diverse peoples may come to see and experience themselves—even if just momentarily—as a common in relation to a commons, a collected if not a collective."[16] Importantly, Honig does not imply that public things unify or bring people together in consensus. Rather, in gathering diverse people around them, they function to make more palpable the difference, plurality, and agonism that Honig believes is the defining characteristic of public life: "Even when they are divisive, they provide a basis around which to organize, contest, mobilize, defend, or reimagine various modes of collective being together."[17] Thus, public things do the work of Arendt's famous "table" of public life, providing occasions for people to gather, appear to one another, speak and act, disagree, be collective. For Honig, the increasing neoliberal co-optation of public things is tantamount to the loss of democratic life itself.

I propose to take Honig's notion of "public thingness" and apply it to a revaluation of the arts and cultural production. If forms of cultural production such as cinema are understood to be "public things" in this sense, then their value to public life lies in their capacity to gather people together in agonistic engagement and conflicted collectivity. This "public thingness" of cinema and its wider field of cultural production is evident in my examination of the Thessaloniki festival, its history, and the ways that history is put to use in the present. Beginning from its inception, but particularly in the 1970s and early 1980s, the festival served as a space for the practice of a particular kind of critical, agonistic publicness: protest, opposition, and resistance, often political in nature. This way of being public differs from the classic model of the liberal-bourgeois public sphere, organized on the principle of rational critical discourse, with its emphasis on "*politesse* and consistency over unruliness and difference."[18]

The kind of publicness practiced in the space of the festival during the 1970s and 1980s was closer to public life as imagined by Oskar Negt and Alexander Kluge in their book *The Public Sphere and Experience*. According to Miriam Hansen, the dimensions of public interaction that Negt and Kluge stressed in their reconceptualization of the public were heterogeneity, difference, conflict, and contradiction:

> While Habermas's notion of public life is predicated on formal conditions of communication (free association, equal participation, deliberation, polite argument), Negt and Kluge emphasize questions of constituency, concrete needs, interests, conflicts, protest and power. . . . The issue for Negt and Kluge is . . . whether and to what extent experience is dis/organized from "above"—by the exclusionary standards of high culture or in the interest of property—or from "below," by the experiencing subjects themselves, on the basis of their context of living. The utopia of such a self-determined public sphere, which is ultimately a radical form of democracy, involves not just the empowerment of constituencies hitherto excluded from the space of public opinion, but also a different principle of organization, a different concept of public life. As a "counterconcept" to both bourgeois and industrial-commercial variants of publicity Negt and Kluge develop the notion of a 'proletarian' public sphere.[19]

The notion of a "different concept of public life" that not only allows but is constituted through conflict and critical engagement would have been especially appealing in Greece at a time when people were becoming more and more frustrated with the cultural policies of the state, as well as the government's increasing unresponsiveness to the public will, evidenced by the parliamentary approval of deeply unpopular austerity measures dictated by the trio of Greece's international lenders. In contrast to the "bourgeois" model of public life, which glosses over the disruptive potential of collective critical action, and the "industrial-commercial" model, which offers little room for the possibility of political agency, Negt and Kluge's "proletarian" public sphere invites conflict, dissonance, opposition, and resistance. In 2009, as protest and civil unrest were on the rise in Greece, this more contentious form of being public and the history of such agonistic collectivity took on renewed significance within the space of the festival, particularly during the launch for its fiftieth-anniversary commemorative publication.

It was also this unruly form of publicness that the FOG members attempted to enact early in their movement and revive within the space of the festival through their demands that the fiftieth-anniversary edition be transformed from a celebration into a protest. It was generally felt that the festival, as a space of publicness, had lost the sense of local and national political engagement it once had. As historian Antonis Liakos pointed out, with the internationalization of the festival in the early 1990s, it ceased to be a politicized arena and became more of a space in which Greeks could be exposed to global cultural trends. In the second chapter of this book, I examined how the festival today is primarily concerned with staging and picturing publicness, and when the institution does attempt to enact publicness, it is the civil, politely critical public that is being evoked, not the politicized, unruly one. In trying to redefine the festival as a space of protest and opposition once again, the FOG drew attention to the institution's history of conflict, as well as to the potential for cultural institutions more generally to foster heterogeneity, contradiction, difference, and resistance. In this sense, the arts and cultural production demand state support not because they are a means of shoring up, performing, or protecting some essentialist notion of collective identity or because they are a means of accruing capital of various forms, but because they constitute an arena for an agonistic public life, a space in which a vital and critical public sphere—characterized by conflict, disagreement, debate, and contestation—can be put into practice. It is important to remember that this is not an idealized understanding of critical collectivity that excludes potentially problematic notions of national cultural identity or patrimony, or private economic interests. In the particular space of publicness imagined by this "different concept of public life," such ideologies and agendas may be included, coming into contact, interacting, vying, or clashing with other beliefs, investments, and pursuits. However, none of these specific interests or agendas determines the space of the public; the organizing principle of this public is not economic profit, political expediency, cultural identity, or heritage—all of which can be a part of what is debated, contested, and pursued within this space—but rather agonistic publicness itself.

This "different concept of public life" also demands a different understanding of cultural citizenship, or the ways in which subjects engage with and position themselves in relation to the state within fields of cultural production. By the late 1990s, as the Thessaloniki festival became increasingly integrated into the European cultural-capitalist economy, its functioning on local and national levels also changed, so that it constituted a space in which festival-goers could learn how to be citizen-consumers within that larger cultural economy in which the Greek state was so heavily invested—part of what Toby Miller calls "a training in equable citizenship."[20] In this sense, the more politicized, contentious public-cultural sphere was replaced by a more "civil" one that better served state interests by forging "a loyalty to market economics and parliamentary democracy, as well as a sustainable society through the formation of cultural citizens, docile but efficient participants in that economy-society mix."[21] This particular cultural citizen is "the virtuous political participant who is taught how to scrutinize and improve his or her conduct through the work of cultural policy," and who is defined as much by her relationship to supranational (in this case, European) cultural policies as to the nation-state.[22] Against this neoliberal model of cultural citizenship, the early public actions and declarations of the FOG members evoked a different conception of citizenship. In their repoliticization of the festival and their use of that public-cultural space as a means to address and engage critically with the state, they were attempting to enact an agonistic citizenship, a relationship to the state based on dissent and contestation rather than docility and compliance. It is a citizenship conceived in relation to the nation-state but working across different scales: local, national, European. In this reformulation of citizenship, the state is not simply imagined as a patron or framework providing the space and support for public life. Rather, it is envisioned as itself a part of this unruly, conflicted, dynamic publicness.

Such agonism could be seen not only in FOG's early positioning in relation to the state, but also in the filmmakers' relationships with one another, which were characterized by contention as much as collectivity. The movement had the effect of creating a sense of community among Greek independent filmmakers that did not previously exist, as explained to me by Leda, a Greek-American producer and director who was active in the group early on. She attributed this earlier sense of isolation and individualism to the general lack of funding for film production in Greece, and particularly to the meager amounts of public funding made available by the state, which bred a fierce sense of competition and guardedness among filmmakers all vying for a piece of a rather small pie, especially since private funding was even harder to secure. Coming from New York, where she had enjoyed working collaboratively within a dynamic filmmaking community, she had been especially struck by this lack of cohesion. Regardless of her reservations about how successful the FOG movement could eventually be, she was at least happy to see the FOG members coming together over common interests. Similarly, Lucia Rikaki felt that the most exhilarating aspect of the movement was that for the first time she felt she was getting to know her colleagues, and through her involvement in the group, she even started to rebuild relationships with people from whom she had been estranged for many years. She told me about a listserv they had begun in June 2009, which became integral to the group's internal communication; in the first five months alone, more than five thousand email messages had been circulated, and through this continuous online chatter, she felt connected to the more than two hundred and fifty other members all day long. This point was illustrated by her constant checking of her smartphone as we sat over coffee, reading me some of the messages that were coming through and replying to others. It was clear that many messages belonged to long threads, with filmmakers responding to one another and engaging in lively discussions that continued over days, and even weeks.

This growing sense of community, however, did not necessarily mean that the dynamics within the group were harmonious or that the filmmakers operated on a principle of consensus. On the contrary, group members disagreed on issues large and small, and interactions among them were often testy and even combative. This became clear as Lucia shared with me messages from the listserv, covering a wide range of topics: So-and-so has requested to become a member of FOG—should we allow him to join, even though he decided to show his film at the festival? If the new Film Academy gives prizes for documentaries, then how many prizes should be given and in which categories? How should the group respond to the latest public statements made by a few of the political parties in support of the Greek Directors' Guild? FOG is losing some of its momentum in the press—how can the group capitalize on the upcoming Thessaloniki Documentary Festival to regain public attention? The long email threads ensuing from these questions were never conflict-free; the filmmakers bickered, argued, and fought, with some discussions ending in members leaving the group, some returning and others not. This mode of interaction also characterized the FOG meetings that I observed in person, which were usually attended by a core group of about fifty members and took place in different spaces throughout Athens, including offices, theaters, and screening rooms made available by FOG members or sympathizers. These meetings were full of disagreements, misunderstandings, heated debates, and even shouting matches, inevitable among a group of more than two hundred people coming from a variety of backgrounds and experiences. Indeed, a frequent topic of discussion in these meetings, as well as online in email threads, was how to deal with such conflict in order to come to collective decisions on how to act publicly, as a movement. During a break between FOG screenings in Thessaloniki, Antonis Kafetzopoulos reflected on the dynamic within the group:

> The very positive thing about all this is that, for the first time, people among us who had no contact, no relationship whatsoever, met. And we were very suspicious of each other, because the funding system was always very divisive . . . which we got over through discussion and getting to know each other. I can't say that we're all the same, that we all think the same thing. There are differences and also suspicions between the directors and the producers, and different points of view, but there remains something very interesting—even over the last few emails, a fight has exploded in FOG—because they're all at each others' throats, but in the end we end up somewhere without having to vote. At some point, after the fight, the minority understands that the majority wants something else, and we proceed. It's unbelievable. This doesn't happen elsewhere in Greece. It's tremendously rare.

Many of the FOG members with whom I spoke shared Kafetzopoulos's appreciation of this collective dynamic. What is important to note here is that conflict and community were not mutually exclusive. Rather, their convergence or coexistence—indeed, their co-constitution—was a defining characteristic of the group: it was precisely *through* conflict that the community enacted itself. Here, we have an example of the way in which cinema, understood not just as a text or media object but also as a wider field of cultural production, functions as a public thing, occasioning the practice of agonistic collectivity: of being, deliberating, and acting together in conflict.

THE VALUE OF MERENESS

In its internal dynamics, as well as in its early (counter)public confrontations with the state, the FOG movement embodied this "different concept of public life." As I have shown in the previous chapter, however, this agonistic spirit was ultimately undone by the group's embrace of the logic of *homo œconomicus,* as the filmmakers chose to translate their value in terms legible to the neoliberal state. In pushing for continued state funding of their work, the filmmakers based their argument on the notion of cinema's *economic* value, thus articulating its significance to public life, and indeed public life itself, in terms that aligned with the cultural-capitalist policies of the Greek state and the European Union. In doing so, they unwittingly set the groundwork for their own dismissal when, as the recession worsened and state budgets continued to shrink, this economizing logic deemed more and more aspects of public life—including the arts—inessential, dispensable, merely a luxury.

It is to this very notion of "mereness" that I now turn, as the final element in my alternative understanding of the public value of the arts and cultural production. In contrast to the line of reasoning mobilized by the FOG, which insists on the significance of the arts and the economic value they generate, I insist instead on their mereness, or their *in*significance within dominant hierarchies of value. If, as I have argued, fields of cultural production function as spaces for the practice of an agonistic public life, then what is particular to these fields, and what sets them apart from other fields of social practice that might also occasion such agonistic collectivity (e.g., education, healthcare, jurisprudence), is precisely that the arts and cultural production are traditionally considered to be "lesser"—less consequential, less serious, with less at stake than what Bill Nichols has called the "discourses of sobriety": Science, economics, politics, foreign policy, education, religion, welfare— these systems assume they have instrumental power; they can and should alter the world itself, they can effect action and entail consequences. . . . Discourses of sobriety are sobering because they regard their relation to the real as direct, immediate, transparent. Through them power exerts itself.[23]

At best, fields of cultural production such as cinema have traditionally had an ambiguous relation to the discourses of sobriety, and are often excluded from this designation altogether. Indeed, for this reason, they are usually the first to be cut from state budgets in times of need, because they are thought to have less "real" effect on the social, economic, and political dimensions of public life. But I contend that it is precisely *because* they are "less serious" or "less consequential" that the arts constitute a particular, and particularly valuable, kind of public thing. For if public thingness is the capacity to gather people together in conflict, then the higher stakes of more "serious" public things put a limit on this agonism, as it often gets drowned out by the imperative for action in concert and the need for consensus that this imperative usually assumes. The seemingly lower stakes of the arts, however, leave room for attempts at more radically agonistic forms of collectivity; the less consequential something is seen to be, the less pressure there is to arrive at resolution through consensus or agreement, and the more tolerance there is for difference and dissent over compliance and sameness. In this sense, we might see fields of cultural production as the "kids' table" to Arendt's "table" of public life: raucous, messy, less "important," but for this reason, less beholden to the rules, affording more radical ways of imagining and enacting public life otherwise, with more possibility for disrupting the dominant order. In their mereness, the arts may not fit our usual understandings of what is properly "public," but it is their very mereness that allows them to function as spaces for a sustained politics of dissonance, with its more unruly and open-ended forms of collectivity.

In her discussion of public things, Honig primarily works through examples that are rather serious and weighty, what she calls "the infrastructure of modern life—sewage, universities, libraries, reservoirs," as well as the shared resources of "air, water, earth," all of which are under threat.[24] She does, however, address the importance of mereness at different points in her theorization, most evocatively in her discussion of Lars von Trier's 2011 feature film *Melancholia,* in which the members of a bourgeois family, beset by different forms of depression and alienation, grapple with the threat of Earth's impending collision with a rogue planet. Reading the film as an allegory for the catastrophe of neoliberalism and potential responses or resistances to it, Honig identifies *play* as the key to resisting and enduring catastrophe. In the film's closing scene, as the planet Melancholia hurtles toward Earth, the trio of mother, aunt, and child takes refuge in a small, makeshift teepee. Sitting in a circle in the skinless structure made of twigs, offered by the aunt to her nephew as a "magic cave," the three hold hands and await the end of the world. While the teepee-cave may seem to be merely a plaything, incapable of offering any real protection, Honig suggests otherwise, arguing that the teepee's power springs from its simultaneous association with past ruin and future survival: "Perhaps the teepee's capacity . . . to scramble the teleologies and temporalities of progress and maturation that surround and constitute us, are what make the magic cave magical. Perhaps there is power, after all, in the teepee that seems useless—no more than a house built of sticks—in the face of catastrophe. Built in play, perhaps it might meet the democratic need or at least stand for the need to meet it."[25] Her valuing of "useless" play here is in the same spirit as her championing, at an earlier point in the book, of "piecemeal" rather than "wholesale" forms of resistance and political action. Pushing back against what she sees as the totalizing views of theorists like Brown, who see little possibility for resistance to the neoliberal takeover of life and mind, Honig points to small-scale political and activist movements, such as those built around issues of food sovereignty or indigenous/tribal autonomy, as examples of "a kind of political action rarely reported in the headlines but nonetheless (or . . . *therefore)* an important current rival to a momentarily dominant paradigm that claims, falsely, that such rivals have been long since left behind."[26] While such movements are dismissed by some as forms of withdrawal rather than resistance, or as too small and scattered to be effective, Honig sees them as "experiments in living that vivify the imagination and help others to enact alternatives too."[27] What they imagine and enact are what Jacques Rancière refers to as alternative "politicities," or ways of being and acting politically, and the logics or "figures of community" that such politicities inscribe. It is not in spite of their mereness, but rather *because* of it, that such movements are able to counter the seemingly totalizing logic of *homo œconomicus*.

This notion of mereness as something to be valued resonates with the idea, in Arendt's *The Human Condition,* of "uselessness" as a defining characteristic of art and one of its strengths. Arendt defines a work of art as something that is neither necessary to the continuation of biological life nor functional in the sense of a use object. Because they are not subject to the "corroding effect" of either consumption or use, works of art have a material permanence that outlasts and transcends the individual life. For Arendt, this durability is the reason why "works of art are the most intensely worldly of all tangible things," by which she means that art works are the ideal objects to populate the common world, or the "non-mortal home for mortal beings," offering stability as they gather people together in the practice of collective life.[28] In this sense, it is the uselessness, or "essential futility" of art, that grants it its world-stabilizing power.[29] In my understanding of the public value of the arts, I offer a variation on Arendt's formulation: It is their "essential futility," that is, their mereness, that grants them their world-*de*stabilizing power. Because fields of cultural production are traditionally presumed to be relatively inconsequential and therefore can be less subject to the disciplining forces of a dominant order, they can be ideal spaces for practicing a prefigurative politics, disrupting the given distribution of the sensible and the ruling structures of the shared world.[30] Of course, this is not always, or necessarily, the case; in fact, the truly disruptive potential of the arts is rarely fully realized, as they capitulate to or become co-opted by cultural-essentialist or cultural-capitalist logics, as we saw with the FOG movement. But it is precisely because of the unchecked co-optation of public life by neoliberal logic that the disruptive potential of the arts and cultural production is all the more vital, as they provide some of the few remaining spaces for prefiguring and enacting other, more radical ways of being public: destabilizing the world as it is in order to fashion the world as it may be. It is for this reason that when faced with the devaluation of the arts as "merely a luxury," the correct response might not be to insist on the significance of cultural production but rather to insist on its mereness.

My aim is not to categorically privilege mereness over seriousness, dissensus over order. Rather, it is to push back against the traditional dismissal of mereness—of noninstrumentality, of inconsequentiality—and to argue that the arts and fields of cultural production are just as important to public life as the more "sober" fields, precisely because of the unruly and counter-hegemonic forms of politicity and collectivity that their mereness affords. Such dissenting forms of public life are all the more important in Greece today, as the country begins to emerge from its "crisis." After nearly a decade of successive bailouts, multiple changes of government both elected and appointed, and widespread social and economic devastation, the last bailout program officially came to a close in August of 2018. Some have declared the "crisis" over, and the economy is now said to be "in recovery," but it is unclear how exactly "recovery" is defined. While official indicators such as GDP and employment levels are rising, and the country has returned to government bond markets, everyday life in Greece continues to be defined by privation and precarity. Unemployment remains high, especially for Greeks under the age of thirty-five, and the overall unemployment rate is still the highest in the eurozone. Those able to find work often lack job security, are underpaid and overqualified, or unable to get jobs in their field. Meanwhile, pensions and social welfare programs continue to shrink while taxes continue to rise. Although the country no longer officially operates under a bailout agreement, the deeply unpopular austerity measures imposed by foreign lenders as the conditions for past bailouts remain in effect, with no end in sight. It appears that the European Union, the European Central Bank, and the International Monetary Fund succeeded in securing the "structural adjustments" they so doggedly pursued. Under these current conditions, the "crisis" is said to be over, but only because "normalcy" has been redefined in neoliberal terms. It is not surprising, then, that the larger "trouble" I described at the beginning of this book continues to characterize life in Greece. Even after the 2015 election of the populist left-wing coalition party SYRIZA, which ran on an anti-austerity platform, the sense of discord and disconnect between state and citizen, and contestation over the terms of public and political life, remain acute. In fact, perhaps the most spectacular demonstration of this trouble came at the hands of SYRIZA when, in July 2015, the newly elected government held a high-stakes referendum on austerity measures demanded by the troika in exchange for an extension of bailout funds. Public sentiment was unequivocal, with more than sixty percent of the voting population rejecting the lenders' terms, but one week after this famous "no" vote, Prime Minister Alexis Tsipras caved to international pressure and agreed to a bailout extension with terms even harsher than those rejected in the referendum. Some saw this as a betrayal, while others viewed it as inevitable, but in either case, the underlying conditions are unmistakably clear: a broken relationship between state and citizen, a disconnect between public will and public (i.e., state) decision-making, and a state of contestation over the terms of collective life, all of which are only exacerbated by the country's continued neoliberal restructuring.

Against the backdrop of this ongoing trouble, cultural production continues. Not surprisingly, given the extreme asymmetries produced by neoliberal policies, the country's cultural landscape has in recent years become dominated by private wealth in an increasingly visible way. The vacuum left by the decimation of public funding for the arts has been filled by high-profile organizations like the Onassis and the Niarchos foundations, which have bankrolled massive cultural venues, including some that now house public cultural institutions, and arts funding programs that have become indispensable for many artists, organizations, and institutions in Greece. Big-name art collectors like Dimitris Daskalopoulos and Dakis Ioannou occupy increasingly important positions in the country's cultural infrastructure, often through their own arts foundations, such as Daskalopoulos's NEON and Ioannou's DESTE Foundation for Contemporary Art. Joining such foundations at this far end of the spectrum of scale, visibility, and funding are large international public-private hybrids like *documenta*—one of the largest international art events in the world, usually held every five years in Kassel, Germany—which decided for its fourteenth edition, in 2017, to split its mammoth exhibition between Kassel and Athens. Despite deep connections to the corporate world and the high-end art market, such large-scale cultural institutions often align themselves with dissenting and counter-hegemonic politicities. For example, *documenta 14*, titled "Learning from Athens," was conceived as a critical engagement with the global political and social "trouble" crystallized in the Greek "crisis," espousing radically democratic, anti-capitalist, and anti-fascist politics. In curatorial statements, press conferences, and programming decisions, the monthslong exhibition and its accompanying yearlong Public Program were presented as "a space for cultural activism" and an intervention "against the transformation of the public into a marketing target," focusing on "micropolitical self-organization, collaborative practices, and radical pedagogy" with the aim of working toward "a radical transformation of the public sphere."[31] Despite these good intentions, *documenta 14* was met with much criticism and controversy in Greece, where it faced accusations of everything from poor organization and lack of transparency to cultural insensitivity and even cultural neocolonialism.[32] After the exhibition closed, *documenta* became mired in a debt crisis of its own, when it was revealed that the organization ran a deficit of €7 million, leading to a very public dispute between the show's curators and its state funders, pitting notions of artistic freedom against demands for fiscal responsibility. In a review of *documenta 14*, Andrew Weiner diagnoses the underlying problem with such large cultural institutions as "an issue of scale: not only the ever-lengthening roster of platforms and venues and artists and publications and archives and events and broadcasts and and and . . . but also the epoch-defining ambition of the curatorial arguments."[33] With half of its more than €40 million cost supported by the state, and the other half by sales, private donors, and corporate sponsorships from the likes of Deutsche Bank and Volkswagen, *documenta* is necessarily entangled in a neoliberal cultural economy that trades in publi*city* and a disavowal of mereness, thus countering and complicating the organization's professed investment in the micro-political and radically alternative forms of publicness. As Weiner puts it, cultural organizations with so much financial and symbolic capital at stake are perhaps not "too big to fail" but rather "too big to really succeed."[34]

At the opposite end of the spectrum in size and significance are countless small-scale arts initiatives that continue to emerge and operate in Greece today. Some are more or less formal, more or less ephemeral, than others. Some are run on shoestring budgets, pieced together through donations, participant contributions, or modest grants from the state or private institutions such as those mentioned above, while others have no budget at all. Many grow out of specific communities, activist movements, or radical political and anarchist groups, and are part of a longer tradition of such DIY cultural practices in Greece.[35] I close this book with a snapshot of one such arts initiative centered on cinema, a small documentary filmmaking workshop in Athens that illustrates the relationship between the arts, mereness, and public life that I have traced in this book.

The workshop, called Inner Landscapes (*Esoterika Topia*) because of its emphasis on personal filmmaking, is organized and led by documentary filmmakers Christos Karakepelis and Natasa Segou. Each fall, they gather between five and ten participants, some of whom are untrained or nonprofessional media practitioners and others who have never worked in media, and meet weekly for about six months. For a few hours each Sunday afternoon, the group meets at KET—a small basement multiuse performance space in Kypseli, a quiet working-class and immigrant neighborhood a little outside the city center—to watch and discuss documentaries and related readings, and to work together to develop their own respective nonfiction video projects. Christos usually leads the seminar-style screenings and discussions, while Natasa oversees the developing projects and meets regularly with participants during the week for one-on-one consultations. Workshop participants are actively involved in one another's projects, reading and discussing early treatments, assisting others with research and production, and giving feedback on footage and at different stages of editing. In the process, they often become close friends, staying in touch long after the workshop ends. Christos and Natasa also take on key roles in the participants' projects, in everything from conceptualization, research, and script development to the production and postproduction stages, helping to organize shoots and operate equipment, often providing equipment themselves, assisting with the coordination of postproduction, and consulting during the edit. And they continue to work on participants' projects after the end of the workshop, in some cases for years.

All this work takes places with few resources and little support. The workshop's only source of funding is €600 in fees paid by each participant, with some paying less owing to economic hardship or because they are repeat participants. This small pool of money is split between the instructors and the space that hosts them. All equipment and media used during the workshop or in the production of projects is provided by the instructors or the participants. This gives the seminar a somewhat scrappy, DIY sensibility that is matched by its informal, even haphazard, organization. Sometimes meetings are disorganized, poorly attended, or canceled or rescheduled at the last minute, not because participants are not committed, but because there is very little organizational support, and because everyone involved, participants and instructors alike, have day jobs, if they are fortunate enough to have steady jobs at all. Despite all the work that goes into the projects each year, most go unfinished. Since 2014, the workshop's first year, only a handful of films have been completed.

One of these films, titled *Amygdaliá,* or "almond tree" in Greek, had its premiere at the Thessaloniki Documentary Festival in March 2019.

Dreamlike in its structure and the visual and sonic associations it activates, *Amygdaliá* is an essay film reflecting on foreignness and belonging in contemporary Greece, bringing together a collage of idiosyncratic visual impressions with the voices of five women narrators who have experienced their own difference in the country in disparate ways. With its handmade feel and its focus on current social issues through a personal lens, *Amygdaliá* is representative of the kinds of projects that are produced in the context of the workshop. More importantly, beyond the form and content of the film, the story of its development and production is representative of the forms of collectivity, or "figures of community," that are forged in such small-scale forms of cultural production. The filmmaker Christina Phoebe Thomopoulos is an artist and activist whom I met earlier in my research. Christina has a job producing media for a national research center, and as an activist, she works primarily on issues around racism, women's rights, and migrant struggles. She first started developing the idea for *Amygdaliá* in 2011, upon returning to Greece after studying in the United States and grappling with her own feelings of estrangement, while also becoming more and more involved in activist work around the economic crisis and its effects on the country's immigrant population. Untrained as a filmmaker, she began to shoot bits and pieces of video from her everyday life on a consumer DSLR camera, but soon realized that she needed help with the filmmaking process and turned to the documentary workshop in 2014. As the concept for the project took shape during workshop discussions, fellow participants, together with other friends, assisted on shoots and then watched and provided feedback on the footage during workshop meetings. At the same time, other aspects of the project were also developed collectively in other settings. For example, the script for the poetic voice-over was developed collaboratively as part of a workshop on foreignness and difference at Embros Theater, a self-organized cultural space in Athens where Christina was active at the time. After the documentary workshop ended that year, Christina, Natasa, and Christos continued to work on the film, with work waxing and waning depending on available time and resources, and the film was finally finished in 2018, after they received a small grant from the NEON foundation to cover the costs of the last stages of postproduction.

When talking to Christina about the process of making *Amygdaliá*, what I found most striking is the extent to which she narrates it as a process of making community. While she is attentive to the film as a text and to questions of form and content, she understands the film equally in terms of the relationships, intimacies, conflicts, and negotiations that birthed the film, and the social bonds it occasions. This notion of a film functioning as a holding environment for collective life is reflected in the hopeful question posed by the narrator toward the end of the film and centered in its poster: "Can a film be like a nest? Where we can sit among the twigs and protect the light." Like Honig's teepee, a nest is a place of gathering that is itself a gathering of disparate things, an assemblage of pieces foraged and found, as well as a place of collective care, however ephemeral or temporary. Thus, by imagining cinema as a nest, this question displaces the usual emphasis on film as text, object, or product to emphasize instead the world that gathers around and through it. This displacement of emphasis was captured eloquently by Christos in talking about his own filmmaking practice. Explaining to me why his films take so long to make, as he and Natasa immerse themselves in the communities and lives of their films' subjects, Christos asserted that the relationships forged with those subjects and with his filmmaking collaborators mean as much to him as the film itself, if not more. "The point is elsewhere! (*Allou einai to zitima!*)," he declared, meaning that for him, the point of the filmmaking process, its meaning and value, lies beyond the film, in the forms of collectivity that it affords.

This sentiment was all the more palpable at an informal screening and gathering for past workshop participants. Curious to learn more about the work that had been produced in the context of the workshop, I proposed and then organized this event at KET in December 2017. What became clear to me in the process of preparing for this screening was that most of the projects developed in the workshop had not been finished, in part because participants did not have the resources to complete their films, but also because many were not primarily artists or filmmakers, and completing their films was simply not a priority for them. What they did value, however, was the community they experienced in the workshop, which was evident in the warm and lively reunion that took place that evening, and was also a focal point in many of the one-on-one conversations I had with previous workshop participants. One explained to me that the workshop's small scale and limited resources means that participants are necessarily involved in one another's projects, working together at every stage. In addition, because the workshop focuses on personal filmmaking, this means that participants witness and engage in what are often deeply intimate, challenging, and personally meaningful aspects of one another's lives. For the most part, these working relationships exist outside the circuits of economic valuation and exchange, and many of these film projects will likely remain unfinished. Thus, for most of the participants, the true value of the workshop lies not in the film as a bearer of potential capital, whether economic or symbolic, but in the social bonds that the filmmaking process precipitates. In this sense, the film projects serve as occasions to gather and be collective, as does the workshop itself.

These collaborative projects are not without their share of conflict, misunderstandings, disagreements, and noise. Nor are they entirely free of investment in cultural economies of different kinds and scales. For example, in the five years since the workshop was started, three feature-length documentaries, including *Amygdaliá*, have been completed precisely because the directors of these films worked hard to take their initial projects and expand the scale of their production beyond the limits of the workshop.[36] All three of these films were able to secure external funding, each from a different source, and the range of funding sources for these projects interestingly reflects the broader shape of the arts funding landscape in Greece today: one was supported by a private production company; another received support from both private and public sources, including the Greek Film Center and national public television; and *Amygdaliá* received a grant from the arts foundation NEON, as well as support from a private production company late in the postproduction stage. These films are the exception rather than the norm for projects developed in the context of the workshop, but their production and exhibition histories do make clear that they are not necessarily free of investments in, or aspirations to, different forms of capital. As is more often the case, the workshop, its participants, and their projects move between mereness, on the one hand, and various cultural-economic entanglements, on the other—sometimes occupying both spaces at once. My intention here is not to condemn or disavow such entanglements; on the contrary, as I have argued elsewhere, they are both unavoidable and even necessary.[37] Nor do I wish to romanticize or idealize the mereness of small-scale arts initiatives. Rather, my aim is to push back against what is so often the devaluation or outright erasure of the mereness of cultural production in order to highlight the political importance of that mereness for public life.

The Inner Landscapes workshop occupies a point on the cultural map of Greece today that is far from the much larger, more visible cultural initiatives and institutions that dominate that map. Small, low-profile, and largely invisible to most cultural economies, the workshop is not "public" in the usual senses: the group meets privately, operates without state funding, and neither has nor aims for a wide reach. It also differs from organizations like *documenta* in that it does not explicitly claim for itself a radical politics of publicness; in fact, the workshop does not profess any particular politics at all. In its mereness, though, it enacts a counterpoliticity, a figure of community that resists the neoliberal logic of the market-state. Here again, we see the intersection of scale and publicness in the field of cultural production. Perhaps the value of such "mere" cultural practices for public life lies precisely in the fact that there is so little at stake, at least according to the dominant hierarchies of value: not much money or resources and, at least for a time, not much symbolic capital either. Gathered at the kids' table—with the kinds of community its insignificance allows, and the relationships of mutual care that its inconsequentiality affords—maybe we are a little more free to practice, even if just momentarily, more radical forms of collective life.

Notes

INTRODUCTION

1. The Greek word for "culture" used in the op-ed is *politismos*, which, as discussed at greater length later in this chapter, has a number of overlapping meanings. As in English, it can have as broad a meaning as "civilization," in the sense of a society or way of life particular to a people or a geographical area, as well as the more narrow definition of the arts or forms of cultural production. In the op-ed, which is concerned with the health of Greek cultural institutions, this latter, narrower definition of "culture" is used.

2. Panagopoulous, "Ameses lyseis."

3. Karkagiannis, "Tourismos mesa ston politismo."

4. Honig, *Public Things.*

5. Pakulski, "Cultural Citizenship," 73.

6. Stevenson, *Cultural Citizenship,* 334–38.

7. See Flores and Benmayor, *Latino Cultural Citizenship;* Rosaldo, "Cultural Citizenship and Educational Democracy" and "Cultural Citizenship in San Jose"; and Toruellas et al., "Affirming Cultural Citizenship in the Puerto Rican Community."

8. Ong, "Cultural Citizenship as Subject Making," 737–38. See also Ong, *Buddha is Hiding.*

9. Miller, *Well-Tempered Self,* xii.

10. Siu, "Diasporic Cultural Citizenship," 13.

11. Miller, *Cultural Citizenship,* 51.

12. Rosaldo, "Cultural Citizenship in San Jose," 58.

13. For more on cultural citizenship, particularly in the field of media studies, see Apter, Kaes, and Roderick, *Mobile Citizens, Media States;* Miller, *Technologies of Truth;* and Stevenson, *Culture and Citizenship.* On cultural citizenship,

Europe, and EU cultural policy, see Balibar, "Is European Citizenship Possible?"; Craith, "Culture and Citizenship in Europe"; Delgado-Moreira, *Multicultural Citizenship of the European Union;* Habermas, "Citizenship and National Identity"; Shore, "Inventing the 'People's Europe'"; and Shore and Black, "Citizens' Europe and the Construction of European Identity."

14. Bourdieu, *Field of Cultural Production,* 29.

15. Elliott, Silverman, and Bowman, *Artistic Citizenship,* 3–7.

16. Martin, "Artistic Citizenship," 2.

17. Ibid, 4.

18. Ibid., 5.

19. Ibid.

20. Ibid.

21. Ibid., 11.

22. Ibid., 12.

23. Ibid., 4.

24. In *The Human Condition,* Arendt quotes Werner Jaeger to describe the *bios politikos* in the ancient Greek *polis:* "The rise of the city-state meant that man received 'besides his private life a sort of second life, his *bios politikos.* Now every citizen belongs to two orders of existence; and there is a sharp distinction in his life between what is his own *(idion)* and what is communal *(koinon)."* See *Human Condition,* 24.

25. See Herzfeld, *Ours Once More, Anthropology through the Looking Glass,* and *Place in History;* and Lowenthal, "Classical Antiquities" and *Heritage Crusade.*

26. Roitman, *Anti-crisis,* 11–12.

27. Ibid., 2.

28. Papataxiarchis, "Pragmatism Against Austerity," 229.

29. Ibid., 230. See also Butler, *Gender Trouble.*

30. Ibid., 26.

31. Ibid., 230.

32. "Ζημιές δεκάδων εκατομμυρίων ευρώ στα εμπορικά καταστήματα από τις ταραχές," at http://news.in.gr/economy/article/?aid = 966466 (accessed April 1, 2019).

33. Examples of such holidays include October 28, or *OCHI* ("No") day, when student and military parades celebrate the day Greece famously refused to surrender to Italian invasion in 1940; or November 17, when thousands march in the streets to commemorate the day in 1973 when the *Polytechneio* and its students fell to the military dictatorship. During my fieldwork, when strikes and protests grew more frequent with the worsening economic crisis and political instability, on more than a few occasions friends would suggest that we "meet at the protest" rather than for a coffee, and on protest days local pharmacists in my neighborhood would have on hand extra supplies of surgical masks and Maalox, which protesters heading to the march, encouraged by the pharmacists, would rub on their faces to counteract the effects of tear gas. In Greece, protest can feel fairly run-of-the-mill.

34. Ananiadis et al., "Η 'atakti skepsi,'" 6.

35. Ibid., 8.

36. The term "lifestyle," used as an adjective, was one that many people I spoke to in the field used to describe what they saw as the consumer society that became dominant in Greece in the late 1990s and 2000s. It is taken from the "lifestyle" magazines that also became popular at the time, which promoted conspicuous consumption and luxury goods (e.g., women's magazines, decor, shopping, tourism).

37. The main campaign slogan used by PASOK in the lead-up to the 2009 emergency elections was "The Citizen Comes First" (*Prota o Politis*), splashed across posters, billboards, and in television commercials. One PASOK campaign commercial during this period emphatically declared, "We imposed absolute transparency in our income and expenses. . . . No tolerance for 'dirty' money. We spoke cleanly and clearly, and that which we said we put into practice. That's how we want to govern."

38. Warner, *Publics and Counterpublics,* 29.

39. Ibid., 30.

40. For decades, a civil servant position has been considered highly desirable, guaranteeing a decent salary, job security, possible political connections, and potentially even positions for one's children. But with the pressure of the economic crisis, the public sector began to be characterized as bloated, filled with complacent and unnecessary bureaucrats occupying lifelong positions, inefficient, corrupt, and draining the state budget. As the Papandreou government began to overhaul the public sector in 2010, people's opinions on the matter once again centered on the relationship between the state and its citizens; among my friends and research subjects, some expressed dismay at the swift cuts to paychecks and sudden threat to job security, while others were skeptical that the state would actually dismantle such an important part of its patronage system. Yet others confided half-jokingly that they knew they had lived for too long on the largesse of the state.

41. Brown, *Undoing the Demos,* 17–21.

42. Ibid., 22.

43. Ibid., 39, 108.

44. Butler, *Notes Toward a Performative Theory of Assembly,* 55.

45. Ibid., 89.

46. Arendt, *Human Condition,* 50.

47. Warner, *Publics and Counterpublics.*

48. Honig, *Public Things.*

49. Ibid., 5–6.

50. Loverdou et al., "Changes Are Coming," and Kontrarou-Rassia, "Apo ti theoria stin praksi."

51. Since 2010, with the near bankruptcy of the Greek state, the festival has stopped receiving funding from the Ministry of Culture. Instead, it now survives primarily on EU grants and private sponsorships, and its annual budget is a fraction of what it was in 2009.

52. The most notable are *Dogtooth* (dir. Giorgos Lanthimos, 2009), *Strella* (dir. Panos Koutras, 2009), and *Plato's Academy* (dir. Filippos Tsitos, 2009). *Dogtooth* premiered at the 2009 Cannes Film Festival, where it was awarded the Un Certain Regard prize and subsequently nominated for an Oscar for Best

Foreign Language Film. *Strella* premiered at the 2009 Berlin Film Festival, while *Plato's Academy* had its premier at the Locarno Film Festival, where it won an award for Best Actor. The success of these films would mark the beginning of a renaissance of Greek cinema internationally.

53. Honig, *Public Things,* 92.

CHAPTER I

1. My decision to approach the festival in this way, as part of a broader field of cultural production and practice, is in line with recent developments in Greek film studies, and particularly in Greek film historiography. These fields have produced rich scholarship for decades, especially Greek-language scholarship, but they have notably matured in recent years, in both Greek and English. One major strain within this new scholarship moves away from the more traditional focus on film texts and auteurs to consider larger social, political, and economic histories of cinema, for example, Skopeteas, "Greek Cinema in the 1990s"; Papadimitriou and Tzioumakis, *Greek Cinema;* Paradeisi and Nikolaidou, *From Early to Contemporary Greek Cinema;* Loukopoulou, "'Campaign of Truth'"; Sifaki, "Cinema Goes to War"; as well as much of Lydia Papadimitriou's recent work on contemporary Greek film production and distribution. My approach to the Thessaloniki Film Festival is in conversation with such work and contributes to this growing literature.

2. Chapter in Elsaesser, *European Cinema,* 70–82.

3. Ibid., 83.

4. Ibid., 86.

5. Iordanova and Rhyne, *Film Festival Yearbook 1,* 3.

6. Iordanova and Cheung, *Film Festival Yearbook 2,* 1.

7. Stringer, "Regarding Film Festivals," 108–9.

8. de Valck, *Film Festivals,* 84–85. See Hardt and Negri, *Empire.*

9. Key to my approach is the use of ethnographic methodologies, which have recently come into more frequent usage in the field of film festival studies. Initially, the field was dominated by more systemic approaches to studying the global festival circuit, as well as analyses of larger festival structures and programming trends. However, ethnography offers the advantage of allowing for more fine-grained knowledge about cultural institutions as they are actually lived and experienced, as well as the complex ways in which they are entangled in other larger social and political processes. For this reason, ethnographic methodologies also afford a better perspective on the specific ways multiple geopolitical scales intersect within such institutions. This is especially true in the case of sustained ethnographic research focusing on a single festival, as in this study. For more on ethnography and film festival studies, see Lee, "Being There, Taking Place," and Vallejo and Peirano, *Film Festivals and Anthropology.*

10. See Herzfeld, *Anthropology through the Looking Glass* and "Absent Presence."

11. For more on the ideological and cultural constructions underlying early Greek nationalism, see Gourgouris, *Dream Nation,* and Herzfeld, *Ours Once More.*

12. For a discussion of the Hellenic-Romeic distinction, see ibid., 18–21.

13. Herzfeld, *Ours Once More*, 15.

14. For more on the complex articulations of contemporary cultural practices and notions of (belated) modernity in twentieth-century Greece, see Calotychos, *Modern Greece*, and Faubion, *Modern Greek Lessons.*

15. Xanthopoulos, *Pavlos Zannas*, 17.

16. Ibid., 5.

17. Ibid., 17–19.

18. Ibid., 6.

19. Makedoniki Kallitechniki Etaireia "Techni," *Techni sti Thessaloniki*, 20.

20. Xanthopoulos, *Pavlos Zannas*, 7.

21. Makedoniki Kallitechniki Etaireia "Techni," *Techni sti Thessaloniki*, 20.

22. Xanthopoulos, *Pavlos Zannas*, 54–55.

23. Aktsoglou, *30 Chronia*, 7.

24. Xanthopoulos, *Pavlos Zannas*, 9.

25. Kokonis, "Is There Such a Thing as a Greek Blockbuster?," 40–44.

26. Valoukos, *New Greek Cinema*, 28–31.

27. Delveroudi, "O Modernismos ston Elliniko Kinimatografo."

28. For further discussion of these filmmakers and their position in Greek film history, see Karalis, *History of Greek Cinema*, and Mitropoulou, *Ellinikos Kinimatografos.*

29. Karalis, *History of Greek Cinema*, 143. See also Valoukos, *New Greek Cinema*, 71–75.

30. The state awards system was controversial from its inception, with some accusing the system of being fixed or corrupted, while others felt that there was no reason for the festival to be affiliated with the state awards, which were seen as an imposition by the Ministry of Culture on a festival that already had its own award system. For further discussion of the State Film Awards and their central role in the FOG boycott, see chapter four.

31. For more on the relationship between the festival's national and international identifications over the course of its institutional history, see Papadimitriou, "Hindered Drive toward Internationalization."

32. For more on Thessaloniki's participation in the European Capitals of Culture program, see chapter four and Deffner and Labrianidis, "Planning Culture and Time in a Mega-Event."

33. Papadimitriou, "Greek Cinema as European Cinema," 221–23.

34. According to Augé, "non-places" are marked by a particular spatio-temporality that arises in the late twentieth century: "If a place can be defined as relational, historical and concerned with identity, then a space which cannot be defined as relational, or historical, or concerned with identity will be a non-place. The hypothesis advanced here is that supermodernity produces non-places. . . . A world where people are born in the clinic and die in hospital, where transit points and temporary abodes are proliferating under luxurious or inhuman conditions . . . where a dense network of means of transport which are also inhabited spaces is developing." Although Augé is careful to note that non-places do not exist in a pure form, he nevertheless maintains that "non-places are the real measure of our time; one that could be quantified . . . by totaling all

the air, rail and motorway routes, the mobile cabins called 'means of transport' (aircraft, trains and road vehicles), the airports and railway stations, hotel chains, leisure parks, large retail outlets, and finally the complex skein of cable and wireless networks that mobilize extraterrestrial space for the purposes of a communication so peculiar that it often puts the individual in contact only with another image of himself." See *Non-places*, 77–79.

CHAPTER 2

1. Appadurai and Breckenridge, "Why Public Culture?," 5.
2. Ibid, 6.
3. Arendt, *Human Condition*, 48.
4. Ibid., 66.
5. de Valck, "Drowning in Popcorn," 103–4.
6. Warner, *Publics and Counterpublics*, 121.
7. Ibid., 86–87.
8. Hansen, *Babel and Babylon*, 2–4.
9. Ibid., 5.
10. The Balkan Fund Script Development program was closed after the 2010 festival due to budget cuts. One of the main organizers of the program explained to me that it was not possible for them to justify continued spending on such programs during economically difficult times.
11. There is a growing body of literature on such "festival films." See Falicov, "'Festival Film'"; Talbott, "Familiar Difference of World Cinema"; and Wong, *Film Festivals*, 65–128.
12. Schwartz, *It's So French!*, 57–58.
13. Schwartz describes the early significance of paracinematic events at the Cannes festival, which already in its first decade became known as much for its black-tie parties, receptions, celebrity appearances, and media rituals as for the films it showcased. Some critics were quick to disparage these paracinematic elements, complaining that they had nothing to do with cinema. Others enjoyed the frivolity as much as the films, while still others understood the festival to be the sum of its rituals, film-related or not (see Bazin, "The Festival Viewed as a Religious Order"). Regardless of one's position, it was undeniable that the extra-cinematic activities and media coverage, together with the actual films, were fundamental to establishing the festival's international reputation and appeal, a fact of which the organizers were well aware. Schwartz quotes Robert Favre Le Bret, the director of the Cannes festival until 1968, writing about the importance of the paracinematic: "If the Festival is recognized worldwide, it is much less due to film reviews . . . than to all the extra-cinematic events. Whether we like it or not, this is what gives the Cannes meeting its appealing shape and provides an alluring atmosphere that pleases all the foreign guests and provides their memories with lively and brilliant images." See Schwartz, *It's So French!*, 72–73.
14. Boorstin, *Image*, 11.
15. Schwartz, *It's So French!*, 73. For further reading on media events, see Dayan and Katz, *Media Events*, and Couldry, Hepp, and Krotz, *Media Events in a Global Age*.

16. Ibid., 73–74.

17. At the 2009 closing ceremony, this audience changeover was so pronounced that French actress Anne Consigny—on the stage to introduce the closing film, Alain Resnais's *Les Herbes Folles,* in which she starred—was taken aback by the number of audience members racing to the exits even as she was about to speak, and she joked that perhaps she should perform a striptease on stage to keep audience members in their seats!

18. Theodorakis, "Oi Alloi Protagonistes."

19. Thessaloniki International Film Festival, *Street Cinema,* 5.

20. Thessaloniki International Film Festival, *Geniki Synelefsi,* 5.

21. Writing about the iconography of Cannes, Schwartz notes the importance of showing not just the stars but also the photographers as another way of "picturing publicness": "Chalais' [Reflets de Cannes] team filmed not only the event being covered, but also the press coverage of an event. There are countless images of the photographers taking pictures in the television broadcasts; thus the television cameras filmed the subject of the photos and the subject being photographed at the same time. The television programs emphasized what could already be found in the still photographs, which often had trouble getting their subjects without photographing photographers as well. . . . The television's camera 'eye' reveals the fabrication of the event as an event by showing the photographers at work . . . the coverage of coverage." See *It's So French!,* 86.

22. Arendt, *Human Condition,* 50.

23. Beltrán, "Going Public," 597.

24. Arendt, *Human Condition,* 57.

25. Honig, "Toward an Agonistic Feminism," 159.

26. Wong, *Film Festivals,* 159–89. See also Wong, "Publics and Counterpublics."

27. Ibid., 164–74.

28. Ibid., 176–88.

29. Warner, *Publics and Counterpublics,* 123.

CHAPTER 3

1. Parts of this chapter were previously published in Lee, "Festival, City, State."

2. Thessaloniki International Film Festival, *Why Cinema Now?,* 4.

3. Thessaloniki International Film Festival, *Geniki Synelefsi,* 4.

4. Holdsworth, "Rethinking Cinema," A16.

5. From the fifth episode of the five-part series "Festival 50 Eton" (Festival of 50 Years), which aired on the national state television channel ET1 (November 10, 2009).

6. Thessaloniki International Film Festival, *Why Cinema Now?*

7. Kornetis, "No More Heroes?" See also Kornetis, "1968, 1989, 2011" and "The End of a Parable?"

8. Nora, "Between Memory and History," 8.

9. Wood, "Memory's Remains," 127.

10. Nora, "Between Memory and History," 12.

11. Turner, *Celebration*, 16.

12. Ibid., 129.

13. Grimes, "Lifeblood of Public Ritual," 282.

14. Bernbeck, "*Lieux de Mémoire* and Sites of De-Subjectivation," 258.

15. Xifilinos, "Kato apo fota kokkina koimatai i Saloniki," 1.

16. Legg, "Contesting and Surviving Memory," 482.

17. Bernbeck, "*Lieux de Mémoire* and Sites of De-Subjectivation," 255.

18. It is important to note that everyone on the team was local. Except for me, everyone was born and raised in Thessaloniki or in northern Greek cities close by, and all had spent their adult lives as Thessalonicans. This project could easily have been carried out in Athens, which might have even been more convenient, as the main offices are there and Athina would have been able to meet with the research/editorial team more often. I would argue that the deliberate decision to keep the group locally based reflected the fact that the history of the festival is grounded in Thessaloniki and its institutions, but also had the effect of producing a book aimed at a local public.

19. In the end, the publication was structured in three parts: an opening section with captioned photographs and reproductions of posters from each edition; the main section with entries for each year; and three appendices—one with information about the State Awards, one briefly describing the history of the Olympion building and detailing the year-round activities of the festival organization beginning in 1992, and one listing the festival administrations (Board of Directors and General Assembly) beginning in 1998. The entry for each festival edition details films shown in all the various programs; side-bar events (exhibitions, panels and round-table discussions, masterclasses, concerts, honorary ceremonies, book presentations, parties); publications; facilities and screening rooms; juries; prizes; the names of the festival president, festival director, and Minister of Culture; and in later years, the Industry Center activities. Each entry also includes a section called "At a Glance (*Me mia matia*)," which presents supplemental information and anecdotes. All of this information is presented in the form of lists and bullet points.

20. Thessaloniki International Film Festival, *50 Chronia*, 2–6.

21. Rentzis, *Case of the '77 Greek Film Festival*.

22. Nora, "Between Memory and History," 7–8.

23. Ibid., 15.

24. Wood, "Memory's Remains," 146.

25. Yalouri, *Acropolis*, 73.

26. Boym, *Future of Nostalgia*, 41–48.

27. Miller, *Well-Tempered Self*.

CHAPTER 4

1. Parts of this chapter were previously published in Lee, "Being There, Taking Place."

2. NET, "Katalipsi."

3. See Hallin and Papathanassopoulos, "Political Clientelism," and Papatheodorou and Machin, "Umbilical Cord."

4. Rancière, *Dissensus*, 38.

5. Ibid., 39.

6. Taken from a special brochure published by the Athens-based weekly magazine *Athinorama* in conjunction with the FOG screenings in Athens (Nov. 5–12, 2009), which included screening schedules and film notes.

7. The so-called Melina's Law, named after its champion and architect Melina Mercouri, had been in place since 1986. Law 1597/1986, "Prostasia kai anaptyxi tis kinimatografikis technis, enischysi tis ellinikis kinimatografias, kai alles diataxeis" [Protection and development of cinema art, support of Greek cinema, and other ordinances].

8. Dartzali, "Kinimatografistes stin Omichli."

9. "Kinimatografika kondylia."

10. In 2009, the official numbers were about €6 million for the festival and about €3.5 million for film production. Many filmmakers complained that even the production funds they were awarded by the Greek Film Center were never actually disbursed.

11. Venardou, "Oi tainies pou den tha doume," 9.

12. See Corless and Darke, *Cannes*, 121–44; Cowie, *Revolution!*, 197–207; Harvey, *May '68*.

13. Warner, *Publics and Counterpublics*, 119–20.

14. Mouffe, *Democratic Paradox*, 86.

15. Ibid., 97–99.

16. Ibid., 102–3.

17. Ibid., 104.

18. The FOG filmmakers' work collectively represented a wide variety of forms, styles, and approaches: documentary, narrative, feature length, short, experimental, and commercial. While the "manifesto" outlining their five basic demands addresses the need to support "artistic," "creative/auteur-driven," and "polyphonic" cinema, this language remains vague, and it is used in the context of calling for a balance between such "artistic" cinema and more commercial films. And while some of the filmmakers told me in private that they were particularly concerned about making sure that the new law contained provisions to support more "experimental" work, this was always in the larger context of seeking more general reforms, and it was never a talking point in the group's public events or presentations. This is in contrast to other filmmaker movements that chose to use film festivals as platforms for publicizing their agendas—for example, the Young German Filmmakers and the "Oberhausener Manifest" presented at the Oberhausen Short Film Festival in 1962. Like the FOG filmmakers, the "Oberhausener" sought changes to funding structures and other administrative and policy issues, but articulated their movement in terms of a "new style of film," distinguishing this from what was considered the old, conventional "Papa's Kino" that dominated film production in Germany at the time. Their demands for reform aimed specifically at providing better conditions for this "new film" to flourish. See Hagener, "A New Wave Without Films?"

19. Elsaesser, *European Cinema*, 83.

20. Ibid., 82.

21. Czach, "Film Festivals, Programming, and the Building of a National Cinema," 86–87.

22. Harbord, *Film Cultures,* 73.

23. In the years 2005–2009, more than €1.25 million in state funds was given to support film industry unions. See "Kinimatografika kondylia."

24. "Kinimatografistes stin Omichli," at http://feleki.wordpress.com/2009/06 /30/κινηματογραφιστές-στην-ομίχλη (accessed on April 1, 2018).

25. Foucault, *Birth of Biopolitics,* 267–69.

26. Brown, *Edgework,* 42.

27. Ibid., 43.

28. Law 3905, "Enischysi kai anaptyxi tis kinimatografikis technis kai alles diataxeis" [Support and development of cinematic art and other ordinances].

29. Brown, *Edgework,* 40.

CHAPTER 5

1. Karkagiannis, "Tourismos mesa ston politismo."

2. Ibid.

3. In 2009, the total cost of the Balkan Fund program was €120,000. See Thessaloniki International Film Festival, *Geniki Synelefsi,* A14.

4. Karkagiannis, "I aftotelis aksia tou Politismou."

5. Yalouri, *Acropolis,* 73. See also Hamilakis, *Nation and Its Ruins.*

6. My use of this term differs somewhat from Slavoj Zizek or Mark Rectanus (see Rectanus, *Culture Incorporated*), both of whom are concerned with the way that corporations are increasingly involved in philanthropic and cultural activities for the usual purposes of economic profit. It also differs from the idea of the culture industry as articulated by members of the Frankfurt School, which centers on the cultural commodity as the product of industrial forms of organization, mechanical reproduction, and distribution, again driven by the pure profit motive.

7. Bourdieu, *Rules of Art,* 142.

8. Ibid.

9. Bourdieu, *Field of Cultural Production,* 39.

10. Yalouri, *Acropolis,* 47.

11. https://ec.europa.eu/programmes/creative-europe/actions/capitals-culture_en (accessed April 1, 2019)

12. For more on cultural capitals, see Johnson, *Cultural Capitals,* and Patel, *Cultural Politics of Europe.*

13. Rhyne, "Film Festival Circuits and Stakeholders," 16.

14. For more on state cultural policy and its relation to the market, see McGuigan, *Culture and the Public Sphere.*

15. Brown, *Edgework,* 57–59.

16. Honig, *Public Things,* 16.

17. Ibid., 24.

18. Miller, *Well-Tempered Self,* xi.

19. Hansen, "Unstable Mixtures, Dilated Spheres," 201–2.

20. Miller, *Well-Tempered Self,* x.

21. Ibid., xii.

22. Ibid., xxi.

23. Nichols, *Representing Reality,* 3–4.

24. Honig, *Public Things,* 92.

25. Ibid., 82–83.

26. Ibid., 21.

27. Ibid., 22.

28. Arendt, *Human Condition,* 167–68.

29. Ibid., 173.

30. For more on prefigurative politics, see Boggs, "Marxism"; Breines, *Community and Organization;* Day, *Gramsci is Dead;* and Graeber, *Direction Action.*

31. "Public Programs" at www.documenta14.de/en/public-programs/ (accessed April 1, 2018).

32. For critical perspectives on *documenta 14,* see Demos, "Learning from documenta 14"; Weiner, "Art of the Possible"; and Yalouri and Rikou, "documenta 14 Learning from Athens."

33. Weiner, "Art of the Possible."

34. Ibid.

35. See Souzas, *"Stamata na milas gia thanato, mwro mou."*

36. Like *Amygdaliá, Antoni's Voice* (dir. Christos Kapatos, 2018) and *Happy Princes* (dir. Panos Deligiannis, 2017) premiered at the Thessaloniki Documentary Festival.

37. Lee, "Beyond the Ethico-Aesthetic," 146.

Bibliography

Aktsoglou, Babis, ed. 30 *Chronia: Festival Ellinikou Kinimatografou* [30 Years: The festival of Greek cinema]. Thessaloniki: Thessaloniki Film Festival, 1989.

Ananiadis, Grigoris, Lina Ventoura, Giorgos Malamis, Vangelis Bitsoris, Efthimios Papataxiarchis, Stefanos Pesmazoglou, and Elli Droulia. "H 'atakti skepsi' ws gnostiki prosklisi, i, apopeira katanoisis enanti tou apotropiasmou kai tis exidanikefsis" ["Disorderly thought" as invitation to thought, or, an attempt at understanding, as opposed to disgust and idealization]. *Synchrona Themata* 103 (2008): 6–8.

Appadurai, Arjun, and Carol A. Breckenridge. "Why Public Culture?" *Public Culture* 1, no. 1 (1988): 5–9.

Apter, Emily, Anton Kaes, and D. N. Roderick, eds. *Mobile Citizens, Media States*. Special issue, *PMLA* 117, no. 1 (2002).

Arendt, Hannah. *The Human Condition*. Chicago: University of Chicago Press, 1958.

Augé, Marc. *Non-places: Introduction to an Anthropology of Supermodernity*. Translated by John Howe. London: Verso, 1995.

Balibar, Etienne. "Is European Citizenship Possible?" *Public Culture* 8 (1996): 355–76.

Bazin, André. "The Festival Viewed as a Religious Order." Translated by Emilie Bickerton. In *Dekalog 3: On Film Festivals*, edited by Richard Porton, 13–19. London: Wallflower Press, 2009. Originally published as "Du Festival considéré comme un order," *Cahiers du Cinéma* 8, no. 48 (June 1955): 6–8.

Behar, Ruth. "Ethnography and the Book that was Lost." *Ethnography* 4, no. 1 (2003): 15–39.

Beltrán, Cristina. "Going Public: Hannah Arendt, Immigrant Action, and the Space of Appearance." *Political Theory* 37, no. 5 (2009): 595–622.

Bernbeck, Reinhard. "*Lieux de Mémoire* and Sites of De-Subjectivation." In *Between Memory Sites and Memory Networks: New Archaeological and Historical Perspectives,* edited by Reinhard Bernbeck, Kerstin P. Hofmann, and Ulrike Sommer, 253–78. Berlin: Edition Topoi, 2017.

Boggs, Carl. "Marxism, Prefigurative Communism, and the Problem of Workers' Control." *Radical America* 11, no. 6 (1977): 98–122.

Boorstin, Daniel. *The Image: A Guide to Pseudo-Events in America.* New York: Vintage Books, 1992.

Bourdieu, Pierre. *The Field of Cultural Production.* New York: Columbia University Press, 1993.

———. *The Rules of Art: Genesis and Structure of the Literary Field.* Translated by Susan Emmanuel. Stanford, CA: Stanford University Press, 1996.

Boym, Svetlana. *The Future of Nostalgia.* New York: Basic Books, 2001.

Breines, Winifred. *Community and Organization in the New Left: 1962–1968.* New York: Praeger, 1982.

Brown, Wendy. *Edgework: Critical Essays on Knowledge and Politics.* Princeton, NJ: Princeton University Press, 2005.

———. *Undoing the Demos: Neoliberalism's Stealth Revolution.* New York: Zone Books, 2015.

Butler, Judith. *Gender Trouble: Feminism and the Subversion of Identity.* London: Routledge, 1990.

———. *Notes Toward a Performative Theory of Assembly.* Cambridge, MA: Harvard University Press, 2015.

Calotychos, Vangelis. *Modern Greece: A Cultural Poetics.* New York: Berg, 2003.

Corless, Kieron, and Chris Darke. *Cannes: Inside the World's Premier Film Festival.* New York: Faber and Faber, 2007.

Couldry, Nick, Andreas Hepp, and Friedrich Krotz, eds. *Media Events in a Global Age.* London: Routledge, 2010.

Cowie, Peter. *Revolution! The Explosion of World Cinema in the Sixties.* New York: Faber and Faber, 2004.

Craith, Máiréad Nic. "Culture and Citizenship in Europe: Questions for Anthropologists." *Social Anthropology* 12, no. 3 (2004): 289–300.

Czach, Liz. "Film Festivals, Programming, and the Building of a National Cinema." *The Moving Image* 4, no. 1 (2004): 76–88.

Dartzali, Despina. "'Kinimatografistes stin Omichli': Den eimaste enantion tou Festival" ["Filmmakers in the Mist": We are not against the Festival]. *Macedonia,* November 8, 2009.

Day, Richard. *Gramsci is Dead: Anarchist Currents in the Newest Social Movements.* Ann Arbor, MI: Pluto Press, 2005.

Dayan, Daniel, and Katz, Elihu. *Media Events: The Live Broadcasting of History.* Cambridge, MA: Harvard University Press, 1992.

de Valck, Marijke. "Drowning in Popcorn at the International Film Festival Rotterdam? The Festival as a Multiplex of Cinephilia." In *Cinephilia: Movies, Love and Memory,* edited by Marijke de Valck and Malte Hagener, 97–109. Amsterdam: Amsterdam University Press, 2005.

———. *Film Festivals: From European Geopolitics to Global Cinephilia.* Amsterdam: Amsterdam University Press, 2007.

Deffner, Alex M., and Lois Labrianidis. "Planning Culture and Time in a Mega-Event: Thessaloniki as the European City of Culture in 1997." *International Planning Studies* 10, nos. 3–4 (2005): 241–64.

Delgado-Moreira, Juan M. *Multicultural Citizenship of the European Union.* Burlington, VT: Ashgate, 2000.

Delveroudi, Eliza-Anna. "O Modernismos ston Elliniki Kinimatografo" [Modernism in Greek cinema]. Lecture, Macedonian Museum of Contemporary Art. Thessaloniki, May 13, 2009.

Demos, T. J. "Learning from documenta 14: Athens, Post-democracy, and Decolonization." *Third Text: Critical Perspectives on Contemporary Art and Culture* 2017. http://thirdtext.org/demos-documenta. Accessed April 1, 2019.

Elliott, David J., Marissa Silverman, and Wayne D. Bowman, eds. *Artistic Citizenship: Artistry, Social Responsibility, and Ethical Praxis.* New York: Oxford University Press, 2016.

Elsaesser, Thomas. *European Cinema: Face to Face with Hollywood.* Amsterdam: Amsterdam University Press, 2005.

Falicov, Tamara L. "The 'Festival Film': Film Festival Funds as Cultural Intermediaries." In *Film Festivals: History, Theory, Method, Practice,* edited by Marijke de Valck, Brendan Kredell, and Skadi Loist, 200–219. London: Routledge, 2016.

Faubion, James. *Modern Greek Lessons: A Primer in Historical Constructivism.* Princeton, NJ: Princeton University Press, 2001.

Flores, William, and Rina Benmayor, eds. *Latino Cultural Citizenship: Claiming Identity, Space, and Rights.* Boston: Beacon, 1996.

Foucault, Michel. *The Birth of Biopolitics: Lectures at the Collège de France, 1978–79.* Translated by Graham Burchell. New York: Palgrave Macmillan, 2008.

Fraser, Nancy. "Rethinking the Public Sphere: A Contribution to the Critique of Actually Existing Democracy." In *Habermas and the Public Sphere,* edited by Craig Calhoun, 109–42. Cambridge, MA: MIT Press, 1992.

Gourgouris, Stathis. *Dream Nation: Enlightenment, Colonization, and the Institution of Modern Greece.* Stanford: Stanford University Press, 1996.

Graeber, David. *Direct Action: An Ethnography.* Oakland, CA: AK Press, 2009.

Grimes, Ronald. "The Lifeblood of Public Ritual: Fiestas and Public Exploration Projects." In *Celebration: Studies in Festivity and Ritual,* edited by Victor Turner, 272–83. Washington, DC: Smithsonian Institution Press, 1982.

Hagener, Malte. "A New Wave Without Films? The Curious Case of the Young German Film." Paper, Annual Meeting of the Society for Cinema and Media Studies. Los Angeles, CA, March 20, 2010.

Hallin, Daniel C., and Stylianos Papathanassopoulos. "Political Clientelism and the Media: Southern Europe and Latin America in Comparative Perspective." *Media, Culture, and Society* 24 (2002): 175–95.

Hamilakis, Yannis. *The Nation and Its Ruins: Archaeology, Antiquity, and National Imagination in Modern Greece.* Oxford: Oxford University Press, 2007.

Hansen, Miriam. *Babel and Babylon: Spectatorship in American Silent Film.* Cambridge, MA: Harvard University Press, 1991.

————. "Unstable Mixtures, Dilated Spheres: Negt and Kluge's The Public Sphere and Experience, Twenty Years Later." *Public Culture* 5, no. 2 (1993): 179–212.

Harbord, Janet. *Film Cultures*. London: SAGE, 2002.

Hardt, Michael, and Antonio Negri. *Empire*. Cambridge, MA: Harvard University Press, 2001.

Harvey, Sylvia. *May '68 and Film Culture*. London: British Film Institute, 1978.

Herzfeld, Michael. *Ours Once More: Folklore, Ideology, and the Making of Modern Greece*. New York: Pella Publishing Company, 1986.

————. *Anthropology through the Looking Glass: Critical Ethnography in the Margins of Europe*. Cambridge: Cambridge University Press, 1987.

————. *A Place in History: Social and Monumental Time in a Cretan Town*. Princeton, NJ: Princeton University Press, 1991.

————. "The Absent Presence: Discourses of Crypto-Colonialism." *The South Atlantic Quarterly* 101, no. 4 (2002): 899–926.

Holdsworth, Nick. "Rethinking Cinema: Fest Topper sees Creative Answers in Global Crises." *Variety*, November 9–15, 2009.

Honig, Bonnie. "Toward an Agonistic Feminism: Hannah Arendt and the Politics of Identity." In *Feminist Interpretations of Hannah Arendt*, edited by Bonnie Honig, 135–66. University Park: Pennsylvania State University Press, 1995.

————. *Public Things: Democracy in Disrepair*. New York: Fordham University Press, 2017.

Iordanova, Dina, with Ragan Rhyne, eds. *Film Festival Yearbook 1: The Festival Circuit*. St. Andrews: St. Andrews Film Studies, College Gate Press, 2009.

Iordanova, Dina, with Ruby Cheung, eds. *Film Festival Yearbook 2: Film Festivals and Imagined Communities*. St. Andrews: St. Andrews Film Studies, 2010.

Johnson, Louise. *Cultural Capitals: Revaluing the Arts, Remaking Urban Spaces*. Burlington, VT: Ashgate, 2009.

Karalis, Vrasidas. *A History of Greek Cinema*. New York: Continuum, 2012.

Karkagiannis, Antonis. "Ameses lyseis" [Immediate solutions]. *H Kathimerini*, October 6, 2009.

————. "Tourismos mesa ston politismo" [Tourism through culture]. *H Kathimerini*, October 11, 2009.

————. "I aftotelis axia tou Politismou" [The independent worth of culture]. *H Kathimerini*, October 18, 2009.

"Kinimatografika kondylia: Osa pairnei o anemos" [Film funding: Gone with the wind]. *Eleftherotypia*, January 29, 2010.

Kokonis, Michalis. "Is There Such a Thing as a Greek Blockbuster? The Revival of Contemporary Greek Cinema." In *Greek Cinema: Texts, Histories, Identities*, edited by Lydia Papadimitriou and Yannis Tzioumakis, 37–53. Bristol: Intellect, 2012.

Kontrarou-Rassia, N. "Apo ti theoria stin praksi" [From theory to practice]. *Eleftherotypia*, October 6, 2009.

Kornetis, Kostis. "No More Heroes? Rejection and Reverberation of the Past in the 2008 Events in Greece." *Journal of Modern Greek Studies* 28, no. 2 (2010): 173–97.

———. "1968, 1989, 2011: Reconsidering Social Movements, 'Moments of Change,' and Theoretical Framing over Time." *Historein* 13 (2013): 57–70.

———. "The End of a Parable? Unsettling the Transitology Model in the Age of Crisis." *Historein* 15, no. 1 (2015): 5–12.

Lee, Toby. "Festival, City, State: Cultural Citizenship at the Thessaloniki Film Festival." In *Coming Soon to a Festival Near You: Programming Film Festivals,* edited by Jeffrey Ruoff, 89–100. St. Andrews: St. Andrews Film Studies, 2012.

———. "Being There, Taking Place: Ethnography at the Film Festival." In *Film Festivals: Theory, History, Method, Practice,* edited by Brendan Kredell, Skadi Loist, and Marijke de Valck, 122–37. Abingdon: Routledge, 2016.

———. "Beyond the Ethico-aesthetic: Toward a Re-valuation of the Sensory Ethnography Lab." *Visual Anthropology Review* 35, no. 2 (2019): 138–47.

Legg, Stephen. "Contesting and Surviving Memory: Space, Nation, and Nostalgia in *Les Lieux de Mémoire.*" *Environment and Planning D: Society and Space* 23 (2005): 481–504.

Loist, Skadi, and Marijke de Valck. *Film Festivals/Film Festival Research: Thematic, Annotated Bibliography.* Accessed April 1, 2019. http://filmfestivalresearch.org/index.php/ffrn-bibliography/

Loukopoulou, Katerina. "'A Campaign of Truth': Marshall Plan Films in Greece." In *Cinema's Military Industrial Complex,* edited by Haidee Wasson and Lee Grieveson, 321–38. Berkeley: University of California Press, 2018.

Loverdou, Myrto, Maria Thermou, Isma M. Toulatou, and Giannis Zouboulakis. "Changes are Coming." *To Vima,* October 11, 2009.

Lowenthal, David. "Classical Antiquities as National and Global Heritage." *Antiquity* 62 (1988): 726–35.

———. *The Heritage Crusade and the Spoils of History.* Cambridge: Cambridge University Press, 1988.

Makedoniki Kallitechniki Etaireia "Techni." *Techni sti Thessaloniki: Keimena gia ton kinimatografo* [*Techni* in Thessaloniki: Texts on cinema]. Thessaloniki: Makedoniki Kallitechniki Etaireia "Techni" and Thessaloniki Film Festival, 2002.

Martin, Randy. "Artistic Citizenship." In *Artistic Citizenship: A Public Voice for the Arts,* edited by Mary Schmidt Campbell and Randy Martin, 1–22. New York: Routledge, 2006.

Mazower, Mark. *Salonica, City of Ghosts: Christians, Muslims, and Jews, 1430–1950.* New York: Alfred A. Knopf, 2005.

McGuigan, Jim. *Culture and the Public Sphere.* London: Routledge, 1996.

Miller, Toby. *The Well-Tempered Self: Citizenship, Culture, and the Postmodern Subject.* Baltimore: Johns Hopkins University Press, 1993.

———. *Technologies of Truth: Cultural Citizenship and the Popular Media.* Minneapolis: University of Minnesota Press, 1998.

———. *Cultural Citizenship: Cosmopolitanism, Consumerism, and Television in a Neoliberal Age.* Philadelphia: Temple University Press, 2007.

Mitropoulou, Aglaïa. *Ellinikos Kinimatografos* [Greek cinema]. 2nd ed. Athens: Papazisi. 2006.

Mouffe, Chantal. *The Democratic Paradox.* London: Verso, 2000.

NET. "Katalipsi sti NET tin ora ton eidiseon apo neous gia ti dolofonia tou Grigoropoulou" [Youth occupation of NET during the news broadcast for the murder of Grigoropoulos]. YouTube video, 1:44. Posted by "synoro1," December 16, 2008. Accessed April 1, 2019. https://youtube.com/watch?v= PK9lpMk7fiY&noredirect=1

Nichols, Bill. *Representing Reality: Issues and Concepts in Documentary.* Bloomington: Indiana University Press, 1991.

———. "Discovering Form, Inferring Meaning: New Cinemas and the Film Festival Circuit." *Film Quarterly* 47, no. 3 (1994): 16–30.

Nora, Pierre. "Between Memory and History: Les Lieux de Mémoire." Translated by Marc Roudebush. *Representations* 26 (1989): 7–24.

Ong, Aihwa. "Cultural Citizenship as Subject Making: Immigrants Negotiate Racial and Cultural Boundaries in the United States." *Current Anthropology* 35 (1996): 737–62.

———. *Buddha is Hiding: Refugees, Citizenship, the New America.* Berkeley: University of California Press, 2003.

Pakulski, Jan. "Cultural Citizenship." *Citizenship Studies* 1, no. 1 (1997): 73–86.

Panagopoulos, Panagiotis. "Ameses lyseis" [Immediate solutions]. *H Kathimerini,* October 6, 2009.

Papadimitriou, Lydia. "The Hindered Drive toward Internationalization: Thessaloniki (International) Film Festival." *New Review of Film and Television Studies* 14, no. 1 (2016): 93–111.

———. "Greek Cinema as European Cinema: Co-productions, Eurimages, and the Europeanization of Greek Cinema." *Studies in European Cinema* 15, nos. 2–3 (2018): 215–34.

Papadimitriou, Lydia, and Yannis Tzioumakis, eds. *Greek Cinema: Texts, Histories, Identities.* Bristol: Intellect, 2012.

Papailias, Penelope. "Witnessing the Crisis." *Beyond the "Greek Crisis": Histories, Rhetorics, Politics.* Cultural Anthropology Online, Editors' Forum/Hot Spots, October 25, 2011. Accessed April 1, 2019. http://culanth.org/fieldsights/witnessing-the-crisis.

Papataxiarchis, Evthimios. "Pragmatism Against Austerity: Greek Society, Politics, and Ethnography in Times of Trouble." In *Critical Times in Greece: Anthropological Engagements with the Crisis,* edited by Dimitris Dalakoglou and Georgios Agelopoulos, 227–47. London: Routledge, 2018.

Papatheodorou, Fotini, and David Machin. "The Umbilical Cord That Was Never Cut: The Post-Dictatorial Intimacy between the Political Elite and the Mass Media in Greece and Spain." *European Journal of Communication* 18, no. 1 (2003): 31–54.

Paradeisi, Maria, and Afroditi Nikolaidou, eds. *Apo ton Proimo ston Synchrono Elliniko Kinimatografo: Zitimata Methdologias, Theorias, Istorias* [From early to contemporary Greek cinema: Questions of methodology, theory, history]. Athens: Gutenberg Publications, 2017.

Patel, Kiran Klaus, ed. *The Cultural Politics of Europe: European Capitals of Culture and European Union since the 1980s.* London: Routledge, 2013.

Periodiko K. "Polites zitoun to logo: Gia ta kommata, tous politikous, kai ta themata pou tous "kaine" [Citizens sound off: On political parties, politicians, and the issues that matter to them most]. *Periodiko K,* October 4, 2009.

Porton, Richard, ed. *Dekalog 3: On Film Festivals.* London: Wallflower Press, 2009.

Rancière, Jacques. *The Politics of Aesthetics: The Distribution of the Sensible.* Translated by Gabriel Rockhill. London: Continuum, 2006.

———. *Dissensus: On Politics and Aesthetics.* Translated by Steven Corcoran. London: Continuum, 2010.

Rectanus, Mark W. *Culture Incorporated: Museums, Artists, and Corporate Sponsorships.* Minneapolis: University of Minnesota Press, 2002.

Rentzis, Thanasis, ed. *H ypothesi tou festival ellinikou kinimatografou '77: To xroniko tou typou mera me ti mera* [The case of the '77 Greek film festival: A chronicle of the daily press]. Self-published, 1977.

Retzios, Tasso. "To telos tis . . . festivalikis metapolitefsis" [The end of . . . the festival regime change]. *Angelioforos,* November 13, 2011.

Rhyne, Regan. "Film Festival Circuits and Stakeholders." In *Film Festival Yearbook 1: The Festival Circuit,* edited by Dina Iordanova and Regan Rhyne, 9–22. St. Andrews: St. Andrews Film Studies, College Gate Press, 2009.

Roitman, Janet. *Anti-crisis.* Durham, NC: Duke University Press, 2014.

Rosaldo, Renato. "Cultural Citizenship and Educational Democracy." *Cultural Anthropology* 9, no. 3 (1994): 402–11.

———. "Cultural Citizenship in San Jose, California." *PoLAR* 17, no. 2 (1994): 57–64.

Rozakou, Katerina. "'Koinonikotita' kai 'koinonia allilengiis': H periptosi enos ethelontikou somateiou" ["Sociality" and "society of solidarity": The case of a volunteer organization]. *Elliniki Epitheorisi Politikis Epistimis* 32 (2008): 95–120.

Ruoff, Jeffrey, ed. *Coming Soon to a Festival Near You: Programming Film Festivals.* St. Andrews: St. Andrews Film Studies, 2012.

Schwartz, Vanessa R. *It's So French! Hollywood, Paris, and the Making of Cosmopolitan Film Culture.* Chicago: University of Chicago Press, 2007.

Shaffer, Marguerite S., ed. *Public Culture: Diversity, Democracy, and Community in the United States.* Philadelphia: University of Pennsylvania Press, 2008.

Shore, Cris. "Inventing the 'People's Europe': Critical Approaches to European Community 'Cultural Policy.'" *Man* 28, no. 4 (1993): 779–800.

———. *Building Europe: The Cultural Politics of European Integration.* London: Routledge, 2000.

Shore, Cris, and Black, Annabel. "Citizens' Europe and the Construction of European Identity." In *Anthropology of Europe: Identities and Boundaries in Conflict,* edited by Victoria A. Goddard, Josep R. Llobera, and Cris Shore. 275–98. Oxford: Berg, 1994.

Sifaki, Eirini. "Cinema Goes to War: The German Film Policy in Greece During the Occupation, 1941–44." In *Cinema and the Swastika: The International*

Expansion of Third Reich Cinema, edited by Roel Vande Winkel and David Welch, 148–58. New York: Palgrave Macmillan, 2011.

Siu, Lok. "Diasporic Cultural Citizenship: Chineseness and Belonging in Central America and Panama." *Social Text* 19, no. 4 (2001): 7–28.

Skopeteas, Yannis. "Greek Cinema in the 1990s: Modes of Practice and Modes of Production." *Journal of the Hellenic Diaspora* 37, nos. 1–2 (2011): 179–94.

Souzas, Nikos. *"Stamata na milas gia thanato, mwro mou": Politiki kai koultoura sto antagonistiko kinima stin Ellada (1974–1998)* ["Stop talking about death, baby": Politics and culture in the anti-establishment movement in Greece (1974–1998)]. Thessaloniki: Naftilos, 2015.

Spinou, Pari. "Epta erotimata zitoun apantisi" [Seven questions demand answers]. *Epta,* October 18, 2009.

Stevenson, Nick. *Culture and Citizenship.* London: Sage, 2001.

———. *Cultural Citizenship: Cosmopolitan Questions.* Maidenhead: Open University Press, 2003.

Stringer, Julian. "Global Cities and the International Film Festival Economy." In *Cinema and the City: Film and Urban Societies in a Global Context,* edited by Mark Shiel and Tony Fitzmaurice, 134–44. Oxford: Blackwell Publishers, 2001.

———. "Regarding Film Festivals." PhD diss., Indiana University, 2003.

Talbott, Michael. "The Familiar Difference of World Cinema: Film Funds, Film Festivals, and the Global South." PhD diss., New York University, 2015.

Theodorakis, Stavros. "Oi Alloi Protagonistes: Dimitris Eipidis" [The other protagonists: Dimitris Eipides]. *Ta Nea,* October 22–23, 2011.

Thermou, Maria. "Ena ypourgeio se apognosi" [A ministry in despair]. *To Vima,* September 27, 2009.

Thessaloniki International Film Festival. *50 Chronia Festival Kinimatografou Thessalonikis: 1960/2009* [50 years of the Thessaloniki Film Festival: 1960/2009]. Thessaloniki: Ianos, 2009.

———. *Street Cinema: O kinimatografos stous dromous tis polis* [Cinema in the city streets]. Thessaloniki: Thessaloniki International Film Festival, 2009.

———. *Why Cinema Now? The 50th Thessaloniki International Film Festival.* Thessaloniki: Thessaloniki International Film Festival, 2009.

———. *Geniki Synelefsi, Fevrouarios 2010: Dioikitikos Apologismos* [General assembly, February 2010: Administrative report]. Thessaloniki: Thessaloniki International Film Festival, 2010.

Toruellas, Rosa M., Rina Benmayor, Anneris Goris, and Ana Juarbe. *Affirming Cultural Citizenship in the Puerto Rican Community: Critical Literacy and the El Barrio Popular Education Program.* New York: Centro de Estudios Puertorriqueños, Hunter College, 1991.

Turner, Victor, ed. *Celebration: Studies in Festivity and Ritual.* Washington, DC: Smithsonian Institution Press, 1982.

Vallejo, Aida, and María Paz Peirano, eds. *Film Festivals and Anthropology.* Newcastle upon Tyne: Cambridge Scholars Publishing, 2017.

Valoukos, Stathis. *Neos Ellinikos Kinimatografos (1965–1981): Istoria kai Politiki* [New Greek cinema (1965–1981): History and politics]. Athens: Aigokeros, 2011.

Venardou, Evanna. "Oi tainies pou den tha doume" [The film we won't see]. *Epta,* September 27, 2009.

Warner, Michael. *Publics and Counterpublics.* New York: Zone Books, 2002.

Weiner, Andrew. "The Art of the Possible: With and Against Documenta 14." *Biennial Foundation,* August 14, 2017. http://biennialfoundation.org/2017/08 /art-possible-documenta-14/. Accessed April 1, 2019.

Wong, Cindy Hing-Yuk. *Film Festivals: Culture, People, and Power on the Global Screen.* New Brunswick, NJ: Rutgers University Press, 2011.

————. "Publics and Counterpublics: Rethinking Film Festivals as Public Spheres." In *Film Festivals: History, Theory, Method, Practice,* edited by Marijke de Valck, Brendan Kredell, and Skadi Loist, 89–103. London: Routledge, 2016.

Wood, Nancy. "Memory's Remains: Les Lieux de Mémoire." *History and Memory* 6, no. 1 (1994): 123–49.

Xanthopoulos, Lefteris, ed. *Pavlos Zannas.* Athens: Thessaloniki Film Festival and Aigokeros, 1999.

Xifilinos, Demosthenes. "Kato apo fota kokkina koimatai i Saloniki" [Under red lights, Thessaloniki sleeps]. *Exostis* 28 (2010): 1.

Yalouri, Eleana. *The Acropolis: Global Fame, Local Claim.* Oxford: Berg, 2001.

Yalouri, Eleana, and Elpida Rikou. "Documenta 14 Learning from Athens: The Response of the 'Learning from documenta' Research Project." *Field: A Journal of Socially-Engaged Art Criticism,* issue 11 (2018). http://field-journal.com/issue-11/documenta-14-learning-from-athens-the-response-of-the-learning-from-documenta-research-project. Accessed April 1, 2019.

Index

Founded in 1893,
UNIVERSITY OF CALIFORNIA PRESS
publishes bold, progressive books and journals
on topics in the arts, humanities, social sciences,
and natural sciences—with a focus on social
justice issues—that inspire thought and action
among readers worldwide.

The UC PRESS FOUNDATION
raises funds to uphold the press's vital role
as an independent, nonprofit publisher, and
receives philanthropic support from a wide
range of individuals and institutions—and from
committed readers like you. To learn more, visit
ucpress.edu/supportus.